The Uncommon Path

of Awakening Authentic Joy

First published by O Books, 2009
O Books is an imprint of John Hunt Publishing Ltd., The Bothy, Deershot Lodge, Park Lane, Ropley,
Hants, SO24 0BE, UK
office1@o-books.net
www.o-books.net

Distribution in:	South Africa
	Alternative Books
UK and Europe	altbook@peterhyde.co.za
Orca Book Services	Tel: 021 555 4027 Fax: 021 447 1430
orders@orcabookservices.co.uk	
Tel: 01202 665432 Fax: 01202 666219	Text copyright Mick Quinn 2008
Int. code (44)	
	Design: Stuart Davies
USA and Canada	
NBN	ISBN: 978 1 84694 208 2
custserv@nbnbooks.com	
Tel: 1 800 462 6420 Fax: 1 800 338 4550	All rights reserved. Except for brief quotations
	in critical articles or reviews, no part of this
Australia and New Zealand	book may be reproduced in any manner without
Brumby Books	prior written permission from the publishers.
sales@brumbybooks.com.au	
Tel: 61 3 9761 5535 Fax: 61 3 9761 7095	The rights of Mick Quinn as author have been
	asserted in accordance with the Copyright,
Far East (offices in Singapore, Thailand,	Designs and Patents Act 1988.
Hong Kong, Taiwan)	
Pansing Distribution Pte Ltd	
kemal@pansing.com	A CIP catalogue record for this book is available
Tel: 65 6319 9939 Fax: 65 6462 5761	from the British Library.

Printed by Digital Book Print

O Books operates a distinctive and ethical publishing philosophy in
all areas of its business, from its global network of authors to
production and worldwide distribution.
This book is produced on FSC certified stock, within ISO14001
standards. The printer plants sufficient trees each year through
the Woodland Trust to absorb the level of emitted carbon in
its production.

The Uncommon Path

of Awakening Authentic Joy

Mick Quinn

BOOKS

Winchester, UK
Washington, USA

CONTENTS

Early acclaim for

The Uncommon Path

"With *The Uncommon Path*, Mick Quinn gives us a program to achieve genuine happiness, and he does so in an informative and gripping way. I highly recommend this book to anyone who is willing to let go of his or her suffering and achieve authentic joy."

Gary Renard: Bestselling author of *Your Immortal Reality* and *The Disappearance of the Universe* (Hay House).

"Mick Quinn's style is clear and direct and places you in a frame of mind from which to comprehend deeper and higher levels of yourself. This is because he speaks between the lines, sometimes even in the things he doesn't say - like silence making music. I highly recommend his excellent book."

Raquel Torrent: Psychologist and Integral Therapist, founder and Ex-president of the Spanish Integral Association.

"*The Uncommon Path* is nourishment for your soul and practical advice for your success. This book inspires change by helping you understand yourself and how you relate to the world around you. Reading it is a joy, and applying its principles is a way to define your purpose and goals in life. I am honored to commend it to you."

Ed Bobrow: Author of 8 books, contributing author to: American Management Association's Marketing Handbook, and former Adjunct Associate Professor at New York University.

"His narrative is eminently readable and lively. I have been most impressed by both his subject matter and his presentation."

Dr. Patrick Murray: M.A, M.Litt. PhD (NUI) PhD (T.C.D.)
H.D.E. Lecturer, historian and author.

"Reading Mick Quinn's material was like a breath of fresh air to me at the time when I first encountered it, or like a 'buzzsaw' that went cross-grain through my beliefs and assumptions."

Rogier F. van Vlissingen:
Author of *Closing the Circle*.

"The Uncommon Path is such an important work."

Lama Ole Nydahl: Author and founder of over 500 Diamond Way meditation centers worldwide.

BOOKS BY MICK QUINN

Poder Y Gracia (Power and Grace)
Corona Borealis Publishing,
Malaga, Spain
(2007)

FOR FURTHER INFORMATION:
For workshop schedule with the author and his wife
Debora Prieto please visit
www.mickquinn.com
info@mickquinn.com
USA: 1 888 350 2353

To my lovely wife Debora Prieto ~ The light of my life.

FOREWORD

I have never cared much for traditional self-development books. The reason is that many of them offer the ultimate, the definitive or the only path leading to success or achievement in their particular field. The author is often someone of note, a respected authority, or someone who has made it big. It seems that once you make your mark in our fast-paced, global, success-obsessed-action-centric-results-driven world, you've earned the right to tell others how the world works so they, too, can enjoy the delicious fruits of success. To me this all seems frighteningly simplistic. What we have are thousands of self-development books that deliver answers – better yet, keys for opening the doors to the good life. The good life invariably means money, comfort, respect, or the effortless fulfillment of all our wishes and desires.

So along comes a new writer by the name of Mick Quinn. He was born in a small town in the middle of Ireland, the product of a working-class family of humble roots. Like so many overachievers before him, Quinn went out into the world to make his mark and to attain success. This self-confessed serial entrepreneur started one business after another. After each business became wildly successful, he sold it and started another. In a few short years, just as he achieved the American – make that Irish – dream he abandoned it and began to reflect on life and, yes, an idea for a book appeared. But Quinn did not produce another how-to-get-rich-and-successful book, he wrote a timeless one about the foundation of true success – *awakening to our eternal motives*.

In *The Uncommon Path*, Quinn bares his soul and delivers a universally powerful, yet intimate message. It is perfectly clear that this book is based upon Quinn's own experiences and journeys, and deeply rooted in a life that vacillated greatly between material, emotional, and spiritual scarcity and abundance.

In *The Uncommon Path*, Quinn shows us how to renounce ego-motives in our conversations and relationships, so that we may challenge the conditioned image we have of ourselves. In doing so, we create the conditions for our own awakening. And as Quinn points out, this process of decentering conditioning and aligning values with pure intentions is very different from the objectives and outcomes common to traditional self-improvement programs. This work delivers you to your destiny – whatever that may be for you. Refreshingly, *The Uncommon Path* has nothing to do with the size of your equity portfolio or your IQ. *The Uncommon Path* is about realizing a *way of life* that is far more durable, fulfilling, and self-sustaining than just gaining worldly success. In Quinn's own words, it's about "Recognizing awakened choices, so you can consistently evolve through the levels of your own consciousness." To achieve this, you have to open your mind and heart to other possibilities, those that are far greater and far more challenging than building the *dream* life – yet are just as attainable and sustainable.

The Uncommon Path is about the discovery of your full potential. The principles Quinn writes about here are the principles by which he lives each day. If you're willing to take a chance and release the ego, climb into a mysterious roller coaster, and enjoy the ride of your life, you, too, can realize an awakening to joy, and a life based on the expression of your full potential.

It is very clear to me that this work and Buddha's teaching are on the same wavelength and that *The Uncommon Path* delivers practical suggestions that are most effective in today's world.

I would like to think that Quinn would pass on Buddha's timeless wisdom. If he makes good on the promises he outlines in his opening chapters, readers will transcend lifetimes of yearning for authenticity and purpose. If this book helps just one person's life, it will have succeeded and when *The Uncommon Path* touches millions, it will truly be a miracle.

Bob Weinstein
Nationally Syndicated Columnist and Author
New York City, May 2008

Preface

Late one afternoon, in the rolling surf of Race Point Beach, Massachusetts, a medicine bottle mysteriously appeared. It was as if the note held inside was the direct response to a frantic request I had just made to the universe:

"If there is anything else out there, please send me a sign!"

As those final words left my lips, I felt something touch my toes. Within that bottle, the note read:

"To find the world's greatest treasure, walk on the beach in the sunset, look toward the west and see The Greatest Treasure."

That bottle and its contents were the catalysts for this book. This 'coincidence' confirmed that the most profound and unfathomable aspect of life was not immediately visible to the eye. The simplicity of the message also revealed that transcending all unnecessary suffering was entirely possible. But the question was: how?

My subsequent search for answers took me on a 'spiritual path' through three continents, to many different teachers, *Siddha* masters, and spiritual groups. The search yielded knowledge, but little relief from the burden of my questions, until spiritual teacher Andrew Cohen said, *"Enlightenment is the relationship you have to the experience you are already having."*

Following my first awakening to the true force of conditioning in 2001, I realized that some roads lead to *home* a whole lot quicker than others. In this book I do my best to identify the part of each one of us that does not know how lost it is in conditioned ideas, concepts and beliefs. *The Uncommon Path* is not for the faint-hearted. The sincere aspirant finds that the admission of *freedom* is merely the beginning of the path. Should you be willing to face millennia of conditioning with the intention to awaken, then that outcome is already guaranteed.

The discovery and expression of our full potential for the sake of humanity is the greatest challenge we can offer ourselves.

3

Acknowledgments

I am deeply thankful to Andrew Cohen, Dennis Genpo Merzel, and Ken Wilber for their enduring teachings, infinite wisdom and love.

I also wish to thank the many partners, guides and teachers, without whom this work would not have been possible: Shirley R. Phelps, Robert Yehling, Linda Ann Knox, Amanda Mayer, Laura López, Juan Carlos Subias, Merce Nerbot Muns, Rogier F. Van Vlissingen, Harriette Halepis-Groulx, Susan Sarao, Maria Balachich, Cathryn L. Craig, MBA, Brenda L. Miller, Bobbi de Haan, Amy Conger, Thomas J. O'Connor, Linda Corene, Sue Tinkle, Lisa Hagan, Patricia Hampton, Dan Britt, Cynthia Duryee, Tara and Joshua, Susan Rose, Norah Quinn, Nofi Gurelneck, Elizabeth Chauncey, Susan Massaro, Carly Thorne, Carolyn Myss, Eckhart Tolle, Jean Klein, Lama Ole Nydahl, Frederick Lenz, Anthony Robbins, Peter Masefield, Ed Bobrow, Don Beck, Thomas Leonard, David Brazier, Andrew Harvey, Gregg Braden, David Whyte, Neale Donald Walsch, Stephen Mitchell, Thomas Byrom, Mihaly Csikszentmihalyi, Michael Murphy, and Rob Berkley of www.groupmv.com, who helped me recognize the power of values in everyday living, business and relationships and whose work I use as the foundation for the values exercises in this book.

Mick Quinn
Salt Lake City, Utah
Barcelona, Spain

A note to the reader

Spiritual practice is about fighting inertia. Since awakening to your full potential can be challenging, there may be times when it seems that I am being uncompassionate in my assertiveness. Sometimes a direct jolt, though uncomfortable, can rouse you to the light shining beyond muted desires to deny your True Nature. It is never my purpose to taunt or harm, though sometimes I can seem unpleasant, which is most certainly not my intention.

To use your awareness to transcend thought requires the development of both *cognition* and *consciousness*. Because the awakened life emerges as the convergence of potentiality and vitality, I attempt to tread a fine line between the two.

Evolutionary Pointers appear throughout this book. They are the signposts of liberation that outline a process of awakened engagement with life. The Evolutionary Pointers significantly shorten the quest for liberation, and simultaneously hush the voices of unreasonable dissent within. A significant portion of your success in uncovering and surpassing concealed conditioning depends on your ability to fully integrate these Evolutionary Pointers into your particular life situations. I also make use of real-life examples to help explain the practical application of this work.

The Uncommon Path is unbound by religiosity and warmly invites you to integrate your current practices and beliefs rather than abandoning that which is most dear and familiar. It is important to remember that the future is always founded upon the levels of development you have attained thus far. You may find that the awakened life compels you - to the best of your abilities - to be cognitively, emotionally, socially, and culturally proficient. Your current competences in each of these areas are most likely to affect your interpretation of my suggestions for growth as they appear throughout the book. *The Uncommon Path* helps you flower while revealing that your 'personal' enlightenment is a humble but majestic beginning.

> EVOLUTIONARY POINTER: To go from sunflower seeds to a swaying meadow of golden petals may require *many* harvests. Complement that which you have already learned, and grow gently.

This book also uses familiar ideas of fear, desire, suffering, values, intentions, right-action, karma, and universal mind, all of which are familiar to you. *The Uncommon Path* then combines and reframes these well-known concepts, merging them with several interrelated assessments to deliver a profound impact on your overall awareness. There are more possibilities to who you *really* are than you can imagine.

> EVOLUTIONARY POINTER: A condition of joy and ease unfolds as you throw yourself wholeheartedly into this work. Of this, there is no doubt. Confidence and trust in your deepest essence blossoms in direct proportion to your engagement.

This work is in a conversation format. Most of these topics have arisen in the classes that I have attended or taught over the past seventeen years. I use the initial 'P' for my 'partner' in this dialogue. I suggest that you read this book from cover to cover and even if you do not complete the exercises the first time through, your consciousness will already have expanded. As you complete the assessments, a period of introspection may be required to assimilate the new possibilities that are arising for you.

Then as you begin to apply your new perspectives to your life and relationships, you may indeed awaken to your eternal motives and glimpse into the immensity of your own potential.

The Uncommon Path places the wisdom of the mystic in your living room.

Finding your home in the Kosmos[1] begins right here!

---

[1] The Kosmos includes the physiophere, the biosphere, the noosphere, and the theosphere.

INTRODUCTION

"We are so accustomed to disguise ourselves
to others that in the end we become
disguised to ourselves."[1]

Intuiting Oneness

MQ: Life is a process of suffering propelled by the illusion of *true* free will.

P: Therefore, by understanding and accepting this false impression, I can let go of all unnecessary emotional and psychological suffering.

MQ: This is correct. Now, ask yourself this question: Would you bequeath your current state of spiritual health upon those you love?

P: Right now... I am not so sure I would.

MQ: Would you confer that condition upon your children?

P: I don't think *they* would be too happy with that!

MQ: You are not alone. These questions are challenging for many people to conclude.

P: Why is it that after all of my attempts to find direction, I am certainly wiser, but not truly at ease with bestowing the level of my attainment to others? Is it possible that there is a part of me that covertly enjoys the anguish of endless questioning?

MQ: I don't think you choose to suffer. But, because you correctly intuit your essential Oneness, you are constantly driven to greatness and to finding purpose.

P: Purpose... I've always wondered what my purpose is. How many of us leave this world without truly knowing? There are many things that I'm good at, but little I seem to have done is of much social value. Purpose implies social value, doesn't it?

MQ: Absolutely. Purpose is what calls you to spring out of bed before dawn to get to work, on whatever that might be. Purpose is what makes you strive through all sorts of obstacles, sometimes with little concern for your personal comfort. Purpose allows you to combine all your most important relationships as *one* toward a goal, which you honestly don't really know you can ever reach. Purpose is the smile you wear, the hand you hold out, the glint in your eye, it's the wind in your sails, the breeze on your face.

P: I sometimes know what you speak of here.

MQ: Yet, despite your finest intentions, you are frequently unable to stabilize a consistent expression of purpose in your life, or peace and unity in your most cherished relationships.

P: True. My intentions are great, but the outcomes of my decisions are rarely aligned with those objectives.

MQ: This is because there are essentially two ways in which you can make choices. Throughout our conversation, we will examine the differences between *conceptual-free-will* and *conscious-free-will*. We will be looking at the ways in which you can include these liberating distinctions so as to express the Oneness you most correctly intuit.

P: With clarity on these differences I can surpass the circles of conflict and confusion?

MQ: Yes. When conceptual-free-will is transcended and included as an essential aspect of conscious-free-will, your glorious purpose is revealed. Otherwise, life may continue to be a process of suffering propelled by the illusion of true free will.

P: But, will this always be so?

MQ: Consider this: What if the range of options available to you in regards to consistently accessing purpose, potential, and the co-creation of a conscious future were entirely limited by individual and collective conditioning, locked within conceptual-free-will, and that you are not aware of this fact?

P: Okay. Good point.

MQ: Then, where is your *true* free will?

P: Are you saying that I have choice, but only up to a certain limit?

MQ: Yes, and that edge never extends beyond pre-set conditioned boundaries, let alone affords you the opportunity to fully awaken.

> EVOLUTIONARY POINTER: To access and apply conscious-free-will means you must have already developed objectivity on the root cause of suffering.

MQ: Only this perspective guarantees your success in awakening to inherited restraints. Otherwise, there is no way you can be sure that concealed conditioning is not enthroned as the charismatic director of your quest to be free from unnecessary anguish.

Untangling Free Will

P: Is *free will* by definition, not constrained by forces, physical or divine?

MQ: Correct: however, what is generally considered to be 'my' free will exists within such a narrow array of options put forth by your conditioned past. This is what I refer to as *conceptual-free-will*. Without objectivity on your immersion in that conditioned past, it should come as no surprise to discover that your access to *true* free will is fully restricted.

P: But, there are many people who say that free will doesn't even exist in the first place.

MQ: Yes. But, resilience in the face of chaos always usurps such false humility.

P: Is free will at the level of conceptual-mind sufficient to satisfy most people?

MQ: Mastering conceptual-free-will is a necessary level of development that we all must go through. It can, however, be troubling to acknowledge that significant choices from your past were not so much a reflection of your individual volition, but of your selections from the alternatives offered by concealed conditioning.

P: As a result, attempting to sustain a consistent course of spiritual development by using the selections of the conceptual-mind is futile, not to mention frustrating!

MQ: Yes. You can only go so far. And this is exactly how concealed conditioning stifles your potential and drains your vitality. If you believe that you can be free, without first identifying and transcending hidden habituation, it has you right where it wants you. Lost, without knowing you are lost.

EVOLUTIONARY POINTER: When concealed conditioning is crafting your motives and values, you remain astray in phases of peace and conflict, pursuit and achievement, gain and loss. When the ego-identity is the only one seeking enlightenment, it commonly misnames that itinerary as *your conscious spiritual path*.

P: And if my conscience does not permit me to bequeath the current state of my spiritual health, I can suspect that hidden habituation may be restricting my growth and development.

MQ: Indeed. Let's start with these two distinctions:

Conceptual-Free-Will:

Conceptual-free-will is the decision-making process of the ego. It appeared in you about the age of four or five when you first became self-aware. Conceptual-free-will stabilized as you developed and matured and it is a necessary level of development that we all must go through. The range of options it offers to you, however, is naturally constrained by the average level of consciousness in the culture in which you grew up. Though you use conceptual-free-will to survive and thrive in this world, it encases you in conditioned limitations, albeit as an accomplished member of that community. Conceptual-free-will offers no possibility of liberation.

Conscious-Free-Will:
Conscious-free-will begins to unfold as you identify the ways in which *conceptual-free-will* has been restricting your development. As you uncover and let go of individual and collective conditioning, you can access conscious-free-will and unleash your full potential. The meaning and purpose of existence stabilizes to the degree that you have transcended and included conceptual-free-will as an object in your awareness. By the consistent application of conscious-free-will, you can co-create an awakened life together with other people in relationships that are completely free from personal conflict. Conscious-free-will allows you to master your destiny for the sake of humanity.

P: Conscious-free-will is *true free will,* which exists beyond the scope of conditioned limits.

MQ: Exactly.

P: What do you mean by *transcend* and *include*?

MQ: Recall a series of thoughts, decisions and responses you had to a situation in your teens. Perhaps it was with a sweetheart or a friend at that time. See how you can now view that entire dynamic as a single entity. It has become an 'object' in your awareness. To transcend is to *let go of* or *go past.* In the case of this particular event, you have *let go* of your attachment to those teenage ways of being, but you have not entirely abandoned the tools you used or what you experienced and learned. In other words, you have *included* all those experiences in that object as part of your new perspective.

P: Thank you.

MQ: To be able to think clearly about your own experience is an essential aspect of your ability to free yourself from unnecessary anguish.

Concealed Conditioning

P: What if concealed conditioning is running my spiritual quest?

MQ: If unconsciousness is plucking at the heartstrings of your freedom pursuits, needless suffering is rife and impossible to escape. Despite a mind-boggling selection of therapies and personal improvement programs, something is gravely amiss: evidence of simple ease and fulfillment. By evidence, I mean not sterile statistics, but the joy of discriminating awareness and the ability to consistently come together with other people in the absence of unnecessary conflict.

P: Otherwise, the struggles persist and the crowd just gets older, and those who were not born when I started on my quest now fill the front rows of the lecture halls in wide-eyed anticipation.

MQ: A sad state of affairs indeed.

P: Could it be worse than this?

MQ: What if the single greatest discovery you make on your quest for true happiness is the extent to which concealed conditioning has been directing that search *away from* contentment?

EVOLUTIONARY POINTER: Your path seems endlessly arduous when you are erroneously convinced that you have accessed one that leads to the end of superfluous suffering.

P: Is this why lasting happiness is so elusive?

MQ: Correct. In fact, many people who are certain that they are advancing toward liberation have yet to take their first step on a path that is not entirely constricted by individual and collective habituation. They remain lost in the pursuit of freedom, unaware that concealed conditioning is leading their quest. Without clarity on this hidden habituation and the origin of the ego-mind that sustains it, living a fully conscious life is next to impossible.

13

P: In that case, to create the conditions for my awakening, I have to first identify the life I have unknowingly constructed and am sustaining because of concealed conditioning.

MQ: Indeed. To awaken is to discover those dialogues and self-conversations, relationships and responses to life that curb the expression of your most natural Self. That's what this work is all about.

P: But, isn't every effort toward sacredness to be encouraged and celebrated?

MQ: Of course, and at every level. But, because the conceptual-mind paints a convincing picture of *the way*, you seldom question if your current path can lead to victory. These unseen influences of hereditary habituation are so forceful that a significant portion of your attention is frequently unavailable to you. When unconsciousness motives are manipulating your words and deeds, you commonly manifest fleeting states of purpose and fulfillment, interspersed with periods of great doubt and confusion. Is this your experience?

P: Yes, it often is like this.

MQ: Let this rollercoaster act as a first sign that concealed conditioning may be at work.

P: And you said that my attention is unavailable because...?

MQ: Because it is unsuspectingly consumed with supporting and defending the beliefs, lifestyles, relationships and choices of the culturally-created-self. Surpassing the covert reins of conditioning exposes your eternal motives resting just beyond those inherited agreements.

P: You mention 'hereditary habituation' and 'inherited agreements'. Are you suggesting that I unsuspectingly acquired them from past generations, just like physical attributes?

MQ: We will look at this in much greater detail in Chapter Two, but yes, because of the accumulated unconsciousness of the world into which you were born, you absorb and express conditioning just as readily as you do your dress style preferences.

It's not so bad, at least now you are beginning to wake up to this likelihood.

EVOLUTIONARY POINTER: You can't find your way until you realize your compass has been compromised — not maliciously — but without you or your ancestors' knowledge.

P: Is the awakened one is sure that *every* aspect of his life is included as his path?

MQ: Yes, every aspect and all of the time.

P: Can you summarize how he might have achieved this?

MQ: Yes. It all happened by itself with no effort whatsoever on his behalf!

P: Really?

MQ: Just kidding! That's just what the unhealthy-ego likes to think. By purposeful discipline, the awakened person has identified concealed conditioning in his words and actions. He also integrated the parts of himself he had denied – his shadow. This prepared him to see past the illusion of separation, first through meditation and contemplation, and now at all times. He knows that from an absolute point of view, we are all *One*, and from a relative point of view, we all are different, and he can truly appreciate that magnificence. He sees we are individuals who can also come together in relationships of Oneness for the sake of humanity.

P: The awakened person is aware of both perspectives: The beauty of Oneness and individual exclusivity of the fully functioning human being. And he can manifest both in this world.

MQ: Yes. He becomes a fully integrated human being.

EVOLUTIONARY POINTER: The glorious expression of your full potential is not going to be a matter of accumulating more knowledge or techniques, but of objectivity on what you *already are* – yourself and your Oneness with the Self. Then freedom emerges from where suffering once thrived.

P: Is this one reason why some folks seem to be *more aware* than others?

MQ: Yes, of course. They are more aware of who they are cognitively, emotionally and as form. They are also more aware of who they are as joy, creativity, potential and as the formless.

EVOLUTIONARY POINTER: A fully functioning human being consistently responds to life from the apex of *form* and *formless*.

P: All of this talk of perspectives and concealed conditioning reminds me of the fable[2] about an eagle who was raised by chickens and so she grew up believing she was not an eagle.

MQ: Yes, and when this mistruth was revealed to her — by another eagle — what do you think she did? Did she listen to the limitations put upon her by the average level of consciousness of the chicken culture in which she was reared? Or did she spread her wings and soar to her full potential beyond the mediocrity to which she had unknowingly succumbed?

P: I hope she had the courage to fly into her full potential.

MQ: Indeed. Understand, however, that your awakening reveals that you are born of majestic potential, and for inconsequential reasons, you may elect to stay in the safety of the 'coop'. Therefore, as you work to awaken, which voices do you habitually pay attention to?

P: But, there are so many voices!

MQ: Which is perfectly normal, so then, first ask: Who's listening?

EVOLUTIONARY POINTER: To awaken, become aware of the *context* in which your desire to soar as your full potential appears.

Consciousness

P: Is consciousness the context?

MQ: Yes, it is the 'background' in which the world of form arises. Consciousness is also the untouchable awareness of your *being*. What can you be aware of? You can be aware of your thoughts, values, emotions and of physical items – also known as the manifested state. You can also be aware of the un-manifested, or original state, from which all phenomena appear and ultimately return – your natural state of pure beingness.

P: If it's my natural state, why is it that I can't access that Presence of being whenever I want?

MQ: It's not that you're unable to access it; you can't ever get away from consciousness! But, we need to go back before the beginning of time to find the answer to your question.

Before the Beginning

P: Okay. What was there before the beginning of time?

MQ: There was only Presence of being unaware of itself. Then, about fourteen billion years ago, something came from no-thing: the big bang. This is consciousness taking shape, as thoughts, intentions, actions and material objects, which if you notice is still happening today. The big bang hasn't stopped. Then, between 4000 and 1500 BC[4], as part of the unfolding of consciousness into form, a rigid reality of images, symbols, concepts, beliefs, superstitions, heavens, hells, ghosts, goblins and gods emerged in the collective thought of human being as the conceptual-mind. And another amazing development occurred during this time. A thought-based 'self' emerged in the mind's-eye of every human. Now each person had access to a *separate sense-of-self*, which was simultaneously identified with, yet somehow separate from all of these ideas and the material universe in which it found itself. This separate sense-of-self could also think about itself and so distinguish one individual from another. The ability to make decisions, at the level of conceptual-free-will, emerged shortly afterwards. Before that there was no 'self' to make choices. Then along came 'you' and 'me'.

> EVOLUTIONARY POINTER: In a significant majority of humanity, consciousness is still lost in pantheonic polygamy.

P: So, for a long time consciousness in me has only been identified with the separate sense-of-self, the ideas and notions of the conceptual-mind and the material world.

MQ: Yes, and the various fears and desires as conditioned by your culture.

P: Is this *separate sense-of-self* what most of us refer to as 'me'?

MQ: That's correct. A person alluding to 'me' very often has mistaken who they truly are for the culturally-created-self. For instance: Look at the amazing diversity in belief systems that exist in our world today. The existence of the concept-based mind in different cultures allowed for the emergence of Buddhism, Christianity, Islam, Hinduism, Sikhism, Judaism and so on. Then, depending on where you were born, you were naturally inclined to identify with the traditions that were most popular to that geography and include that as part of your individuality.

P: Each religion has its own versions of heaven and hell. Which heaven is the right one? Which hell is the right one?

MQ: The answer to both of your questions is *all of them*. They are all equally correct at that level of development. Now, humankind has started to transcend and include the ideas of 'heaven' and 'hell' offered to us by the mythic traditions. Our full potential is only beginning to become known to us.

P: Therefore, my role as a person who is interested in recalling and stabilizing oneness with Presence is to recognize my desire to consciously evolve beyond my own individual and collective conditioning?

MQ: Yes.

The Two Sides of Narcissism

MQ: Therefore, it is best to identify and let go of the *malevolent aspect* of the ego-mind that may have you caught up in heaps of unneeded conflict.

P: Not all aspects of the ego are unhealthy?

MQ: No, not in the least. The healthy aspects of the ego are invaluable because they help us to make important distinctions and navigate this world.

EVOLUTIONARY POINTER: An unhealthy attachment to the ego causes you to be obsessed with defining yourself as *only* the separate sense-of-self.

MQ: We will be coming back to this in the second chapter, but as you can see there is a huge difference between these two aspects of the ego. The part of yourself that you seek to identify in your spiritual practice is this malevolent side of narcissism. From now on, I will primarily use the term *unhealthy-ego* to refer to the part of each one of us that is exclusively fixated on sustaining the separate sense-of-self. The unhealthy-ego accomplishes this by having you believe that you are only the separate sense-of-self, which is simply untrue. You are not *just* that. And remember, the ego does not care about how much *you* suffer because of this identity. It only cares about itself. The unhealthy-ego is a ruthless element of the conceptual-mind that is only concerned about conserving superfluous anguish and staying in charge of your life. It is important, however, that you do not deny the ego completely. To acknowledge its existence in you prevents you from become a living example of its covert manifestations. As we will see in subsequent chapters, it is only by identifying and owning its many manifestations, that you can take full responsibility for its presence in you. Then, you can use *true individuality* for your sake and also to benefit others.

P: Is the unhealthy-ego the same as what Eckhart Tolle[5] describes as the *pain-body*?

MQ: Only in some ways it is the same.

P: Is this because Tolle doesn't really distinguish between the healthy aspects of the ego-mind and its pathological aspects?

MQ: This will become clearer as we progress in our conversation, but for now, look to your own experience. If you completely disown the ego you would be unable to function as a normal person. Therefore, it is good to know there is a difference between its useful parts and the part that just feeds on suffering – the unhealthy-ego.

P: The ego has two sides to it?

MQ: Yes.

P: Then, if consciousness in me is unknowingly fixated on the separate sense-of-self, I will also be manifesting the unhealthy-ego in my life.

MQ: Exactly! Ignorance abounds whenever your attention is distracted from consciousnesses, and this always results in unnecessary emotional and psychological suffering.

The Vice-Grip on Your Spirit
P: The question is never my personal level of development or my individual beliefs?

MQ: Correct, but instead, the inherited attachments you may have unsuspectingly ascribed to and the social and cultural structures that are holding those agreements in place. This vice-grip on your consciousness can exist unnoticed from cradle to grave. It's not the things you want or do not want, have or do not have, that keep you separated from peace of mind and ease of being. The root of suffering rests with the motives for those cravings and also your attachment to the unhealthy-ego that suggests *only* its conditioned desires are valuable. And the wonderful news is that the development of your consciousness — your ability to be aware — is always up to you, whether you are currently awake to this potential or not.

P: A key part of my development therefore, is to reclaim my misplaced consciousness.

MQ: Yes. The first part is to find out how Presence in you is lost in the matrix of the unhealthy-ego and then to release that mislaid attention. Can you see now why it is so important to determine who might be leading that particular quest?

P: Yes. To know that I am headed in a wholesome direction, I need to find out who's in charge. If the unhealthy-ego is running my spiritual development, I won't get very far. And, though conceptual-free-will is phenomenally useful in this world, its scope only extends to the brink of the conditioning into which I was born, never beyond. By using *only* conceptual-free-will for the decisions about my spiritual development, I will stay stuck, so to speak!

MQ: This is true. To bring freedom from all unnecessary suffering within the scope of your decision-making process calls you to transcend and include conceptual-free-will.

P: In order that I may access conscious-free-will?

MQ: Yes.

Verifying The Way

P: I'm not sure if I am fond of the idea that I may have been unknowingly wandering under the influence of concealed conditioning all this time.

MQ: *You* don't like it or is it that the ego-mind is having trouble with this because you are seeing its authority there for the first time?

EVOLUTIONARY POINTER: What can look and feel like a path of genuine development is often a hologram of progress that is well within the confines of what the ego considers safe for its own survival.

P: How can I verify that 'my way' is not exclusively influenced by an unwitting attachment to the ideas and beliefs of the culture into which I was born?

MQ: Consider the following statements:

	YES	NO
1) I have implicit trust in myself and in the process of life.	_____	_____
2) I do not create unnecessary suffering for others or myself.	_____	_____
3) All of my important relationships are free from personal conflict.	_____	_____
4) I interact with other people in relationships free from unhealthy-ego.	_____	_____

P: I can agree with these statements except for number three.

MQ: This is not unusual. Your disagreement — a 'no' response — to one or more of these statements may suggest that you are unsuspectingly sidestepping your full potential. A 'no' reveals that because of concealed conditioning you are still operating, at least in some aspects of your life, at the level of conceptual-free-will.

EVOLUTIONARY POINTER: The path that leads to the end of all unnecessary emotional and psychological struggling is not just a matter of *belief*. Verification is vital.

MQ: On the other hand, your full agreement — a 'yes' response — to each one of these statements, indicates that you are using conscious-free-will to create a victorious course. Curiously, in the timeless moment of choosing your responses, it is possible, regardless of your prevailing life situations, your current opinions and beliefs, or the views of other people, to honestly respond with a 'yes' as a reflection of your genuine aspirations. You can awaken now by answering all four statements positively. How simple is that? And of course you can confirm your four positive answers by the ways in which you respond to life situations as they are presented to you.

P: That would be walking my talk for sure!

Relationships Free From Personal Conflict

P: I am having difficulty grasping that my most important relationships are to be free from personal conflict so that I may verify the potential of my chosen path.

MQ: Start by asking this: Would you choose a life in which all of your relationships were free from bickering and arguments, or one with various degrees of strife in that aspect of your life?

P: But, long-term committed relationships totally free from personal conflict... that's impossible. I don't even see that I have a choice in this matter.

MQ: You always do. But, perhaps that opinion is a reflection of ego-identity? To understand how long-term relationships can be free from personal disagreements you can first become clear that *that is what you want*, regardless of whether you think it is possible. Is that what you want?

P: Yes!

MQ: Great!

EVOLUTIONARY POINTER: Let your awakening begin with the genuine aspiration to awaken.

MQ: In a 2008 radio interview with spiritual teacher Eckhart Tolle, Krista Tippett of American Public Media asked him if there is *"a sign or a symptom of a true shift in consciousness"*. Tolle replied, *"A very good yardstick or criterion is, for example, your relationships with other human beings; do they become more peaceful, do they become free from conflict, are you still contributing to the conflict, or does conflict dissolve in your presence?"*

EVOLUTIONARY POINTER: Holding on to suffering never makes its final release any more exhilarating.

Peter and Rebecca's Story:

Peter and his wife Rebecca taught others how to sustain long-term relationships that were both emotionally rich and completely free from personal conflict. They had worked hard to nurture this amazing development in themselves during their 22 years of marriage. While teaching at a week-long couples' seminar, Peter and Rebecca were introduced to a well-known spiritual teacher, Oji and his wife Patrice, who happened to be teaching a course on psychic abilities at the same center. When Oji and Patrice initially heard about Peter's and Rebecca's work, neither of them could conceive the possibility of intimate relationships that were simultaneously free of personal conflict and also emotionally spicy. Then Peter asked the couple if they had a choice between a life of such relationships and a life in which struggle was common in this area, which one they might pick. Oji said that his preference would surely be the absence of personal conflict. In his wife's opinion, however, personal conflict in relationships was normal and acceptable, and the presence of such anguish was certainly no indication of the level of the consciousness of the partners. Then Oji asked his wife if she might indulge him in exploring this new potential he had just awoken to. When Patrice did not respond, Oji said softly, "I think this would be great for us to try, don't you?" Still she ignored him, so a little later he added with great care, "You know, my dear, I can't possibly do this without you." Patrice then turned to face her husband and in a somewhat irritated tone, replied, "Why are you always trying to blame me for not wanting to take our relationship to the next level?"

P: It is clear to me that Patrice is denying even the possibility that their relationship could be free from struggling and anguish. The unhealthy-ego is enjoying those battles.

EVOLUTIONARY POINTER: The absence of personal conflict in significant relationships is a reality for many people. What part of you might want you to believe it is only a dream?

Convenient and Awakened Decentering

MQ: As you work toward becoming a fully functioning human being[6], there are two distinct phases of transcending the limiting patterns of conditioning. The first is *convenient decentering* and the second is *awakened decentering*.

P: What's the difference?

MQ: Well, let me start by saying that the leading role of the unhealthy-ego in your spiritual search ends when you progress from the first to the second phase. The reason for this is clear:

25

EVOLUTIONARY POINTER: By only wanting to be free from unnecessary emotional and psychological suffering, your wanting eventually becomes an impenetrable obstruction to awakening.

P: Wanting is not enough?

MQ: Wanting to be free is essential, of course, and it is by using ego-based desires that you first get started with your spiritual development. Wanting to be free from this level however, is only the beginning and if you are not careful, you may just get stuck there – in the wanting that is manifested solely by conceptual-free-will.

P: If wanting eventually becomes an obstacle to my development, do I have to accept that a certain amount of suffering is going to be necessary so that I may progress?

MQ: In a way, yes. But not without first gaining a certain degree of objectivity on the root cause of the suffering you wish to accept. You have to be careful here because the unhealthy-ego needs suffering to survive. It wants you to ambivalently accept it *all*. In this way you don't threaten its dominion over your destiny. And as you can see, there is not much point in accepting *what is,* and at the same time blindly continuing to create additional unnecessary anguish for yourself and other people.

P: Again, it's all about distinguishing the voice of the unhealthy-ego in myself.

MQ: Yes, and now to get back to your first question. The difference between these two stages of letting go of concealed condi-tioning is subtle, yet critical. The *convenient decentering* of ego-identity describes the work you do when you first feel the desire to be free. This craving to be free generally means that you make a certain amount of changes for the sake of your peace of mind. These developments may be reflected in feelings of happiness, satisfaction and relief. Nevertheless, the convenient decentering of unhealthy-ego cannot conclude all superfluous conflict and confusion. This is because these activities are based on the motives of the conditioned mind itself, which you are continually enacting with the use of conceptual-free-will.

EVOLUTIONARY POINTER: Convenient decentering describes the unhealthy-ego's endless pilgrimage of self-empowerment workshops. The work is convenient for the unhealthy-ego because its domination of your destiny is never challenged.

P: Therefore, convenient decentering rarely leads to the liberated life.

MQ: Correct. This is because *wanting* to live authentically means that you simultaneously have to deny certain actions and reactions that keep those thoughts of wanting alive. Convenient decentering can certainly comprise the early stages of your search, of your questions, of your suspicion that there is something more than just a lost and lonely separate-self in a vast ocean of meaninglessness. Convenient decentering is pretty important because it propels you toward something higher. You must then be willing and able to surrender your attachment to that level of development and also to conceptual-mind, at least temporarily.

In other words, it is only when you let go of all beliefs of how the *start* of a truly awakened life should look, that you can see your true face.

P: Conceptual-free-will drives me at the outset of my quest, but I have to transcend and include it in order to go on to the next level of development.

MQ: Yes. 'You are *here*, awakening is *there*'. That's how the unhealthy-ego always sees it.

27

> EVOLUTIONARY POINTER: Spirit is you – with or without your thoughts of wanting.

MQ: Even profound spiritual experiences that stun the conditioned trance into short-term submission are frequently incapable of stabilizing you on a path of authenticity and transparency.

P: What is transparency?

MQ: It means that the motives and intentions for your relatedness are perfectly clear and visible to the people with whom you are interacting. The forcefulness of the unhealthy-ego swiftly recovers from such encounters, often before you have interpreted them correctly.

P: Correctly?

MQ: To interpret means to *bring out meaning in action*. To correctly interpret a glimpse into your own unfathomable nature is to subsequently adopt new values and intentions for living, ones that can liberate you from your oneness with the conceptual-mind. Mostly what happens after a spiritual experience is that hidden habituation quickly clambers back into the driver's seat and begins to refute your full potential, even though it was perhaps radiantly revealed. If you are wondering why the promise of peace and purpose that once motivated your search may now seem impossible to stabilize, here is the reason:

> EVOLUTIONARY POINTER: Your awakening cannot unfold, even when you have the best intentions, when concealed conditioning is your silent partner.

P: And awakened decentering is...?

MQ: The work you do to let go of individual and collective conditioning and your attachment to the ego, but as a *free person*! We will be coming back to this by the end of the second chapter, so please be patient.

The ego's Dharma[7]

P: There is no doubt that traditional self-development practices and the convenient decentering of the unhealthy-ego help us improve our relationships and upgrade our careers and addresses.

MQ: True indeed. Yet, after a thirty-year quest for inner peace you may wonder why the only obvious changes are the cosmetic ones. Deep-seated issues often remain unresolved, such as: What is my purpose? Why do I suffer? How can I express my potential together with other people?

P: Why, after billions of dollars spent to awaken, have so few done so?

EVOLUTIONARY POINTER: The vast majority of the available self-help programs are based on the feeble motives of the unhealthy-ego; therefore, they are fundamentally objective-less.

MQ: Self-help that is designed and developed by the unhealthy-ego is circular and ultimately useless, except in keeping the insanity of unnecessary suffering alive.

P: I am having a vision now of a 'chicken coop' conference offering a high-priced motivational lecture on the secrets of long-distance flight. Seems silly, right?

MQ: Well, yes and no. At that level of development such training might be necessary. How else is the student going to learn that the secrets this slick seminar leader is selling are a ruse? The student only realizes this after he tries on this new theory by exploring it in his own life. When he realizes he still can't 'fly', he may then suspect the instructor can't either.

EVOLUTIONARY POINTER: The development of the unhealthy-ego by the unhealthy-ego does not change the future. It only causes *you* and those around you to suffer today.

P: So, teachers who are unknowingly infected with unhealthy-ego are going to bring more suffering to their students?

MQ: Yes. The developmental plans of the unhealthy-ego cannot awaken you because these requests for transformation are already locked into conditioned safety zones of limitation, compromise, and mediocrity. The spiritual marketplace is replete with guides and gurus who thrive on the inquisitive nature of those who suffer so unnecessarily. When the unhealthy-ego is coaching itself in you, it always gives safe guidance to predictable outcomes, frequently using feelings and the attainment of personal goals as the primary gauges of progress.

EVOLUTIONARY POINTER: A prerequisite to getting off the treadmill of the unhealthy-ego's dharma is first recognizing how fast you are running.

P: Thanks! The unhealthy-ego-mind has little or no interest in my awakening.

MQ: None whatsoever. And rightly so, for the malevolent ego knows that freedom serves ease of being, joy and humanity – but *not* the ego. To preserve itself, the unhealthy-ego offers you the comfortable illusion of progress toward your awakening instead. Then to nourish this goal-less fantasy, concealed conditioning provides countless resources so that you may hone your skills in relationships, finances and family, in meditation, manifesting your dreams and in healing destructive habits. The unhealthy-ego then labels all of these activities as part of *your conscious path.*

P: Therefore, the lesser-self cleverly avoids detection when I am convinced that I am *already centered on* an authentic path, by persuading me that activities motivated by *its* cravings and aversions are an integral part of my spiritual development.

EVOLUTIONARY POINTER: It is possible that a significant portion of your efforts toward self-emancipation are directed and curtailed by concealed conditioning for its own benefit, not *yours!*

MQ: There's a popular New Age magazine that recently stated: *"You could spend your whole life going from one spiritual workshop, diet, or fitness or program to another without ever realizing that the whole enterprise is based not so much on self-improvement as on self-loathing. The guru culture of self-loathing will persist until the wisdom of the ages is passed to the reader not only with the promise of light and love, but with the tools and the evolutionary call to awaken to selfless responsibility and dignity."*[8]

P: *The Uncommon Path* suggests a set of practical tools with which I can respond to that *evolutionary call?*

MQ: Absolutely! And responding to the evolutionary call reveals that what is commonly referred to as conscious self-development can be nothing more than a kaleidoscope of metaphysical distractions, orchestrated by concealed conditioning to keep you well clear of an authentic path.

Determining Your Interest

MQ: Your interest in awakening is a precious commodity. Protect and nurture it because curiosity can easily transmute to cynicism. Shield it from the voices of the skeptics.

EVOLUTIONARY POINTER: Consistent interest can awaken you to the process of life beyond the hidden orchestrations of the ego-identity. Never renounce that possibility.

MQ: The success of any journey depends on the leader of the expedition, the maps you are following, and the consciousness of the mapmaker. The degree to which you expand your perspective beyond inherited limitations depends upon how inquisitive you are about that possibility. Therefore, it is important for you to determine if your interest in awakening is genuine, and not just another deception of your attachment to an ego-identity.

P: How do I differentiate authentic curiosity from a pointless ego-based charade?

MQ: Look at this question:

EVOLUTIONARY POINTER: If freedom from all unnecessary emotional and psychological suffering called for the alteration of almost every aspect of your current lifestyle, and the basis for the majority of your important relationships, would you be eager to make these changes?

P: In other words, how excited am I to identify and let go of all unnecessary emotional and psychological suffering?

MQ: That's it! How interested are you? To an awakened person, this question would reveal just how lost they once were in the maze of individual and collective conditioning, without even knowing they were lost! Look now to your own response to this question. Does it include a sense of excitement or a glow of anticipation – no matter how muted or subdued?

P: It does, but it is only a glimmer.

MQ: No matter how slight, you can know that this interest is indisputably genuine.

P: And what if concealed conditioning is influencing my response to this question?

MQ: If that were the case, you would likely refute the need for such radical transformations. The reason for this is that the unhealthy-ego would like you to believe that it can get you to enlightenment by its process of convenient decentering: A nip here, a tuck there; certainly nothing too drastic.

EVOLUTIONARY POINTER: The unhealthy-ego makes personal development seem plausible, but depicts evolutionary transformation as daunting and unattainable; and maybe even unnecessary.

P: This brings into question the entire basis for my interest in spiritual development.

MQ: That's the point, right? If the foundation for your interest in spiritual development is not to fully awaken to the unhealthy-ego's role in your life, then what is it? Remember, the malignant ego will have you wait forever to get started, or it will have you start and stop, start and stop. The logic of concealed conditioning always insists that you maintain a clear line between your *real* life and your *spiritual* life.

P: And this sustains an even wider gap between reality and potential.

MQ: Yes, and this gap is a no man's land of hesitation, procrastination and sadness, in which liberation does not exist. While you do your best, work on yourself, think happy thoughts, perform good deeds, and mean well, you may still be missing what it is to be truly alive.

Missy's Story: Missy was married, had a son in college and she had recently survived breast cancer. She was well loved by all her friends and she had a deep interest in self-development and personal enlightenment. Despite years of seeking, she often had trouble living the joy of the great teachings to which she had been exposed. As she explained this quandary at an event with a well-known spiritual teacher, Missy described herself as having great clarity on her "conscious spiritual journey." The teacher said to her, "Please describe an average week in your life." Missy happily recounted a busy schedule which included: riding and taking care of her two horses, socializing with her friends, keeping a nice home, preparing food for her son, working with a personal trainer and a motivational coach, and volunteering one night a week at the local YMCA. She also said that she liked to read, attend a yoga class, and meditate when time permitted. The teacher asked what she liked to read. Missy replied, "Self-help and spirituality books, *Cosmopolitan* magazine and romance novels". The teacher paused for a moment, and then replied, "Of all these activities, which ones do you think most clearly represent your conscious spiritual journey?" Missy quickly responded with great conviction, "All of them." The teacher then asked her, "If you were to replace the existing top-two most time consuming aspects of your current spiritual path – so that you may create more time to, perhaps, focus on a regular discipline of meditation – which two activities might they be?" Missy thought for a moment. In a most pragmatic tone she answered, "Since I spend most of my time either with my horses or socializing with my friends, I would say those are the two most important parts of my conscious spiritual journey. Are there not many paths to God?" "Absolutely," the teacher continued, "by looking at the evolution of consciousness in humankind as a ladder, it becomes clear that the 'top rung' is always evolving. Reading from the bottom up, this hierarchy of paths currently looks something like this," pointing to a list[10] that was displayed on a screen behind him.

- Integral Spirituality, Collective Individualism.
- Evolutionary Enlightenment, Natural Hierarchies.
- Personal Enlightenment and the 'Now'.
- Human Equality, Human Rights, Pluralism, Relativism.
- Global Economy, Scientific Rationalism, Materialism.
- Nations, Mythic Gods, Authoritarian, Fundamentalist Religions.
- Tribal Order, Magic, Superstition, Great Mother, Great Goddess.
- Pre-Egoic, Survival Groups, Questing for Food, Water and Shelter.

"As you can see, Missy, there are many paths as God. This means that some paths are more evolved than others, which doesn't make one right and another wrong, just different." "Where are you, with your socializing and your horses on this hierarchy?" As Missy pondered her place she said in a surprised tone, "Well, it seems that I thought I had reached the pinnacle of my development, but perhaps I am living from about the mid-point of my full potential."

MQ: Each step is necessary for that level of development. But, when the unhealthy-ego is in control of your evolution, events and activities that have much more to do with personal affirmation, comfort and security appear as integral aspects of a conscious spiritual journey. You will discover, as our conversation progresses, that such concepts and notions solely comprise the reverent path of the culturally-created-self, not the uncommon path of the *Real You*. These concepts and notions of the unhealthy-ego only ensure that your most profound aspects remain neatly tucked away.

In that same radio interview with Tolle we spoke of earlier, the NPR interviewer also said, *"Someone might imagine they are very spiritual and yet still very preoccupied with themselves,"* to which Tolle answered, *"Yes"*. Missy's story introduces us to the first tenet of the unhealthy-ego's dharma: *Everything I do is part of my spiritual path.* A significant majority of your actions *can become* truly spiritual, of course, but only when you are certain that the malicious ego-mind is not the warden of your will.

P: Therefore, it is by identifying how the ego's dharma has been concealed in my awareness that I can access my conscious-free-will so that I may transcend those misguided signposts to freedom.

MQ: Yes.

P: Therefore, it's not enough to just believe that I am a spiritual being having a human experience?

MQ: No. It's only a great place to start. Lacking the evidence for Presence, however, might also mean that you are a little lost like Missy.

P: The greatest evidence of Presence is the ability to come together with other people in the absence of personal conflict.

MQ: Yes.

We are not absolved of confirmation for authenticity and transparency by the mere presence of conviction.

1   Francois de La Rochefoucauld (1613–1680).

2   A story by author Jamie Glenn.

3   According to many great scientists, such as Lemaitre, Einstein and Hubble.

4   Ken Wilber: *The Atman Project*, Quest Books, 1980 and *Up From Eden*, Quest Books, 1996.

5   *The Power of Now* by Eckhart Tolle, New World Library, 1999.

6   From the Big Mind/Big Heart Process by Dennis Genpo Roshi.

7   Dharma – from Buddhism means the cosmic law underlying all of life.

8   From Marketdata Enterprises Inc, February, 2004 – "Excerpted from a popular new age magazine".

9   http://speakingoffaith.publicradio.org/programs/tolle/

10   List is derived from Spiral Dynamics – Graves/Beck and from Integral Theory – Wilber.

Chapter 1

AN OVERVIEW OF
THE FOUR INSIGHTS

"Few things are impracticable in themselves;
and it is for want of application, rather than of means, that men
fail to succeed."[1]

The Four Insights of Awakening Conscious-Free-Will

MQ: The Four Insights awaken *conscious-free-will* by helping you identify the ways in which conditioning has concealed itself in your life. They also allow you to consciously direct your intention to awaken, to experience completion within, and subsequently to engage with others in awakened relationships as a fully functioning human being. The Four Insights are the tools of transformation:

1) Renounce Conditioned Motives
2) Reclaim Your Consciousness
3) Recall Your Origin of Oneness
4) Relate as Your Full Potential

P: The co-creation of a glorious tomorrow becomes possible when the formations in my consciousness are capable of constructing more than just a wretched yesterday?

MQ: Yes. Let's start with this quote:

"It is now some years since I detected how many were the false beliefs that I had from my earliest youth admitted as true, and how doubtful was everything I had since constructed on this basis; and from that time

I was convinced that I must once and for all seriously undertake to rid myself of all the opinions which I had formerly accepted, and commence to build anew from the foundation, if I wanted to establish any firm and permanent structure..."[2]

MQ: The opinions you have accepted may be very different from those of René Descartes in the quote above.

P: This is true.

MQ: But, beyond the particulars of those ideas, freedom rests in identifying the mechanism of acceptance. To rid yourself of *false beliefs* is also to see that the *permanent structures* upon which you can *build anew* already exist in consciousness. Imagine a high mountain range that has no trails at all. The first few people who traversed those peaks experienced great difficulty. But, when the paths are well-trodden, the going is much easier. In the same way, there are structures already existing in consciousness that you can include in your perspective, so that you, too, may live an awakened life. Just adapt the ways that are already in existence and apply them to your life situations.

P: It is by recognizing these preexisting *permanent structures* in consciousness that my own awakening can be realized and expressed?

MQ: Exactly. The Four Insights reveal those preexisting *permanent structures* in consciousness upon which you can confidently construct an awakened experience from amongst your own life experiences and situations.

P: I can do this regardless of my current level of development?

MQ: Yes. You can complement and supplement your current perspectives. Let's look at the insights, now, one by one. The First Insight helps you identify the hidden motives of the unhealthy-ego as part of your broadening perspective. The First Insight is designed to bring concealed conditioning into the light of awareness where it cannot survive. This takes care of the past. The Second Insight provides you with the means to reclaim your consciousness from habituation in the future.

P: Therefore, by recognizing conditioning today, I can mitigate its appearances tomorrow.

MQ: Without this essential practice of reclaiming consciousness, your finest attempts to awaken are continually overpowered by the values and intentions of the culturally-created-self, thereby ensuring the reappearance of painful symptoms.

EVOLUTIONARY POINTER: Eckhart Tolle said that reclaiming our consciousness is *"one of the most essential tasks on the spiritual journey."*[3]

MQ: The assessments and exercises contained in the First and Second Insights demonstrate how everyday life situations, deemed to be irrelevant to your awakening are, in fact, quite critical. The first two Insights bring the influences of individual and collective conditioning to your attention. This, however, is only one half of the task of awakening. The other half is to offer your consent to transcend and include these hidden influences in your new perspective. Therefore, the exercises and their related chapters are purposely placed toward the latter part of the book. This will allow for both subtle and profound leaps in your awareness, before you begin to apply the Insights in your particular life circumstances. Integrating these developments in your life delivers to you the *"self-knowledge of the unconscious motivations of behavior"*[4]. Your awakening, for the sake of humanity, begins there.

P: And then I can come together with other people to consciously co-create the future as an expression of acting beyond the hidden motives of the unhealthy-ego.

MQ: Yes, you can. Small networks of such highly conscious individuals are now just forming in our world. When the time is right, you may become one of those brave pioneers if you wish.

The Dalai Lama's Shoes

MQ: But, before we get too excited about the imminent appearance of a courageous life, it is good to know that the development of your awareness, beyond an initial effortless growth phase, is entirely volitional. Let me explain. According to Ken Wilber, American philosopher and author of over 25 books, each person's *stage of development* at birth is identical – zero. Their *state of consciousness*, however, may vary greatly. A Dalai Lama at birth may possess a higher consciousness than average, but he still has to grow through similar stages of development just like the rest of us.

P: They too, had to learn to read, write, and tie their shoes.

MQ: For sure. And the internationally acclaimed author, David R Hawkins, PhD explains that the average person hardly ever develops past the most common level of awareness of the culture into which they were born[5]. And if they do, it can be relatively insignificant.

P: But, in our early years, we will naturally evolve through many stages of growth?

MQ: Yes.

EVOLUTIONARY POINTER: The natural development of our awareness peaks and stops in our second decade at about the average level of the culture into which we were born.

P: Are you saying that the development of our awareness stalls out in our early to mid-twenties?

MQ: Yes, for some unknown reason that's what happens. Just look to your own experience. Then, later in life, especially if we have sufficiently tasted the pangs and sorrows of the human experience, the development of our consciousness may start up again. But this could be thirty or forty years later.

P: And, in the meantime?

MQ: Well, since you are mostly identified with the separate sense-of-self, you unknowingly obsess over the endless cravings of the unhealthy-ego as well as trying to fulfill the demands of society and culture. All of this activity adds to the grand distraction from Oneness and the expression of my potential. These mid-life years can also be a time of much unnecessary struggling.

P: And, after all of this, while I may have sixty or seventy years of life experiences, I still view reality from a twenty–three-year-old's perspective?

MQ: Yes. In light of that possibility, the Four Insights offer you solace, should it be your wish to make great leaps in both your *states of consciousness* and in *stages of development* – regardless of your personal history or current age. These disciplines offer you an avenue to the expression of awakened potential and even the possibility of mastering the double-knot!

P: The enlightened master never trips over his own bootlaces?

MQ: Well, only if he has rooted out all of his shadow! But, let's come back to that later.

The First Insight – Renounce Conditioned Motives

MQ: The First Insight points toward conditioning that has concealed itself in the motives of everyday situations. As I mentioned earlier, a significant number of these circumstances are frequently overlooked as being relevant to your awakening. Because of this oversight, many actions and reactions are exclusively compelled by the unhealthy-ego. This, of course, is detrimental to an outcome of clarity and contentment. Yet, curiously, many of these drives are related to seeking ease of being and also peace in your relationships.

EVOLUTIONARY POINTER: If you are not aware that the unhealthy-ego is supporting your reasons for acting, you will never be able to escape its influence.

MQ: The assessments in the First Insight are based on Ken Wilber's *Four Quadrants*[6], which he developed during thirty years of work with Integral Theory:

1) **Subjective**: Inside me/Inside the 'I' – *Thoughts, emotions, feelings, sensations, concepts, values, prayer, contemplation, meditation and introspection.*

2) **Inter-Subjective**: Inside Us/Inside the 'We' – *Relationships, Belief Systems* and *Culture.*

3) **Objective**: The outside of 'I'– *Body, Energy, Health, Medicine and the Sciences*

4) **Inter-Objective**: Interacting with social structures – *Economics, Environment,* and *Social Systems.*

MQ: Each of these four assessments contain individual statements. While by no means comprehensive, these statements are sufficiently inclusive for you to discern the occurrence of covert conditioning in your beliefs, words, actions and relationships. Each conditioned situation that you uncover, no matter how minor, stands in stark contrast to your attempts to stop struggling with the mind and also with the consequences of the past. According to the Buddha, liberation is the end of karma. The First Insight makes this big claim: *It is the beginning of the end of karma.* Because many of your responses to life are unsuspectingly based on conditioned motives, you are constantly creating both "good" and "bad" karma, as opposed to simply acting without creating *any* karma. And, don't worry, we'll look at karma in Chapter Six.

P: I am recreating the 'wheel of suffering' without even knowing it. Therefore, the purpose of the statements contained within the First Insight is not to search for the causes or meanings of the unhealthy-ego-motivated situations?

MQ: That is true, though let's not deny their significance. Instead, we will shift the focus from restriction to transcendence. When you clearly identify that the unhealthy-ego has a vested interest in your destiny, you are given an opportunity to let go of that limitation. When you apply the First Insight to your life, your perspective will broaden – from identification to objectivity and from restriction to transcendence.

EVOLUTIONARY POINTER: When you renounce previously hidden motives of the unhealthy-ego, you will end the painful consequences of those situations. A powerful momentum is created through this process, and those impelled by the voice of genuine aspiration are unstoppable.

P: The First Insight lets me see if I am unsuspectingly acting on the half-baked wisdom I inherited from a world that is clearly not at ease.

MQ: Yes, those suggestions that also sustain the un-awakened state of endless spiritual seeking.

P: Is it possible that even those who deem themselves *spiritually advanced* may be completely unaware of acquired ego-drives functioning in both their worldly and ethereal pursuits?

MQ: That's entirely possible. And, your question introduces another tenet of the ego's dharma: *If I think I am a spiritual person, it must be true.*

P: This explains why I seem to endure unpredictable cycles of confusion and doubt. The unhealthy-ego is manipulating my purpose and simultaneously draining my awareness without my knowledge. And thus, it keeps me focused on sustaining the optimal conditions for *its* survival — unnecessary suffering — even amongst my 'more' spiritual relationships.

MQ: Petty politics and personal conflict, even in the sangha[7], are all based on concealed conditioning.

EVOLUTIONARY POINTER: The motives of the unhealthy-ego promote responses and reactions to life that are psychologically, emotionally, physically and spiritually draining.

MQ: When the true force of inherited motives is clouded in complexity, you will consistently create a future that looks and feels much like your past. As you gain more and more clarity on the unhealthy-ego, you can begin to move beyond its urges by disregarding the thoughts that support those patterns.

P: But, shouldn't it be more about noticing, accepting, and then *changing the pattern* of my thoughts?

MQ: The ego's dharma professes that you should try to change the patterns of your thoughts. Following this naïve instruction ensures a constant struggle with the mind. This, as you will see in the fifth chapter, is the trap that sustains unneeded psychological suffering, and the favorite food of the unhealthy-ego.

EVOLUTIONARY POINTER: Joy lies in your journeying, but only when your motives for that adventure are not inherited from those who are still unknowingly adrift in an ocean of endless confusion.

P: Okay. So, does that mean that I am not going to engage with people who are lost in conditioned and limited patterns and conversations?

MQ: Of course you are going to engage with such people, but now you will do so with full awareness.

P: It's a much different matter to be communicating with the unhealthy-ego and knowing that is what you are doing, as opposed to speaking and listening *as* the unhealthy-ego.

MQ: It is like night and day. You will then act and respond when appropriate, in the right measure, and with the right reason. The good news about disregarding thoughts is that you are *already* an expert at this! You disregard irrelevant thoughts all the time without even knowing it. This natural skill can be applied to the unhealthy-ego's demands with great precision; but only after you know *exactly* what is to be disregarded.

P: Then, as I develop my ability to disregard thoughts, it will take me one or two seconds to recognize those thoughts, that if acted upon, will be conducive to awakened living.

MQ: And the rest can be disregarded confidently.

EVOLUTIONARY POINTER: As you identify and disregard conditioned patterns of cognition, your awakening blossoms and the unhealthy-ego loosens its grip and retreats to an easier prey.

MQ: We will be coming back to this topic of disregarding thought in Chapter Five.

The Second Insight – Reclaim Your Consciousness

MQ: The Second Insight helps you uncover concealed conditioning in your values. Your values are core psychological structures by which you make decisions. Consequently, your values, and the way in which they are arranged, greatly influence your future; therefore, they also have a profound impact on the world around you and on the future of humanity. The Second Insight also reveals a fascinating relationship between values, intentions and destiny. The root of the word *intention* is *to lean forward*; it is the picture you hold in your mind of the many possible outcomes of an action you are about to take. *Intention* is the aim or anticipated outcome of an action you are considering. Your intention is the future un-manifested, where creativity meets probability. Your values guide your intentions to fruition. Therefore, if you have an objective to awaken, it will be most effective when guided by a supportive values structure. But, very often, the way in which you are conditioned to arrange your values, is wholly contrary to such a wonderful intention. If you try to set forth your intentions to live with courage and authenticity based on an inherited arrangement of your values, those objectives will recurrently flounder on the rocks of self-deceit and denial.

EVOLUTIONARY POINTER: The liberated life is the outcome of your intention to *not just be* an automatic expression of the unhealthy-ego.

P: If I want to awaken to Presence, autonomy and communion, then it is unwise to navigate by a decision-making process given to me by a world that shows little evidence of that goal.

MQ: Correct! Though you always mean well, inherited values and the way in which they have been arranged for you are incapable of supporting your purest aims to awaken.

P: Inherited value spheres are arranged to support conceptual-free-will. This arrangement of my values simply doesn't allow me to access conscious-free-will.

MQ: This is true. You can't awaken by just using conceptual-free-will. The goal, therefore, of the Second Insight is to liberate you from the effects of *hand-me-down* decision-making methods. With the help of a ten-part exercise, which will be outlined in the tenth chapter, you will examine your life situations to find out what is important to you; what you truly *value*. In doing so, you will realize the values you use when making major decisions. This discovery also allows you to see if these essential guiding principles have been set according to the limits of individual and collective standards. Fortified with this clarity, you can then align your existing values with your intention to live an awakened life. When the arrangement of your values is capable of guiding your pure intention to awaken, that *is* the outcome.

P: What are some ways to know if concealed conditioning is manipulating my values and value structures, hence limiting my ability to access conscious-free-will?

MQ: If you answer 'yes' to any of the following questions, it is likely that the unhealthy-ego has somehow infiltrated the arrangement of your values:

1) Do you experience unreasonable fear and anxiety when faced with big decisions?
2) Are your priorities continually shifting, despite your best efforts to focus?
3) Do you change your mind about important choices you made in the past?
4) Do you often regret the choices you made?
5) Do you put off major decisions until the last minute?
6) Do you seem to poll your peers to see what they think about your options?
7) Do you look for the options that may provide the most predictable outcomes?
8) In decision-making, do you seek the most emotionally rewarding results?
9) Do you sometimes feel as if you have too many choices?
10) Do you feel as if you have no choices at all?
11) Do you have great intentions, yet seem to be in a cycle of the same old habits and patterns?
12) Are you surrounded by a majority of people who constantly change their minds?

P: The Second Insight shows me how my values may have been arranged by the ego to suit *its* ends – and not *mine*? It also reveals how it is possible that 'my' values have been crafted by the ego to support conceptual-free-will and to destroy the power of conscious-free-will?

MQ: That's it. And this takes us to the core of conceptual-free-will. When your values are selected and organized according to the needs of the culturally-created-self, they will certainly be capable of creating a moderate or even a successful material life, and yet, they are hopelessly inadequate in supporting an awakening.

P: The Second Insight stabilizes the conditions for awakening by diluting the grip the unhealthy-ego has on my choice-making process.

MQ: Yes. The Second Insight helps you to transcend and include conceptual-free-will as part of a new decision-making process. It does this by allowing you to align your *existing* values with your desire to evolve so that you can access conscious-free-will. Now, you are capable of making important decisions based not on the conditioned restrictions of conceptual-free-will, but on the liberated potential of conscious-free-will.

EVOLUTIONARY POINTER: When the arrangement of your values supports the clarity of your intention to awaken, you will reclaim consciousness that would otherwise be dissipated in struggling with conditioned consequences in the future.

MQ: Subsequently, a newfound clarity emerges on previously veiled opportunities to consciously co-create the future.

P: Together with other people?

MQ: Yes. Making *awakened choices* becomes possible when our attention is no longer consumed by the unhealthy-ego at the very moment of that decision, toward a value structure that supports an intention to be free. Therefore, by transcending and including the unhealthy-ego, we also displace it as the primary director of our destiny.

EVOLUTIONARY POINTER: By generating, identifying and responding to awakened choices, the possibility of awakened living becomes a reality.

MQ: It is possible, too, that you will realize that up to this point in your life, the outcomes of all your major decisions could never have reached beyond the boundaries of conceptual-free-will. Therefore, be humble and be gentle with yourself as you work with the Second Insight.

EVOLUTIONARY POINTER: Conceptual-free-will masquerad-ing as conscious-free-will cannot release you from the plight of the past, no matter how hard you try.

MQ: Discovering that perhaps the unhealthy-ego has imprisoned your values also uncovers this tenet of the ego's dharma: *I freely choose my own experiences.* The secret is that you don't know that those choices have always been limited by conceptual-free-will.

P: I see what you mean. I choose my own experiences, which of course are locked within the perimeters of conceptual-free-will.

EVOLUTIONARY POINTER: When you are unaware of your exclusive identification with the ego and you say 'my free will', you are generally referring to ego-based *conceptual-free-will.*

MQ: To support the limitations of conceptual-free-will, conditioning segregates values into distinct and concurrent groups related to various *life domains* such as: Career, Home, Family, Relationships,

Source of Income, Spiritual Seeking, Hobbies and so on. Because you are generally unaware of this arrangement, the use of multiple sets of values to guide your choices, within and between each of your life domains, is considered to be normal. For instance, a working mother has different sets of values associated with her spouse, her extended family, her career and her children. Not only does each value sphere have its own agenda, but each group also is presided over by its own primary value. Because of these multiple primary values, important decisions are difficult to make and harder still to stand by. Can you see the conflict that can arise at the times of making important life decisions?

P: Yes, indeed.

EVOLUTIONARY POINTER: The Second Insight reveals that you have been conditioned to create multiple sets or groups of values to guide your decision-making process.

MQ: Therefore, conflict arises not only before but also after major choices. In this way the unhealthy-ego can orchestrate and prolong unneeded disharmony and reinforce existing conditioned perspectives. When multiple and divergent values are directing and supporting your quest for contentment, the search never ends.

P: Is this why my future mostly mirrors my past? Despite a new job or relationship, overcoming an addiction, a spurt of creativity, a new spiritual teaching or technique, I cannot awaken to potential, let alone prolong, authenticity and unity in my life and relationships.

MQ: You've hit the nail on the head.

EVOLUTIONARY POINTER: Values arranged by the unhealthy-ego lead you in circles.

P: Is the ego's dharma all about going around and around?

MQ: Pretty much. As in spending forty or fifty years hoping that someday you will awaken, while making choices according to concealed conditioning. Clarity of values reveals that many who consider themselves followers of a conscious path spend significantly more time following the unhealthy-ego instead. What the culturally-created-self refers to as a 'balanced life' is often one of grave compromise, denial and suffering. And, if things don't go your way, you can always *change your mind!*

EVOLUTIONARY POINTER: 'Changing your mind' is the unhealthy-ego's way of giving you the illusion that you are in control of your destiny.

P: Do you mean that the conditioned mind's version of balance leans heavily toward its own self-preservation?

MQ: Heavily? It is entirely slanted that way. Recall the first tenet of the ego's dharma from our story of Missy in the previous chapter: *Everything I do is part of my spiritual path.* All of our activities can most certainly be part of your spiritual path; yet, when the unhealthy-ego is impinging on your values, that is rarely the case.

The Second Insight reveals how the life of an awakened person is centered on a single hierarchy of values. The primary value of this single hierarchy is identifiable, consistent, and applied *first* to all major decisions, before the other values. The remaining — or non-primary — values will vary in their hierarchical positions according to details of each decision, but the conscious primary value always comes first. As we will see in the full chapter on The Second Insight later in the book, these non-primary values can include *money, learning, entertainment, travel* and so on.

EVOLUTIONARY POINTER: An awakened person's single hierarchy of values contains a primary competent value, which completely reflects and directs his intention to live at the edge of his full potential.

P: I can see now why clarity of values is important if I want to manifest my intentions to be free.

MQ: Yes, because *conditioned intentions* (those objectives of the unhealthy-ego) and *conscious intentions* – (those objectives of the Higher Self and the Higher We), are never alike.

EVOLUTIONARY POINTER: Clarity of values becomes essential because the intentions of the unhealthy-ego and those of the Higher 'We' are drawn to completely different outcomes.

P: The intentions of the unhealthy-ego are primarily concerned with the 'already manifested'.

MQ: The conceptual-mind — the mind that needs to know and understand — is most certainly necessary because you are in a body and have to relate with the world. And that's fine, as long as you are not exclusively identified with the conceptual-mind. On the other hand, the intentions of the Higher Self and the Higher 'We' are to *co-create* our future as the conscious conduits of that creativity, in the recognition of being the process itself... and in this body.

P: That's big!

MQ: Yes, but isn't that what you wanted? The awakened life!

P: Clarity of values allows me to become an agent for conscious evolution?

MQ: Yes.

P: This is good to know!

MQ: Therefore, you can embrace transformation for the sake of humanity with unbending confidence because you know that your intention is *always* going to be your outcome.

P: Always?

MQ: Absolutely. That's the uncommon path. By integrating such an awakened decision-making structure into your daily life, you can align who you *think* you are with what you *do*. Conscious-free-will gives the fully integrated human being the power to co-create a new reality as an integral aspect of the Higher 'We'. This topic of consciously co-creating a new world is discussed in the last chapter of the book.

EVOLUTIONARY POINTER: As you continue to evolve your consciousness — by making awakened choices — eventually it becomes clear that you are *compelled* to authenticity.

The Third Insight – Recall Your Origin of Oneness

MQ: Let's move on now to an overview of the Third Insight.

P: Okay.

MQ: Did you know that according to renowned French author and spiritual teacher, Jean Klein, the desire to meditate is predicated by deep, restful sleep? The Third Insight, therefore, is supported by the First and Second Insights. Identifying unhealthy-ego-motives with the help of the First Insight and reclaiming your awareness from conditioned outcomes using the Second Insight allows you to break free from the weight of the past and the burden of the future. This goes a long way toward letting you sleep really well.

P: Sounds great!

MQ: Therefore, the Third Insight outlines the lesson of *stillness meditation*.

EVOLUTIONARY POINTER: Meditation is the state in which the need for answers disappears because the questions, the questioner and all possible answers have temporarily enfolded.

MQ: Stillness meditation will work just as well for you if you have no prior experience with it or if you already have twenty years of sitting practice. Frequently though, the less familiarity you have of this art, the better off you are.

P: Why is this?

MQ: You have to be careful that you are not 'sitting' with such great expectations that they are restricting the possibility of your awakening. As we will see later, life-long meditators are often sitting amongst inherited restrictions. In spiritual development, whether your interest is in expanding your awareness, widening your perspective, increasing your depth, or discovering and expressing your full potential in community with other people, the practice of meditation is *essential*.

P: Essential?

MQ: Yes. You can always tell how serious someone is about spiritual advancement by inquiring about the consistency of his or her personal practice.

P: How so?

MQ: Often, when you ask this question, the unhealthy-ego will hastily respond with a long list of very convincing excuses for incon- sistency.

P: Because it loves busyness and hates emptiness?

MQ: Yes. Stillness meditation is a way to explore potential beyond the limited perspective of the rational and individual body/mind/personality. Please imagine this: *"A strike of lightning on a moonless night, where in the flash, you see true reality, if only for a few seconds"* [8]. The darkness of a moonless night symbolizes a way of living that is weighted down by concealed conditioning. The short flash represents your ever-present state of completion, which is revealed when the body is gently poised in stillness.

P: Can a spiritual experience ease all existential uncertainties? Can just one taste glimpse shift how I express myself, away from being a spokesperson for the unhealthy-ego?

MQ: A momentary immersion in the power and grace of your own consciousness can cut lifetimes from your quest for authentic joy. Often called *One Taste*, your Origin of Oneness is never forgotten and it leaves an indelible trace within. It is instantly recognized as 'more real' than any previous experience in the world.

EVOLUTIONARY POINTER: One short glimpse into your true nature can also convey a potential-packed purpose, as you recall, even for a brief moment, your Origin of Oneness with Completion, Oneness with Creativity, Oneness with Fullness, Oneness with Emptiness, your True Self.

MQ: The Third Insight is founded upon a motionless body. In this radically simple practice, you do not have to worry about the mind and the emotions. They will eventually follow the extent of your physical calm. Your thoughts and feelings have no influence over your body beyond that which you permit. Physical stillness is all that is needed for the state of meditation to become apparent. With dedication to a regular practice, you will notice that the constant mental busyness you are witnessing is *not at all* who you are.

P: The logic is simple then: Be still and be who you are.

MQ: In stillness meditation, you learn to rest evenly in equilibrium and alertness, while watching body and breath, desire and aversion appear and disappear of their own volition. Meditation is to discover what awareness is, to expand *who* is aware, and to experience *bare attention unborn as the direct experience of your True Self.*

The resplendent potential of all sentient beings unfolds as the canvas upon which phenomenal worlds appear. In stillness meditation, you discover that you are *that* impression of space and openness and not just the ever-changing hues of concepts and forms.

EVOLUTIONARY POINTER: Meditation is revealed as your *natural state*, whether sitting with your eyes closed or walking around living your life.

MQ: As the state of meditation arises, it is plainly obvious to you. This is because you recognize it as your *True Self*. And then you, the witness of that infinite majesty will eventually get lost there. In stillness mediation the subject and the object merge; the observer and the observed blend in a state of already fullness, already emptiness; the ecstatically familiar, yet eternally unknowable "One".

P: This does not make much sense to me right now.

MQ: It will make perfect sense when the time is right for you. Meditation awaits your practice.

EVOLUTIONARY POINTER: The purpose of meditation is to align your intention for *being* with the body in stillness, in order that consciousness can pay attention to itself.

P: To be honest with you, I am somewhat jaded with the results of past meditation practices. I mean, I struggle with thoughts such as: "Meditation doesn't work for me," "I've tried this practice before and it is too difficult," "Meditation has nothing new to offer me" or "Who has the time to practice?" Can you speak about resistance to practice?

MQ: Please be wary not to fall prey to cynicism or to the voices of the unhealthy-ego. Be careful to disregard these suggestions that may be arising as objects in your awareness. Let them be and let that be another lesson in objectivity: This is the conditioned mind attempting to skewer you with harmless thoughts. Because the ego is stuck in clock-time, it thinks that meditating is wasteful because this practice is directing you toward a depth that is timeless and out of its range of control. We will also look at the concept of clock-time and also how a discomfort zone of resistance indicates a wholesome direction, later in the book.

P: How can I help quell these voices of dissent until they fade into the joy of One Taste?

MQ: Ask yourself this question: Are you absolutely certain that your current way of being in the world does not just lead to the inevitable end of the unhealthy-ego in you, as opposed to the end of unnecessary suffering in you?

P: When is the end of the unhealthy-ego in me?

MQ: It occurs a little while after the time of physical death.

P: Therefore, my meditation is the *conscious* experience of Oneness that includes my exclusive identification with the separate sense-of-self?

MQ: Yes. This also allows you to transcend and to include the separate sense-of-self as an object in that awareness.

P: And transcending and including the separate sense-of-self as an object in awareness allows *conscious-free-will* to emerge.

MQ: Yes. Can you also see that the First and Second Insights are fully supported by the Third Insight?

P: Yes, I can. But, the struggle against doing nothing while in meditation still persists.

MQ: Do you know that there are people at lower stages of development who may never encounter opposition to meditation? This is because they have yet to encounter and go beyond ways of *being* that are already included in your development. The discipline of searching and practice begins in the dualistic-mind. You intuit

Oneness, but the conceptual-mind can't get you there. Nonetheless, it is important that you pay attention to the cues of consciousness toward your full potential. You become ready to transcend and include the conceptual-mind and all those cherished notions by simply being still.

EVOLUTIONARY POINTER: Stillness meditation is the invitation of consciousness to experience the origin of your most authentic Self.

P: And if I ignore this invitation, I am placing my interest in the voices of the unhealthy-ego ahead of my interest in stillness, and that is not such an awakened choice.

MQ: I agree. According to the conditioned mind, salvation is always *there* – never *here*.

EVOLUTIONARY POINTER: All you have to do in stillness mediation is *nothing*. In your *real* life, the unhealthy-ego loves it when you do nothing; but, in meditation, it will defy your every attempt at stillness.

MQ: Don't you find this interesting?

P: Yes, indeed.

The Fourth Insight – Relate as Your Full Potential

MQ: The integration of the first three Insights into all aspects of your life sustains the conditions for awakening your full potential for the sake of humanity. Therefore, the Fourth Insight is a *way of being* and not an instruction. It is a spontaneous unfolding, propelled by the degree of your engagement with the First, Second, and Third

Insights. The extent to which you identify and let go of the motives of the unhealthy-ego, use awakened choices to reclaim your consciousness from concealed conditioning, and recall your origin of Oneness in meditation – is clearly demonstrated as the emergence of this new perspective.

There is no limit to your experience of the Fourth Insight; its eminence and inclusiveness are entirely dependent upon your willingness to embrace its potential. In fact, tomorrow is as yet uncreated as your potential is grand. It is in accordance with the depth of your new perspective that the latent expansiveness of who you are finds the room for realization.

Now, in a life free of all unnecessary emotional and psychological struggling, you are fully available to engage in the evolution of consciousness and culture as the central theme of that life. With the unfolding of the Fourth Insight, you find that it is not so much that your worldview has shifted or that you see things in a different way, but, that you are now living in a completely *different* world: A completely different world to those who are asleep in the matrix of individual and collective conditioning. This is the world of *true free will* and infinite possibilities, lived at the intersection of form, creativity and emptiness, in easeful community with other people.

> EVOLUTIONARY POINTER: The Fourth Insight is the emergence of the unity in you; the confluence of self and the Self, the unification of your daily life with your spiritual life.

MQ: Your personal past now looks like that of someone you once knew, but hardly remember. Your personal history is referenced mostly for the worth of your experiences. In the awakened condition, you are free to just *be*. This is because life as you have always known it appears in a context of stillness, ease, enthusiasm[9] and as endless possibilities for the evolution of awareness.

The future, which is co-created in awakened relationships and based on conscious intentions, unites without apprehension into the present. You are most certainly aware of tomorrow, you will continue to make plans and earn a living and the once familiar state of 'looking forward to' does not entirely dissipate. But now all your attempts to influence the future are driven by your recent *objectification* of evolutionary *unconsciousness*. Your eternal motives now work hand-in-hand with those of the fully functional conceptual-mind.

As the path and the goal of your fully integrated humanness stabilize as one, your incentives for living are profoundly revised. You are conscious of the process of being alive on the very edge of discovering *who you are* in each new moment. Who you have become, and your reasons for being are now clearly reflected in what you *do*. The discovery and expression of awakened potential, in harmony with others for the sake of humanity, emerges as a primary interest. You, too, realize that each human birth is precious, that each soul is unique and the suffering of mankind makes perfect sense to you. And, because of this realization you actively seek out and create relationships beyond the limitations of the conditioned-mind. Such relevant relationships provide the ground upon which consciousness can continuously evolve; both individually and collectively, and offer us the possibility of a new reality.

EVOLUTIONARY POINTER: The paradox of the Fourth Insight is that the concepts, beliefs and opinions formerly accepted as accurate are now seen to be *without* significance. Yet, this revelation is the basis upon which your new way of being in the world is founded.

MQ: The Fourth Insight is a perspective that includes the world of time and the timeless ground of being. As the empty promises of perfection, offered by individual and collective conditioning come to a close, there is *"an eighty percent reduction in the thinking process"*[10]. You fall in love with life for the sake of life itself — not for any particular reason — but just because it seems to be natural. And, it matters not if your attention is in the 'now' because you see that enlightenment is the relationship you have with the experience that you are already having, whether that experience happens to be of the present moment, memories of the past or plans for the future.

P: When viewed from the outside, the liberated life can appear as quite ordinary.

MQ: Yes. This is because your day-to-day chores frequently remain unchanged. Yet, in the face of the duty of your new perspective, you will certainly live a stimulating and exciting adventure.

P: How do you know?

MQ: Well, after years of sifting through the empty covenants of ego-identity, you are more than happy to figure out new and creative ways to forward the evolution of consciousness, even while you are taking the dog out for a walk.

P: In the awakened life, do things work out in surprising and unforeseen ways?

MQ: Not more than they do for everybody else. You may also discover that life does not need to change in any way in order to be miraculous.

P: In awakening, your emotions, personal preferences, likes, dislikes and those wacky members of your extended family will still exist, correct?

MQ: Yes, of course. This is another mad idea put out by the ego's dharma. It purports that an awakened person is harmoniously detached all the time; as if they beyond chaos and change, temper and excitement, hurt and consequences, weddings and funerals. Sometimes an awakened person acquiesces to a brief 'courtesy dip' in the unhealthy-ego's sideshow of grumbling, self-pitying, narcissism, and even enjoys doing so.

P: In fact I now become 'more' human…

MQ: Absolutely. You are awakening.

EVOLUTIONARY POINTER: The Fourth Insight in no way denies your humanity. In fact, you see humanity of all of its levels of development as something more precious than ever before.

MQ: The Fourth Insight also reveals that many situations and inter-actions you once found disturbing can now be responded to with all the rightness of concerned dispassion and the directness of compassionate detachment. This is a welcomed final release.

P: The future — dare I say — of humanity, is my responsibility.

MQ: You may. The Fourth Insight reveals that it is only by the union of many awakened individuals that we can resolve the complex matters currently threatening the existence of our planet. Without a great leap in collective consciousness, that can start exactly where you are today, these issues will remain unsolvable. This is because they are a product of the same conditioning that is currently attempting to heal them. Our effectiveness together is beyond the pleas of the unhealthy-ego.

P: Regardless of my reason for awakening, what's important is that I do.

MQ: Yes. To paraphrase the revered Western Zen Master, Dennis Genpo Merzel Roshi, the five main reasons for coming to practice are:

Improvement.
Empowerment.
Seeking Enlightenment.
Helping others with Meditation.
There is no Reason, it is what you do, it is Your Life.

EVOLUTIONARY POINTER: Individual transformation begins your spiritual journey. It is in joining together with others in relationships of nonviolent communication, beyond the attachment to the ego-mind, that the essential catalyst to global transformation is activated and unleashed.

1 Francois de La Rochefoucauld (1613–1680).

2 René Descartes; Written in 1641.

3 *The Power of Now* by Eckhart Tolle. New World Library, 1999.

4 The goal of psychoanalysis according to Otto Kernberg, former President of Freud's International. Psychoanalytic Association.

5 Power Vs. Force by David Hawkins, (Endorsed by Mother Teresa), Veritas and Hay House, 1995 – 2006.

6 These are based on the four quadrants developed by Integral philosopher, Ken Wilber.

7 Spiritual groups.

8 Adapted from Divine Revelations in Pali Buddhism by Peter Masefield: Allen & Unwin, 1986.

9 The root of this word is *God within.*

10 Even the Sun will Die, CD Series by Sounds True; Unabridged edition (July 2002).

Chapter 2

THE WHOLE 'I'

"Minds of moderate caliber ordinarily condemn everything which is beyond their range."[1]

Toward Oneness

P: I have found that consistent transformation is difficult because I often react to life in ways that create additional suffering for me.

MQ: When unconsciousness is driving your actions, awakening your deepest potential can sound like a great idea, but it's virtually impossible.

P: So how do I maintain regularity in such endeavors?

MQ: Let's begin with a look at some distinctions that delve deeply into psychological structures. Creating the conditions for your liberation begins by distinguishing the *Freudian Ego* (which is the self-organizing principle of the psyche) from the *shadow* (which contains the aspects of yourself you have denied or repressed) from the *ego-mind* (which is the part of you that protects the separate sense-of-self). The unhealthy ego is also motivated by conditioned fears and desires of that little-self. Please be wary of any objections arising in your awareness that such efforts are 'unspiritual'. Who's that reacting?

P: The unhealthy-ego is objecting to being identified?

MQ: Yes, that part of us that wants to deny that spiritual evolution and psychological endeavors are not in any way related. Denial, as we will soon see, is never the way out.

P: Okay, I will disregard those thoughts.

MQ: Thank you. The reason for making these distinction is that it is only with a *whole 'I'* that you can act with power and grace in communion with other people.

EVOLUTIONARY POINTER: When a whole 'I' is engaged as an integral part of a whole 'We' the issues of humanity are resolvable. Such purposeful unions deepen ease of being, amplify autonomy and expand the awareness of the group beyond that which previously existed.

P: Is it true that for many people the 'I' is far from whole?

MQ: Yes. Parts of the 'I' have been lost along the way, forgotten, abandoned, subdued, repressed or denied. Therefore, in anticipation of the magnificent collective expression of Oneness and the co-creation of a new reality, let's look at the distinctions that allow the 'I' to become whole.

The Ego and the 'I'

MQ: In the 1920s, Freud described the Ego[2] as a 'sense of self'. As his understanding evolved, he later revised this idea and explained the Ego to be a set of psychic functions related to the gathering and processing of information, memory and defense. The Freudian Ego, therefore, is necessary to survive and thrive in this world.

P: The Freudian 'I' has nothing to do with a sense of self, it is simply a set of functions?

MQ: Yes. And remember, when a fully functioning or whole 'I' is engaged as an integral part of a whole 'We', the grave matters facing our world are finally resolvable.

P: And what if I find that the Freudian 'I' in me is incomplete? Is it difficult to make it whole again?

MQ: Conscious development is only a matter of your interest in doing so.

P: How might I know that parts of the Ego have been broken off or denied?

MQ: Can your subjective experience sometimes be like an unpredictable and erratic rollercoaster ride?

P: Yes, it can be.

MQ: There's one of your indicators. And now, back to our distinctions.

EVOLUTIONARY POINTER: The 'I' or the Freudian Ego is the self-organizing principle of the psyche. The capacity to gather and process information has existed to some degree since human beings first appeared on this planet. It is a functional tool that *pre-dates* the separate sense-of-self and both the healthy and unhealthy aspects of ego-mind.

P: You are pointing out three distinctions here: The *Freudian Ego*, and the *healthy* and *unhealthy* aspects of the ego.

MQ: Yes. And don't confuse the Freudian Ego with the part of ourselves that gives us individuality. We will have more on that later in this chapter. As you can imagine, the Freudian Ego or the 'I' can be at various levels of development in different people. A person with a severely underdeveloped Ego needs to be attended to in a psychiatric care facility.

However, the maturity of this mechanism does not imply its uniqueness in you. For example, in order to pay for your children's education, you rely upon a complex array of psychological functions to determine if increasing your working hours could adversely affect your marriage and relationships outside your family. Another person, in another culture, may employ similar functions to come to terms with the consequences of getting married, with a dowry of only one cow as opposed to three. How you process, manage and subsequently respond to your life situations becomes an expression of the wholeness of the Ego in you at your particular level of development.

P: Therefore, individual responses do not personalize the 'I'.

MQ: This is true and critical to grasp as we move forward. We all use the Freudian 'I', yet our expression of this principle reflects the level of development, but not necessarily the uniqueness of the 'Ego' in each of us. This does not imply that your memories and my memories are not distinct and exceptional. Our perspectives are unique, but not the ways in which we process information.

EVOLUTIONARY POINTER: There is only one Ego. It is not *my* Ego, *his* Ego or *her* Ego; it is *the* Ego.

The Ego – with a Capital 'E'

P: Therefore, a fully awakened person has an Ego or a Freudian 'I' just like you and me.

MQ: Yes and that capacity should be obvious.

P: In other words, their actions should reflect those of a fully functioning human being.

MQ: Yes, direct yet discreet, certain yet open, and powerful yet humble. For example, I was once present when a woman, who is considered by many of her followers to be a *living saint*, instructed her chauffeur to purchase a couple of expensive full-length wool sweaters, saying, "*I want to look good for the TV interviews*". As another example, when Ken Wilber put his home located in the Rocky Mountains on the market, the asking price was just under a million dollars.

P: The same healthy Freudian Ego function is operating well in both of these individuals. Which is great to know because this tenet of the ego's dharma says: *Awakened people shouldn't have expensive tastes.*

MQ: The enlightened person does not identify with or attach himself to these objects, but simply enjoys them for what they are – temporary. The essential point here is not whether we have expensive tastes or not, but it is to be sure that the 'I' is healthy.

Without that, you and I and the awakened person are unable to fully function in this world.

The ego – with a Small 'e'

P: Spiritual discovery is often described as the process of identifying and letting go of the attachment to ego. Is this *ego* the same as this self-organizing principle of the psyche – the Freudian Ego?

MQ: No, not in the least. How can you be attached to a function that existed prior to the 'you' that is getting attached? The *ego* (with a small 'e') you aim to transcend and then include in your spiritual work is different from the Freudian Ego (with a capital 'E'). And this ego (small 'e') has two sides to it, the healthy and unhealthy aspects.

EVOLUTIONARY POINTER: The ego's primary role is to define the separate sense-of-self.

MQ: Clearly distinguishing the Ego from both the healthy-ego and the unhealthy-ego is essential as you progress toward awakening.

P: So the ego's significant function is not the processing or gathering of information?

MQ: No. Those are the tasks of the Freudian Ego. The responsibility of the ego (small 'e') is to promote your separate sense-of-self as unique and primary. The ego is solely comprised within its own thought processes. Its goal in life is to keep all of your thoughts focused on your particular subjective experience or about your subjective experience as being significant, exclusive and personal. The ego wants you to think about yourself, first and foremost.

P: You said the ego is comprised within its own thought processes?

MQ: Yes, it is an autonomous and self-directing object in awareness.

P: You said that there are two sides to the ego. Can you describe some the healthy aspects?

MQ: Sure. The healthy-ego gives us the ability to appreciate the beauty of diversity in people and culture. It is the capacity for individuated thinking and the healthy-ego helps us discriminate one person's life-skills and experiences from another. The ego also empowers the phenomenal facility of choice, albeit at the level of conceptual-free-will. The ego is especially useful if there is ever a need to defend our separate sense-of-self or our 'personal' property. The ego also allows us to feel passion and pride for events that could be considered entirely 'personal'. For instance, tears of joy still stream from the eyes of the awakened one, upon the birth of his first daughter.

P: This means that despite the bad name it's gotten, this ego is not all 'bad'.

MQ: No, not in the least. When we acknowledge the ego and take full responsibility for such an important and beautiful part of ourselves, we prevent ourselves, and those around us, from being subjected to painful projections which otherwise result. Listen to what spiritual teacher Andrew Cohen had to say about the ego:

"The development of ego, the capacity for individuation, is a miraculous, extraordinary, wonder of evolution itself. It's a very sophisticated and highly evolved state that most of us are in. The problem is that we have become infatuated with ourselves to a degree that is extreme. So the ego is good and bad. It's the best thing that ever happened to us in terms of the capacity it gives us for self-liberation and it's the biggest problem we have that we need to get over. We've gotten trapped in the wrong way on the best thing we have." [3]

EVOLUTIONARY POINTER: If you are exclusively identified or obsessed with the 'me' sense, all of the healthy aspects can quickly become pathological, trapping you in the limitations of individual and collective conditioning.

MQ: To develop yourself at the level of awareness and to access your full potential, it becomes necessary to transcend and include the ego-mind and that which it is charged to defend – your separate sense-of-self.

P: Not kill, do away with, or separate from, but transcend and include the ego.

MQ: This is correct. An awakened person does not always *need* to locate the 'me' sense in awareness. He can act as a fully functioning human being for long periods of time without ego-identity.

EVOLUTIONARY POINTER: Though the ego and the 'me' sense are very important parts of your development, they are not so essential to your survival that you have to be exclusively focused upon them all the time.

Suing the Buddha: A fully awakened teacher of evolutionary enlightenment, considered by thousands of people worldwide to be a living Buddha, was holding his annual winter retreat at a teaching center in the mountains of Upstate New York. On a break during the lectures, one of the visiting students was having a hot chocolate, when it fell on him, burning his hand. A massive claim was made by the family of the student who said the injuries were due to sheer negligence on behalf of the center. Though the warning sign was clearly placed on the hot chocolate machine, they claimed it should also have been placed on each individual cup. The multi-million dollar suit named the teacher, his organization and the cup manufacturer as being responsible for these injuries.

MQ: How do you think this enlightened teacher responded to this claim? Did he immediately admit liability and settle out of court for a huge sum? Or did he look to the part of himself that is responsible for the separate sense-of-self, which is the healthy side of the ego, and hire a competent law firm to defend the case?

P: I would think he did just that.

MQ: And you would be correct. Awakened or not, the rules of developed societies are there for all of us to take advantage of when needed.

P: The unhealthy-ego also knows all about hiring attorneys. Just look at the thousands of false slip-and-fall and product-liability lawsuits that are in progress.

MQ: Indeed. But, note the difference between the intentions of an awakened person and the intentions of an un-awakened person who pursues a petty lawsuit. The conscious objective of the awakened person is to protect the sense of authentic individuality and his 'personal' property. The intention of the un-awakened person is unconscious, a futile attempt to compensate for a lack of authentic individuality. The awakened person moves consciously with the healthy-ego, taking steps to protect his rights according to the law. The un-awakened person reacts unconsciously with the unhealthy-ego in order to get whatever he can for himself according to the rules of society or not.

P: The awakened person takes the stand in complete conscious awareness of his actions. The un-awakened person takes his position without any knowledge of the conditioning that has put him there. And when he takes the oath: "Do you swear to tell the truth, the whole truth and nothing but the truth, so help you God?" The unhealthy-ego will answer, "Yes".

MQ: Indeed.

P: I understand now that the ego and the separate 'me' sense are necessary parts of our development, but what happens if I try to deny the ego and/or the separate sense-of-self?

MQ: Well, you may go wandering naked in the streets or simply stop eating, like Ramana Maharshi[4] did, much to the chagrin of those responsible for him.

P: And when I hear someone saying, "He has a big ego," which one is being referred to?

73

MQ: This is generally a reference to a person who has an over-inflated sense of self in the negative sense. Which one do you think is being referred to?

P: The ego (small 'e') of course.

MQ: And which side – the 'healthy' or the 'unhealthy'?

P: Well, that would depend on the level of consciousness of the speaker and the person being referred to.

MQ: Correct. And when you hear this, see if you can qualify if the person means, the healthy-ego, the unhealthy-ego or the Freudian Ego, or if they are projecting shadow, which is a topic we will look at in great detail by the end of this chapter.

P: I can see how people often confuse the Freudian Ego and the ego-mind.

MQ: This is very common. Pay attention the next time someone is speaking about this topic. See if you can tell if he or she is clear about whether he is talking about the Freudian Ego or the ego-mind. If that person can't tell the difference, then it's generally the ego (with a small 'e') talking about itself – a pointless charade.

EVOLUTIONARY POINTER: Because concealed conditioning relishes complexity, without a distinction between the Ego and the healthy and the unhealthy aspects of the ego, your advancement may not be so rapid.

P: To summarize: I will never lose the Freudian Ego, the self-organizing principle of the psyche, because its functions have thousands of uses in my life and in my spiritual development. In fact, I will work to make it more complete. This Ego is not personal and has nothing to do with my sense of self. This Ego works alongside both the healthy and unhealthy aspects of the ego, which setup and defend my so-called 'personal' boundaries. The ego offers me the capacity for individuation, but its malignant side is totally obsessed with fortifying and promoting 'my' thoughts, 'my' past, 'my' future and so on. I must learn to let go of my exclusive identity with the ego as being all that I am.

MQ: By contemplating these distinctions as best you can, based on the examples given and on your own life experiences, you will find clarity emerging. Remember, you have to be willing to jump a few cognitive hurdles in order for this to happen. Failing this, it is most certainly guaranteed that the malignant aspects of the ego-mind will continue to run havoc with your life and relationships.

P: Okay, so the question always comes back to my interest in spiritual development.

MQ: Yes. The awakened life is available to those who show sufficient interest in attaining that level of awareness. There are no barriers to entry.

P: Thank you. I can remember that.

The Unhealthy-ego

MQ: The unhealthy-ego has no interest whatsoever in awakening. At one level of development, it offers you the promise of eternity only as a thought or an idea – 'heaven', for example. The unhealthy-ego will try to convince you that no one can fully transcend and include the ego. It offers such ill-conceived logic as: if the guy next to you also doesn't lose his ego, he will eat your lunch. In other words, it wants you to believe that to be free you have to let go of providing for yourself and your family. This is a grave misunderstanding. The well known French spiritual teacher Jean Klein[5] was a gifted speaker and he was not homeless. Gandhi was an independent thinker and also provided for his family. Gautama Buddha led great communities.

P: These great people thrived in the world proves because they were not completely 'Ego-free'.

MQ: Yes. And as strange as it might sound, to create meaning and purpose, the unhealthy-ego thrives on suffering. It will do everything it can to defer your ease of being. Can you see now why it defends personal conflict as being normal and acceptable? If you take personal anguish away, you are removing a significant avenue from its domination.

The unhealthy-ego also includes characteristics that are considered to be positive, such as: ambition, bravery, courage, pride and flattery, but if you are unconsciously identified with the ego, the unwholesome application of these particular traits allows it to manipulate and schmooze its way to all sorts of positions in your life. The unhealthy-ego then wholly consumes your potential with having and getting as it attempts to satisfy its unquenchable thirst for more, bigger and better. It taps your consciousness by fabricating a world of things-to-do, 'personal issues' to deal with, cherished opinions to defend, and hoards of neighbors to keep up with. The unhealthy-ego is the communal aspect of consciousness found in those who are unknowingly obsessed with transience, self-importance, excuses for limitation and personal disagreement on all levels.

P: Spirit is completely caught up in this false identity?

MQ: In the vast majority of humankind, completely!

EVOLUTIONARY POINTER: The manifestation of the ego in different individuals does not personalize this entity. The location or the language spoken by the ego does not infer its uniqueness either.

MQ: Our absorption in the ego-mind begins early in childhood without our knowledge or the awareness of those who helped indoctrinate us. And then this mental construct continues to be compounded by long-term interactions with family, society and culture. It becomes personalized by our naïve acceptance of inaccurate, albeit well-intended, opinions about the sources of happiness, fulfillment and malcontent. The ego, existing to one degree or another in all of us, perceives itself as a separate and superior entity, and eventually assumes exclusive rights to our thoughts, emotions and actions.

EVOLUTIONARY POINTER: Because the ego assumes full charge in you at an early age, spirit in you becomes focused on the *content* of your life situations. Spirit loses awareness of itself: the eternal *context* in which both form and formless, ego and Ego arise and ultimately disappear.

Spirit Distracted?

P: As a result, I end up lacking both an objective awareness of the ego-mind and a deep sense of my own innate potential.

MQ: This is true. And you have to live in the gap between your 'real' life and your 'spiritual' life. This is a life that often seems to be purposeless.

EVOLUTIONARY POINTER: Krishnamurti said, *"In the gap between subject and object lies the entire misery of humankind"*.

P: Awakening, therefore, is to query the ego's monopolizing of my destiny and also the habitual guidelines I have been following toward the promise of release. I am interested in doing this not because I want to rebel or turn my life upside down, rather I am beginning to question the foundations of what I've been referring to as a map of 'my free will'.

MQ: That's quite right. Discovering that a chart or its maker that you once revered was not holding the whole picture, does not give you the right of rebellious condemnation. Remember, you are here today on the shoulders of all previous levels of development. Awakening is to see both the healthy and unhealthy aspects of the ego-mind as they move in you and in other people. This is why liberation is often referred to as *ego-death*. It is not that the ego dies, but as it lives on elsewhere, you are no longer exclusively identified with it.

EVOLUTIONARY POINTER: The gap between subject and object closes as the ego-mind loses its predominant reign over your attention. Your purpose for being can then find room to blossom.

The Ego-Mind Defends Itself

P: As I discover this concealed mechanism, I suspect that the ego will be greatly disturbed by my audacity for awakening. "How dare you," it may say, "I am the ruler of this roost!"

MQ: This is why the awakened decentering of the conditioned mind is frequently accompanied by intense emotional and psychological pressure. Often, both internal and external hostilities can combine in a bid to thwart the expression of your authentic nature. Be careful not to underestimate this force; though transitory, it can completely derail even the most inspired endeavors. *"Let he who seeks remain always seeking until he finds, and when he finds he will be troubled, having been troubled, he will marvel, and will reign over all."*[6]

EVOLUTIONARY POINTER: The illusion of separation from your Self will die in you without your cooperation.

Tara's Story: Tara was shocked the first time she recognized the unhealthy-ego in another person, especially since it was also clear to her that they had no idea of this manipulation. Tara had just finished explaining to her father how thrilled she was to be resigning from a job she had disliked for many years, divorcing an abusive husband, ending several draining friendships, and beginning a meditation practice. Tara's intention for making all of these awakened choices was to break free from the conditioned mold in which she had been cast. Her father stunned her by asking, "When are you going to see the psychiatrist we recommended about all of this nonsense?" Speaking through him, the malicious aspect of the ego then added, "The reason we want you to go to the doctor is so that, if he says you are crazy to make all these changes, your mother and I will know it is not our fault."

MQ: Remember, the unhealthy-ego can be forthright or reserved, yet it will always be persistent in its resistance to your awakening. It wants you to remain convinced that the power and grace of autonomous community are unavailable to you. It will even question if such a thing even exists.

P: Therefore, its task is much easier if I am battle-weary and weakened from creating and then fighting battles on behalf of the unhealthy-ego.

MQ: Become aware now, as you begin to disprove the fixed notion that you can't let go of all unneeded anguish, that the unhealthy lesser-self will relentlessly campaign to quench your curiosity in the discovery and expression of the infinite possibilities of your humanity.

The Shadow's Trap – Making the 'I' Whole[7]

MQ: To help you transcend and include individual and collective conditioning, you must be sure that the self-organizing principle — the 'I' — is intact. Here's a simple example. Imagine the difficulty that a severely neurotic person might have with sustaining a normal career. For a multitude of reasons, the Freudian Ego in such a person is in a state of disarray. Similarly, if you've been meditating for years or engaged in other lines of spiritual development, and you still can't seem to find your way, it is likely that the Ego in you is, to some degree, un-whole.

EVOLUTIONARY POINTER: The power of 'now' is only available when *all of you* is in the now!

MQ: Except in a few highly enlightened individuals, when the self-organizing principle of the psyche — the Freudian Ego — is incomplete, unnecessary suffering is unavoidable.

P: What is the process of the making the 'I' whole?

MQ: It begins by uncovering the aspects of yourself that you have consciously or unknowingly rejected or denied. This is called your *shadow*. The shadow is a component part of the Freudian Ego. It is the part of the 'I' you have hidden away. It is the lie you tell yourself, mostly unknowingly.

P: Does my shadow contain both positive and negative aspects of myself that I have denied, and not only the negative aspects?

MQ: Yes. You bury both desirable and undesirable aspects of yourself in your shadow. Just because the shadow is out of sight does not mean it is not going to have an affect on your action and those around you. For example, picture a crescent moon; the portion that is in the darkness, though out of sight, is still there. If you run into it, it's going to hurt.

P: Therefore, the presence of the shadow has dire consequences for all aspiring spiritual seekers.

MQ: Very much so.

EVOLUTIONARY POINTER: The shadow impels you to act unconsciously; and you do so *unfailingly*.

MQ: Acting on unconscious motives means that you do so right *before* you recognize a 'trigger'. Thus, creating and sustaining the conditions for the awakened life is very difficult, if not impossible. Even though you may have access to deep states of consciousness and be very knowledgeable in spiritual matters, there will also be a constant struggle with the mind, emotions and the consequences of seemingly insensible actions.

P: Is the shadow a reason why the guru, priest, counselor or coach ends up in the student's bed?

MQ: This is often the case.

P: And then they change their name, move to a different state and hang out a sign that says: "Seeking unsuspecting sustenance to feed the shadow I don't know I have."

MQ: Indeed. You can't find your way if you don't know who's in charge.

P: What if I think that I am fully conscious of the determinants of my actions and reactions?

MQ: Well, if you think that you are clear about the motives behind your moves, consider this story. Early in his career, Freud attended a performance by a well-known hypnotherapist. As part of the act, a man was hypnotized and then asked to open an umbrella. Later, when questioned as to why he did this, the man responded with various reasons such as, "I wanted to see where it was made" or "To see if it functioned properly". Freud realized that the man was completely unaware of his true motives for opening the umbrella, yet he acted with full belief and conviction on what he thought were his real motives. This realization has become a pillar of Western psychotherapy.

P: To sustain the conditions for an awakened life, it is essential that I identify my shadow and then reintegrate it back into the Ego?

MQ: Yes. And, please note that the shadow should not give you cause for shame. Each one of us has fallen prey to the convictions of repression or denial to one degree or another. You will soon have the understanding with which you can forgive yourself and to progress with great ease.

EVOLUTIONARY POINTER: Wholeness of the Ego creates the first condition for freedom.

MQ: My goal, therefore, is to offer a simple method of re-owning the shadow, one that you can start using right away. It is derived from a process that was first developed by Ken Wilber and his team at the Integral Institute.

P: Before we get to the cure, how can I tell if I have a shadow?

MQ: Go outside on a sunny day and look at the ground!

P: Real examples please!

MQ: Okay. Here are some ways to tell if you have shadow:

1) Are you occasionally of the opinion that other people don't care enough?

2) Are there situations in which you just can't stand the way another person is being?

3) Do you blame others for their insensitive ways?

4) Are other people seemingly intolerant of your beliefs and convictions?

5) Do you sometimes despise, even hate aspects of certain situations or people?

6) Do you seem to rush to immediate conclusions about people and situations?

7) Do you get annoyed or reticent, sometimes over the slightest provocation?

8) Do you experience feelings of envy or jealousy?

9) Do you deeply admire someone who seems to have great passion, drive or direction?

10) Is there one person in your life who seems to bring up swells of emotion in you?

11) Do you seem to fall in love at the drop of a hat?

12) Do you experience certain family members as impolite, bitter

or distant?

13) Do insurmountable differences seem to appear after a while in personal relationships?

14) Are you afflicted by unquenchable self-destructive thinking and/or patterns?

P: And, since the shadow by definition is unconscious, speaking about it tends to bring up immediate and forceful responses.

MQ: Yes, so hold on, sometimes it's not pretty!

P: I'll consider myself forewarned!

MQ: Okay, here it goes:

EVOLUTIONARY POINTER: Ninety percent of all emotional responses, whether positive or negative, to another person or life situation, reflect the presence of the shadow in you.

P: Nine out of ten emotional responses I have to the world around me point to shadow in me?

MQ: Yes, I told you it wasn't pretty!

P: If the ninety percent is a reflection of shadow in me, what's the other ten percent?

MQ: Those are authentic emotional responses to the events you are witnessing. In other words, it is fine to despise certain qualities of others, but only if you are absolutely certain they are not a mirror image of your own shadow. A simple rule of thumb to tell the difference between the ninety percent and the ten percent is: If you find that you are obsessed with positive or negative qualities in another person or situation, it is likely to be a snapshot of denied or repressed aspects of yourself – it is a snapshot of the shadow in you.

P: This reminds me of the old adage: 'It takes one to know one'. But, I have always wondered what to do with that knowledge.

MQ: You will find out the answer before this chapter ends.

April's Story: April was newly married, she had a stable job, and lived close to her parents and her only sister. As with most of her friends at that time, April was a light drinker and occasionally smoked marijuana. She also suffered from stress and a debilitating depression would sometimes wash over her. When this occurred, April was often curt with her friends, becoming openly frustrated, sometimes with the simplest of things. To ease the pain, April liked to eat. As a result, she gained quite a bit of weight. In time, tired of being overweight and apprehensive, April went to see an acupuncturist. The series of treatments were not without physical discomfort, but April endured them and then, she lost lots of weight. Though the emotional and psychological symptoms eased for a time, they did not disappear entirely. With her eating habits now changed, the weight stayed off but April, still a light drinker, found herself being drawn to using more drugs to the point where she was selling cocaine to support her habit.

After an acquaintance committed suicide, April quickly dropped this addiction. But, then she began to drink, moderately at first, and then quite heavily. Whenever she had some free time she would go to her favorite bar alone where she would ponder the darkness that seemed to have permanently descended upon her. Sometimes she would get drunk at home all by herself. The pain she was feeling was real, but its source eluded her thinking. The only way April knew how to 'fill the hole' was by drinking. Her marriage was getting worse, since her husband was addicted to cocaine, and her work was suffering because of her poor attitude and consistent tardiness.

P: So shadow causes me to act on unconscious motives, like the man opening the umbrella.

MQ: Yes. A reaction you have to an object in your awareness, be that object a thought, feeling, another person or a life situation, will always be based on a motive that you are simply not aware of. You will, however be convinced you know the real reason why you are acting. You will think you know why you are responding in a particular way, but that's not true. You don't know it is shadow, therefore, you keep reacting in ways that support those painful situations.

P: In other words, because of shadow, I respond unconsciously in ways that support unnecessary suffering. My shadow is exhausting me, making a total mess of my life's purpose and my relationships without my knowing what's happening. Internally I may even be screaming to myself, "Why am I doing this?" or "Why can't I stop?"

MQ: Yes. And you won't be able to stop until you figure out that shadow is propelling you. Your shadow not only has control over your present, but is also creating your future. April did not notice the cycle of unconscious reactions she was in, and responded to the presence of her shadow with some form of 'medication' in a doomed attempt to ease her pain. Healing one symptom did not diminish her shadow. April went from over-eating, to drugs, to alcohol, from one medication after the next. As you can see from this example, trying to get rid of negative inclinations does not work. It is a fine intention, but it is simply insufficient to heal your shadow. Even people who meditate get stuck in similar cycles since that practice does not reach, let alone heal, their shadows. We will return to this topic in Chapter Eleven.

EVOLUTIONARY POINTER: The shadow casually defers you from success in releasing your truest passions. Therefore, its manifestations can only be temporarily disregarded.

Identifying the Shadow

P: Does healing this unconscious aspect of me involve effort?

MQ: Yes, and it also requires much humility. Look what Swiss psychiatrist, influential thinker and the founder of analytical psychology Carl Jung had to say about this: *"The Shadow is a moral problem that challenges the whole ego-personality, for no one can become conscious of the shadow without considerable moral effort. To become conscious of it involves recognizing the dark aspect of the personality as present and real. This act is the essential condition of self-knowledge, and it therefore, as a rule, meets with considerable resistance."*[8]

P: So how do I clean it up?

MQ: You only need to become aware of it. Beyond the simple process of identification, there is little else to do.

P: That's great news!

MQ: Look now to your own deeply felt emotional reactions that seem to originate because of other people or other external stimuli. When these responses appear in you, know that, in nine out of ten cases, you are interacting with buried aspects of yourself. This is the shadow in you.

P: Therefore, when 'this', 'that', or 'they' tick me off, or when 'it' seems to settle over me, I am likely being shown a window into my preconscious mind. I am being shown my shadow.

MQ: Yes.

P: Is this what Eckhart Tolle calls the 'pain-body'?

MQ: The 'pain-body' is negative thinking about 'this' or 'that'. Therefore, such thoughts can act as stimuli, which bring up deeply felt emotional responses in you. The pain-body is one symptom of your shadow.

EVOLUTIONARY POINTER: The present is only the perfect teacher if you are not trying to avoid the thoughts and/or emotions that are arising in that same moment.

MQ: Yes. And be careful not to ignore this gift because the shadow is a closed container, and the only way out is by projection.

P: Projection of what?

MQ: Projection of those deeply felt emotional reactions that are arising in you. You will try to cast them out onto other people or situations in an attempt to be rid of them. For example, you perceive your spouse to be bitter and insensitive. Nine times out of ten what you are seeing is a reflection of the shadow in you.

P: Ouch! In other words, I am bitter and insensitive, but because I don't like that about myself, I deny it and then bury this aspect of myself. This creates shadow. And since I have denied a part of myself, it does not go away, but continues to irritate me. Then, trying to get rid of my shadow, I will project it onto the world and other people. *They* become bitter and insensitive, *not me*!

MQ: Exactly. You unsuspectingly cast your shadow. If you dislike and then shun a characteristic of yours, you will try to put it onto someone or something outside of yourself. This is the only thing you think you can do to get rid of it. For example, if you deny that you are disorganized and confused, you will see disorganization and confusion everywhere. If you shun an admirable characteristic of yours, you will also project that onto someone or something outside of yourself. And if you have denied your own power, you will see other people as manipulative. You may never acknowledge other people's accomplishments. You might even criticize other people for their achievements. At the same time, though, to compensate for your own repressed power, you will seek their approval and you may even be a controlling person.

P: It looks like my projections eventually come back to me.

MQ: Always. In the case of negative emotions and qualities, they usually return exactly as you project them. Nine times out of ten, the aggravation you think is being caused by a life situation reveals anger denied or repressed in you. Depression that seems to come from 'out there' nearly always means a big, fat shadow of repressed anger and/or sadness 'in here'. Positive emotions and qualities, when projected, are often seen in others as the reverse of what you are projecting. For example, attraction toward 'them' is revealing completion denied in you. Jealousy is a shadow of your own repressed potential. We will frequently bequeath our finer aspects so that we don't have to accept responsibility for our buried goodness in our actions and relationships.

EVOLUTIONARY POINTER: If you repress or deny love in yourself, you will encounter those who are needy, when in fact you may be the one who is demanding undue attention as you try to fill the hole of repressed or denied love for yourself.

P: How do I get out of this trap and make the 'I' whole?

MQ: Laying claim to the symptoms of the shadow is the first key to their dissolution.

P: I know that sometimes I feel jealous of the charm and charisma of an acquaintance. That is clearly my shadow that was created by denying my own joy and excitement for living. But, I can also think of things like child abuse, wasting natural resources, my family members forgetting to recycle or a neglected dog down the street. Are these also examples of shadow in me?

MQ: Look carefully and ask yourself: Am I obsessed with positive or negative qualities in another person or situation? If so, it is likely a snapshot of denied or repressed aspects of yourself: the shadow in you. In the beginning of your examination of your shadow, it is good to assume that all emotional responses you have are your shadow. Then, as you gain experience, you will be able to figure out the ten percent of those reactions that are not.

Reintegrating the Shadow

MQ: When an external stimulus stirs a deeply felt emotional response in you, you are being offered an opportunity to dissolve unconsciousness. Once spotted, the process of reintegrating the shadow is fantastically uncomplicated, so much so that you may doubt its effectiveness. Here is what to do:

EVOLUTIONARY POINTER: Acknowledge the particular emotional response and then say to yourself: "This (emotion/feeling/thought) is mine."

P: That's it?

MQ: That's it! Why should it be more complicated? Who do you think might enjoy that?

P: The unhealthy ego?

MQ: Because it can only hide out in complexity.

This simplicity of curing your shadow is based on thirty years of research by the Integral Institute into the human condition. This comprehensive thesis encompasses the findings of the finest minds into human development in both the East and the West.

P: So, in essence, I stop lying to myself!

MQ: Yes. The reason that this is straightforward is because the Freudian 'I' is a self-righting entity. To supply it with the correct information, such as the statement: "This *angst* is mine," allows the 'I' to harmonize and thereby begin to function normally. You stop lying to yourself.

P: With my private statement of acknowledgement and ownership, I, along with the world around me, am freed from the painful symptoms of my unconscious motives. Therefore, the coldness that seems to originate in my spouse is really a reflection of my own lack of concern in every possible way. Or, the frustration I experience on a daily basis is not life giving me a hard time, but a reflection of my disowned aggression toward life. Or, the self-confidence I so admire in my business partner is a reflection of the potential that I am denying in myself.

EVOLUTIONARY POINTER: Reintegrating the shadow, first and foremost, implies that you accept its existence. Then, acknowledge that the arising of positive and negative emotions that seem to come from 'out there' are really coming from 'in here'. Now you have the option to neutralize the force of unconscious motives before they goad you into insensitive responses.

MQ: Remember our story of April's anger from above? She never thought of herself as mean and nasty. She projected those traits outside of herself and then she would perceive them to be coming from the world and other people. April never assumed she was pessimistic. No, she never thought of herself that way. She was not sad and controlling, she was under the impression that it was the world.

P: She felt as if life was unfairly tough on her, though the truth of the matter was that *she* really hated life!

MQ: And, as these thoughts and feelings arose in her, April would deny them, fortifying her shadow. One symptom of the shadow for her was depression, which she tried to cure in various ways. It was a long time before she realized that to dispel this darkness she would first have to acknowledge her anger and sadness and take ownership of it as she felt the depression arising in her. The only way April could be accountable for its presence, and so heal her shadow, was by saying: "This *anger* is mine" or "this *sadness* is mine".

P: It's 'their' fault not 'mine' is usually a reflection of shadow in me.

MQ: Remember the old adage: 'It takes one to know one'. Now you know what to do with this wisdom.

P: Indeed! If I see it 'in them', it's most likely coming from 'in here'!

> **EVOLUTIONARY POINTER:** The parts of yourself that are denied their rightful place in completing the Ego will always show up later as additional conflict and confusion.

Adrian's Story: Adrian found the world of business harsh, yet exciting. He built himself a fine reputation in the financial services industry. As part of his discipline, he studied the lives and strategies of those figures who were revered in that world. But, as he struggled to emulate these great people, his self-esteem began to wane; for no matter what he did, he never felt that he was their equal, in wisdom or status. Beaten up by this struggle, Adrian paid less attention to his work and tried to relieve the pain of his inauthentic emotions in sexual promiscuity. This led to an addiction to sex. Mired by the expense of his compulsion and his faltering company, Adrian now seemed trapped between his high-ticket habit and his low-earning business.

MQ: As we can see in this example, Adrian was projecting his own potential onto his role models, just like April was projecting her anger onto the world. In Adrian's case, these projections were turning around and coming back at him as their reverse, severely battering his self-esteem and self-confidence. The "I'll never be good enough" routine often reflects a shadow of your own repressed potential and inherent goodness. Adrian eventually healed his shadow in the moments of experiencing those inauthentic emotions by repeating, "This *potential* is mine".

P: He was beating himself up with his own denied greatness.

MQ: Adrian was not only repressing his creativity, which he later found out was working with disadvantaged children, but he was also denying he was a sex addict for many years.

EVOLUTIONARY POINTER: When the Ego is incomplete it is only possible to be temporarily present.

MQ: And for those of you who also suffer at the slings and arrows of lust and sexual desire: see it arise, know that it is yours, and say, "This lust and/or sexual desire is mine". Don't get caught in the idea that *it* comes from 'out there'. Don't repress or deny it; acknowledge it, own it, accept responsibility for it and allow it to reintegrate with the Ego. Pushing away parts of yourself that are either too good, too bad or too risky to own only makes them stick around to drive you, and those around you, nuts.

P: It is clear, then, that when the shadow is present, sustained progress toward spiritual authenticity is impossible.

MQ: Which brings us to this point:

EVOLUTIONARY POINTER: When the shadow is *owned* the Ego becomes whole. The *Ego* must be whole before you can let go of your attachment to the *ego* and end the illusion of separateness.

MQ: Now, go live your life and start dissolving your shadow. *"In order to free up your consciousness, you have to own these repressed parts of yourself – you have to take responsibility for all of them, you have to bring light into all the dark and hidden corners of your self, you have to claim ownership of the entirety of your I – before you can authentically transcend ego in the spiritual sense."*[9]

Christopher and Hazel's Story: Christopher and Hazel were married with an 18-year-old daughter and a six-year-old son. Their relationship had not been good since before the birth of their son.

Nonetheless, as many 'good' parents do, they tolerated the dissent between them for the sake of the family. With this new perspective on the shadow, however, Christopher realized that the indifference he thought was coming from his wife might be a reflection of his own indifference. By acknowledging and taking ownership of this aspect of himself, a renewed attitude of genuine caring emerged toward his wife. This went unnoticed at first. Hazel had seen his temporary niceness before, so from his perspective, she remained indifferent. This perplexed Chris a little, but he decided to trust his decisions and continue with his shadow mindfulness.

As he continued the diligence of acknowledging and owning his emotional responses, regardless of their perceived source, Hazel began to sense that "the new Chris" was more than just a passing phase. One day she asked Chris about the changes she was noticing in him. He explained about the work he was doing with the shadow; that the first step in dissolving the symptoms was to take ownership of his own emotional responses, so that he may see if what he was witnessing in other people was really a reflection of the shadow in him or the truth of their own being.*

Then, Hazel said, "It's not you Chris, it's me. The *love* between us has suffered, and at least for me, it died a long time ago. But now we still have to look after the kids and I know I don't want to be alone." Chris' heart sank and in that same moment, he realized that he was not going to be able to save his circumstances simply by being the most caring person he could be.

*... **but there is** *an alternate ending*:
As Hazel realized the truth of Chris' efforts, she sensed a *love* she had long believed had been vanquished by years of bickering and turmoil. Hazel pursued a similar course of acknowl-edgement, acceptance and ownership of her shadow, and in time, the couple united in awakened love. They continued to grow separately and together in ways that surpassed even their wildest imaginations. Soon, the ease and completion that had stabilized

between them flourished as if by its own volition, spreading to their family, their careers and far beyond.

P: The first ending of Chris' story shows that the emotional reaction he was witnessing in his wife was evidence of the verity of that situation. She really did not love him and it wasn't all coming from him.

MQ: Yes, this reveals one of those ten percent cases. The response he was seeing was not a reflection of the shadow in him. With diligence in your own practice of acknowledgement and ownership of the shadow, you are able to tell the difference between the ninety percent and the ten percent with ease. As always, please be gentle and patient with yourself.

This brings up another silly tenet of the ego's dharma: *Without personal conflict you will be incapable of experiencing the full range of human emotions.*

The Unconscious Becomes Conscious

MQ: The emotional residue from dreaming at night can also be neutralized by facing those particular emotional responses and applying this same process. Do this if you wake up in the middle of the night from a dream or before you get out of bed. Your emotional responses to a dream character, be they anger, fear, disgust, worry, happiness, love, power and so on, are likely to be reflections of your shadow. Address the shadow by taking the perspective of the dream character, determining 'its' emotional charge, and then repeating, "This (the emotion/feeling of the external stimuli, which in this case is the dream character) is mine". Self-knowledge is seeing that your emotional and psychological experience is not so much a matter of the world playing with you, or you playing with the world, but of you playing with yourself.

EVOLUTIONARY POINTER: Creating the conditions for your liberation begins by distinguishing the *Freudian Ego*, which is the self-organizing principle of the psyche, from the *shadow*, which is the aspects of yourself that you have denied, from your attachment to the *ego-mind*, which is the part of you that is dedicated to the protection and defense of your separate self-sense.

P: Once differentiated, the Ego can be fully developed, the shadow can be reintegrated, and my attachment to the ego-mind can be disregarded. Only then can I end the illusion of separation with Oneness.

MQ: Well said! And without such clarity, a seeker forever remains a seeker. Even the best intentions are no match for misery. Here's what Ken Wilber has to say about reintegrating the shadow into the Freudian Ego.

EVOLUTIONARY POINTER: *"...try transcending the ego before properly owning it, and watch the shadow grow."*[10]

MQ: Be diligent in this process and all former symptoms will dissolve in their own good time. On the heels of a little persistent tenderness, consciousness can finally move through an unimpeded you, and in that glorious flow a luminescent instrument — the power and grace of the transpersonal[11] *Self*, functioning at its full potential — is made manifest in this world.

EVOLUTIONARY POINTER: A fully functioning human being has integrated both dual and non-dual shadow and so consistently responds to life from the apex[12] of *form* and *formless*.

The Declaration of Freedom

MQ: I invite you now to merge your willingness to acknowledge your most human imperfections with the willfulness to continuously strive for your perfection. Unification of both requires that you accept what is, but with a twist!

P: A twist, I like it!

MQ: When you awaken you are in your life as it is at that moment, correct?

P: Yes, and I would have to accept my life at that moment as that of the one who just woke up.

MQ: Yes. This is the reason the awakened person acts with transparency: there is no longing to be free. They wish instead to be fully accountable. To accept *what is*, is to proclaim that you are free, privately at first and subsequently in your actions as proof of your private proclamation.

P: But there are so many voices telling me that the day-to-day details of my life are not, and never will be, those of an awakened person. How can I just accept *what is*?

MQ: Some of these voices may be expressing the truth, right?

P: Yes, some are.

MQ: That's fine. So, face those truths. But, the rest of those voices are the trap the unhealthy-ego lays for you. As long as you still *want* to be free, it has you. Accepting what is represents a monumental leap beyond the average level of consciousness of the culture into which you were born. Can you imagine that your life is that of the awakened one, not in the past or the future, but what is, now, in this very conversation, now, in the present moment?

P: I can see how the unhealthy-ego will always answer "No".

MQ: Of course, that's its job, so let it do it. You don't have to go along with its logic, do you?

P: No, actually, I don't.

MQ: You see, this is the quintessential awakened choice. Accepting *what is* — your life — as the life of one who just awakened, you find yourself embracing everything in life, including the conditioned mind's never-ending defiance of your unknown potential.

EVOLUTIONARY POINTER: Your statement of freedom is your graduation from *convenient* to *awakened* decentering of conditioning. It puts you on the path of authentic joy. Awakened decentering creates the conditions for the complete unhinging of the illusion of separation.

Jessica's Story: Jessica was an accomplished homeopathic doctor in her early fifties. She had a thriving practice and was much loved by her clients. Her love life had been sporadic and fiery ever since her second divorce a few years earlier. She also had a somewhat intrusive relationship with her extended family. Most of her close friends were periodically at odds with their emotional and psychological states, as she often was. She yearned for freedom, but despite years on a path, she seemed to be at an impasse. How could she surmount the challenges she was facing? Dissolving fifty-two years of conditioned living seemed impossible to her. Then one day, after a very long talk with her spiritual teacher about moving from convenient to awakened decentering of the lesser-self, she surveyed her current life situations, and in a breath, admitted to herself, *"I am free."* Nothing changed visibly, yet this top-down perspective was accompanied by a profound and overwhelming sense of relief and a curious sense of awakened tension. From that point forward, Jessica went about creating the conditions for awakened living as a free person.

<blockquote>
EVOLUTIONARY POINTER: Your statement of freedom releases the desire to consciously evolve.
</blockquote>

P: I am sure things were still challenging for Jessica. But, at least she was uncovering concealed conditioning as a *free* person and not a seeker who still wanted to be free.

MQ: Exactly. Awakened decentering is born of infinite purpose and it begins the instant you admit, at least to yourself, that you are free, regardless of what's happening in your life. *Spiritual finders* walk the path that transcends and includes the culturally-created-self, while *spiritual seekers* are still looking for the beginning of that path. Seekers of the way make changes for the sake of their personal peace of mind. Finders of the way make those same changes for the sake of humanity.

P: This is a subtle but profound distinction.

MQ: Yes, it is. The declaration of freedom ends your tenure as a spiritual seeker and places you firmly on a path of conscious development.

<blockquote>
EVOLUTIONARY POINTER: "I am free" is the last declaration you will make as a seeker.
</blockquote>

P: Doesn't this contradict what you said earlier about the illusion of free will? I mean, is it not an expression of my free will to make my declaration of freedom?

MQ: The statement, "I am free" is just the beginning. It is the very first emergence of conscious-free-will. Subsequent expressions of true free will, or conscious-free-will, always sustain your potential beyond concealed conditioning. A freely functioning human being first wakes up with a lot of work to do: identifying, acknowledging, accepting, then integrating, dissolving, or abandoning all of the aspects of the culturally created self.

P: This work is the consequence of having lived for 20, 30, or 60 years not knowing that I was living in the matrix of false meaning. Is it possible to give an estimate of how long this might take?

MQ: With consistent effort in developing yourself across all aspects of life, regardless of the cost to your 'personal' circumstances, you could estimate about one year per ten years of life experience. Depending on your level of development and conditioning at the outset, for some it may be less, for others it may take a little more time.

P: And of course it all begins with my declaration.

MQ: In this proclamation, you cross from the endless cycles of convenient decentering to the *finite* phase of awakened decentering. Unlike the hardship of inherited ignorance, which frequently amplifies with age, the intensity of awakened decentering is limited.

EVOLUTIONARY POINTER: Your declaration of freedom is *not* an affirmation. Repeating affirmations is often the unhealthy-ego's attempt to deny the conspicuous: the misery of perpetual wanting and the unwillingness to accept responsibility.

P: This also reveals to me that all of my waiting for the right moment, the right person and the right teaching was in vain. It shows that all of my prior pursuing freedom was the mostly the unhealthy-ego leading an impossible charge to transcend itself.

MQ: This is a testament as to how entrenched that concealed conditioning is in all aspects of life. Your next words and actions will determine your fate.

P: True, but isn't my declaration of freedom just the very beginning?

MQ: Yes. And, note that there are no requirements necessary for your declaration of freedom.

Subsequent to your proclamation, you are a *free person* until you say or do something that creates unneeded suffering to another person or yourself. And it's not a matter of making it right after you have faltered, and then making your statement once more. Does it seem impossible to let go of your ego-identity? Sometimes your awakening inflicts anguish that is *necessary*. This is a subtle point, which becomes much clearer as continue with this work.

EVOLUTIONARY POINTER: An awakened choice removes the division between *wanting to be free* and *being free*. Do you choose to make your declaration?

I Am Buddha

P: I am noticing that a part of me is screaming, "Impossible!" "No way!" "This is ridiculous," "It's just not this easy," "This is too good to be true," and "My life is too complicated!"

MQ: Know now that this commentary is normal. The unhealthy-ego wants you to think that supplanting its conceptual-free-will with conscious-free-will is far more complicated than this. The conditioned mind will want to convince you that freedom is *not* a choice, and that if it were, everyone would make that choice. The ego-mind also has a library of reasons why they don't. The reason the unhealthy-ego is recoiling is that you are staring directly at its core. The last thing the ego wants is to have you become present to its existence. When you say, "I am free" there is no ego. In that statement, the ego loses control of your life because it realizes you are taking responsibility for that precious gift.

> **EVOLUTIONARY POINTER:** Beyond your declaration of freedom, the art of expressing your awakening appears as your life.

MQ: And maybe by now you are beginning to appreciate that the ego-mind was a necessary evolution in the consciousness of humanity, but that your continued attachment to it no longer serves the advancement to deeper levels of self-awareness and community.

> **EVOLUTIONARY POINTER:** There is no returning to that place you never left to begin with, or appeared to leave. The ego thus serves a divine purpose[13].

Stepping on the Path

MQ: When someone asked the Buddha, "Are you a god?" he replied, "No, I'm awake."

If you are still sensing that the first step in ousting the unhealthy-ego as the exclusive director of your spiritual development is more demanding than just a proclamation, please consider this question: What kind of difficulty would you like to add to your *declaration of freedom* so that it is sufficiently complex enough to qualify as the birthplace of legitimacy?

P: I know, but to make such a statement as, "I am Buddha," brings all my ideas about enlightenment to the forefront of my awareness. Many of those voices are telling me to wait.

MQ: Of course they are. They only pretend to know what the awakened life is going to be like for you. Waiting for this image to manifest prevents millions from a temporal awakening.

EVOLUTIONARY POINTER: Advancing to your first step of awakened life may not seem like the event you had imagined. But then, what kind of a triumphant entry were you told to expect?

Transcending and including the ego as part of your emerging perspective opens the door to a new reality. *"When you are ultimately truthful with yourself, you will eventually realize and confess that 'I am Buddha,' 'I am Spirit'. Anything short of this is a lie, the lie of ego, the lie of the separate self-sense, the contradiction in the face of infinity."*[14]

The Power to be Yourself

MQ: The whole 'I' opens the possibility of living with power, purpose and grace. *Power* is the capacity to act effectively in complete engagement with life and in autonomous community with other people. True power emerges when all of you — the whole 'I' — is accessible. Power is not synonymous with force. *"Force has transient goals; when those goals are reached, the emptiness of meaninglessness remains."*[15] As you identify the unhealthy-ego, you also surpass its transient goals. There you will find that all of your remaining objectives are eternal. Power permits consistency of direction for the sake of humanity.

EVOLUTIONARY POINTER: Power *transmutes* chaos into harmony.

The Hand of Grace

MQ: Grace is the unmerited assistance from the essence of life. With grace, all things are possible. The whole 'I' moves in accord with your life just as it is, allowing grace to flow, thereby influencing and animating your actions. Grace unifies potential and form. Grace is wildly impersonal. It appreciates your personal tastes, yet does not cherish your particular life situations. And although grace is aware of your knowledge and past experiences, it is mostly disinclined to identify with your history, prevailing emotional states, or personal requirements for reassurance or refuge. Because grace is impervious to the desires and aversions of habituation, the unhealthy-ego — despite its zealous endeavors — cannot even begin to fathom its invincible simplicity.

> **EVOLUTIONARY POINTER:** Grace cares not if you have been a scoundrel, but rather *waits* for you to stop ogling the ego. *Moving your attention* means you must know from where to move it.

MQ: See how often you intuit the presence of grace as it stirs you from the dream of ignorance. *"Wake up,"* Grace says, resting lightly on your shoulder. "I have a busy day," you say. "Wake up," Grace says again. "Not now, I need some time to be alone," you say. *"Thank you, I am infinitely patient,"* Grace replies gently. Curiously, this also reveals this tenet of the ego's dharma, which tells us: *I am not worthy of grace.*

> **EVOLUTIONARY POINTER:** *"Whoso walketh in solitude, and inhabiteth the wood, into that forester shall pass, power and grace."*[16]

The Source of Wisdom

P: In all my striving, true wisdom seems to become more and more obscured. How can I shift that perspective?

MQ: You can demystify the source of wisdom. If you know where wisdom comes from, then you can have all the wisdom you want, right?

True wisdom begins with unshakeable faith in your decision-making structures – your values. Because a wise person is clear about his guiding principles, he accepts complete responsibility for his actions. True wisdom is the gift of advanced discrimination. This is a topic that we will cover in Chapter Ten. Alternatively, you can resign yourself to this tenet of the ego's dharma: *I am not worthy of true wisdom.*

MQ: If the source of true wisdom was really shrouded in secrecy, who could be wise?

P: But, is it not generally thought that wisdom accrues with time and experience?

MQ: This is an incorrect assumption, which persists because the ego glorifies the source of wisdom for the sake of its own salvation. Based on this conjecture, you strive toward a concocted image of wisdom that is divorced from the outcome of your actions.

P: Wisdom is also synonymous with *self-honesty?*

MQ: And being fully accountable can be a difficult matter for many people. This is because the picture that the ego paints of your values — and how in reality they are arranged — are two entirely different matters. Therefore, incompetence frequently replaces the consequences of wisdom. If the source of wisdom is revealed to be uncomplicated, would you accept it immediately?

P: I think so. What is the source of wisdom?

EVOLUTIONARY POINTER: Wisdom comes from paying attention to the consequences of your past actions and then adjusting your intentions for the future accordingly.

MQ: Revising your objectives alters subsequent results. Wisdom is born of frequent judgments. If you judge and do not apply the knowledge you've gathered, you cannot become wise. At the same time, the application of accumulated knowledge without consideration for its consequences also becomes the antithesis of wisdom.

P: And that I am intelligent does not necessarily imply that I am wise?

MQ: Not necessarily. And while intelligence is most closely associated with the mind and emotions, true wisdom transcends intelligence, yet embraces both intellect and body. To paraphrase Ken Wilber: Wisdom is the ability to understand emptiness.

P: So, wisdom denotes higher levels of consciousness animating my words and deeds?

MQ: Yes. A wise person remains still when he sees the malignant aspects of the conceptual-mind moving in himself or in other people. By doing just that, he is wise enough *not* to engage with them based on the consequence of his past experiences.

EVOLUTIONARY POINTER: The wise are aware of, yet unidentified with, the hapless charades of the lesser-self, thus they are spontaneously creative.

MQ: This is the wisdom you can accrue from everyday living. The doorway to your creativity is constantly presented to you as your life experiences. Are you going to respond as you always have?

Or are you, as a *free* person, going to claim great wisdom?

1   Francois de La Rochefoucauld (1613 - 1680).

2   Freud never actually used the word *ego* or *id*. Those are the words of a well-known translation of Freud's work, which replaced the words *I* and *it* that Freud used, with *ego* and *id*, to make him sound more technical.

3   Andrew Cohen: Summer retreat, Montserrat, Spain, 2005.

4   Ramana Maharshi was a highly enlightened sage of the 21st Century.

5   For more see, Beyond Knowledge by Jean Klein – Millennium Publications,1994.

6   Gospel of St. Thomas: Logion 2, Translation by Leloup - Shambhala, 2003.

7   Adapted from Integral Spirituality by Ken Wilber, Published by Integral Books, 2007.

8   Carl Jung.

9   Reprinted with permission from *What Is Enlightenment?* magazine; June-August 2006.

10/13 Integral Spirituality by Ken Wilber, Published by Integral Books, 2007.

11 Transpersonal means beyond personal or *personal plus*.

12 There is a great book called *Big Mind / Big Heart*, by Western Zen Master, Dennis Genpo Merzel, which allows you to get in touch with the voice of the Buddha in you.

14 Eric Cabot Steed (Ahmed al Ashqi Jerrahi Chisti) - Devoted Student of Dr. Alexander P. Hixon, Jr., Ph.D.

15 Power Vs. Force by David Hawkins –Veritas Press, 1995.

16 Ralph Waldo Emerson.

Chapter 3

TWO WAYS TO JOY

"Hypocrisy is the homage which vice pays to virtue."[1]

The Ego-Mind is 4,000 Years Old

P: As I learn to act with power and grace in community with other people, is it unreasonable to expect that the ego-mind will kindly step aside as the primary custodian of my destiny?

MQ: Yes. And here's why. It's taken us 14 billion years to get to this point in our evolution. A new earth is not simply going to appear by the end of next month. And remember, the ego-mind is not the enemy, just your attachment to its commands.

P: But, where did it come from in the first place?

MQ: God made the ego at the end of the sixth day. But, he wasn't happy with it so he fed it to a fish he'd created the previous day. The ego, however, was smart, so it broke free from the belly of the fish and has tormented humanity ever since.

P: Get outta here!

MQ: Seriously though, the evolution of the separate sense-of-self, the ego-mind, and even the mythic traditions were all positive emergences in consciousness, despite the bad rap they often get. Let's look at a brief summary of that development, based on a broad consensus of cultural anthropologists and historians[2].

P: Sounds good.

MQ: We find anatomically modern humans first appearing in fossil records about 200,000 years ago. But, for a long, long time if 'you' and 'I' met, by the entrance of the cave for instance, there would be *no-thing* to say. The fact that 'you' and 'I' were preverbal also meant that we were pretty much thought-less. We were stuck in an unconscious 'now'.

P: I cannot imagine what it must have been like to be twenty years old with a subjective experience of a contemporary six-month old child.

MQ: And at that time, by your twentieth year, you had already reached the end of your life! Then about 50,000 BC, 'you' and 'I' had an initial sense of *a few thoughts.* After another forty thousand years or so, with many more thoughts appearing, fully-fledged language had emerged. From about 8000 to 4000 BC, even though there was role differentiation within our community, there was still no personal sense of 'me', which also meant there was no individual choice.

And realize, too, that there was no personal property, because there was no 'person' to own it. It was not until about 4000 to 1500 BC, due mostly to the improvement in linguistic skills and diversity in communications, that the recognition that 'I am thinking' began to appear between our ears. This quickly led to the amazing birth of self-awareness – a sense of 'I' at the level of my thoughts. This was the very beginning of the separate sense-of-self, of the 'personal me'. At this early stage of the development of the separate self-sense, the ego-mind had not yet appeared.

P: But, because there was separate sense-of-self, 'you' and 'I' could at least now make 'choices'.

MQ: Yes, there now was an 'I' to choose. Then, as the capacity for thinking continued to develop and by giving more and more of our attention and consideration to this separate sense-of-self, the *ego* made its *first* appearance. The ego, therefore, is a collection of highly evolved mental processes that are exclusively focused on this fact: *I can think for and about myself.* The ego-mind is utterly and totally focused on the concept of the little-self.

As this ego-mind solidified with the separate sense-of-self as its center of attention, 'you' and 'I' were now predominantly concerned about me and my thoughts about my 'self'. Curiously enough, it was about this time that the idea of 'personal' property appeared. And since that time, the fully formed ego-mind had been the center of our attention – me and my thoughts about me. Because of this we had entire societies of 'individuals' who had, for the first time since the dawn of time, the capacity of 'choice'.

EVOLUTIONARY POINTER: The amazing emergence of the ego-mind appeared around the globe at about the same time!

P: This was the birth of conceptual-free-will?

MQ: Yes. At the moment of making an important decision, your attention was drawn by the ego-mind to the separate sense-of-self. As you can see, conceptual-free-will is not exactly ideal for transcending the attachment to the ego or the separate sense-of-self.

P: But, there is no denying that the development of self-awareness and the capacity for decision-making was a great advancement in consciousness.

MQ: Great advancements for sure. You see, however, that being attached to me and my thoughts about me can be problematic if you are also interested in spiritual evolution.

P: Yes, the issue of that attachment is clear now. But, before all of these developments, where was our attention, if not on the separate sense-of-self?

MQ: Before the emergence of the separate self-sense our attention was simply fused with nature and the body. Watch a young child figuring out its hand is actually its hand. That's about where we were before thinking, language and the ego-mind emerged.

P: Not so good?

MQ: Well, it's okay for that level of development. But, beyond access to a dim and distance cousin of the modern Freudian Ego, we were extremely unevolved. For instance, the preverbal you could distinguish fear from lust, and there was difference between hunting for one and having to kill enough bears to feed a group. There was some sort of an organizing principle at work. But, at that time, if 'you' and 'I' could eat today, we could live to see tomorrow. There was no 'self', we had little need to think, let alone think *my* thoughts, think *about* my thoughts, or to think about *me*.

P: As a result, if I saw my reflection in the pond I would not know it was 'me'?

MQ: This is true.

P: What happened then?

MQ: As the process of farming emerged about 10,000 BC, a surplus of food was created. This allowed us the time to further develop our cognitive abilities, which included being able to anticipate far into the future. Accordingly, the ego-mind — the mental process that is obsessed with the separate 'me' — devised a plethora of defenses against the end of *me and my thoughts*. The ego was also aware of the inevitability of physical death. As a result, history was chronicled and culture was created by the ego-mind to try to stave off its thoughts of ultimate doom.

P: And so appeared an amazing selection of heavens and hells...

MQ: Yes, that was part of our evolution. Fast forward to the 21st Century and here we are: 'You' and 'I' with a distinct separate sense-of-self and the ego-mind, at the mid-point between unconsciousness and super-consciousness.

EVOLUTIONARY POINTER: It is at this juncture of '*me and my thoughts about myself*' that we have remained, except for some exceptional individuals. This is why the ego-mind is not going to step down easily. Welcome to your world.

P: For a vast majority of humanity, oneness with the ego-mind is unconscious?

MQ: Pretty much and across many levels of development. When unity with the little-mind is seamless, it emerges as a sovereign and superior entity with exclusive rights to your values, obligations, voice, actions, friendships, business partners and bedfellows.

P: This also might explain why so much of contemporary spiritual seeking is just an orbit of the ego-mind.

MQ: Yes. 'You' and 'I' are randomly born into a particular time and place. We eventually become self-aware and then we defend the ideas of this culturally created separate sense-of-self – sometimes to the death.

P: How sad.

EVOLUTIONARY POINTER: *"Having used thought to transcend the body, we have not yet learned to use awareness to transcend thought. That, I believe, will be the next development in men and women."*[3]

The Timeless Lesser-Self

P: Is the ego-mind a fully *autonomous* entity?

MQ: Absolutely. The ego-mind is self-directing, self-sufficient, self-contained, self-reliant, and self-focused. The ego does not need you to exist. It gets smarter, but does not grow old. With every new generation, the ego gains complexity for the sake of its own survival. Some of these advances are quite positive. Note the extension in the average life span over the past century. The unhealthy-ego, however, is interested only its survival, not in you. When the ego says, "I know what's best for you," it is generally talking to itself, not to you! If you are lucky, you get to watch and hear the dialogue. Frequently you just respond to it in the absence of objectivity. You simply think *it* is who *you* are. Even the biological urge to procreate is often misinterpreted by the ego as a personal directive from who is believed to be the creator of its geographic corner of the planet. "The Almighty one wants me to have this child" reflects the audacity of the ego-mind to claim a personal connection to a God.

P: Is this the affliction of the un-awakened state?

MQ: Yes, at this stage of maturity. As the ego prepares for a busy day in Japan, most of its middle-American hosts are in bed. When the little-mind is waking up in Chicago, the ego is oblivious to itself as its Tokyo hosts are soundly asleep. The old axiom, *wherever you go, there you are*, reveals that the ego-mind does not travel, but is already at your destination.

EVOLUTIONARY POINTER: The ego-mind keeps you lost in the pursuit of *immortality tokens*[4]; any kind of experience or object to keep its attention off death – it really doesn't matter what.

P: If I am not clear about the influence of the ego-mind, I can be sure *it* is clear about what its goals are for me. It is only when I begin to recognize its manifestations that I can develop the capacity to free myself from the pathological aspects of its authority. But before that, it is likely that even my finest spiritual seeking is never much more than a narcissistic romp in samsara[5].

MQ: Indeed. Expectation is the opiate of the new age.

Unknowingly One with the Little-Self

MQ: Because the attachment to the ego-mind is seamless, you commonly refer to aspects of this natural evolution in the consciousness of humanity as having characteristics unique to you. This means your identity is exclusively related to what you call 'personal' thoughts, emotions, beliefs and to ideas about your past, and your future. The same ego-mind that exists in you is also present in your oldest friend and in your neighbor across the street. Remember, there is only *one* ego. An individual's entrapment in a historical mold only offers an appearance of distinctiveness. Variety in gender, race and upbringing certainly tempers the expression of the lesser-self, but such wonderful diversity does not make it unique.

P: Are you saying that because I think I am only the lesser-self that when I describe myself, I am not aware that I am merely listing traits of the ego-mind?

MQ: The ego-mind is not at all personal. You can describe the aspects of the culturally-created-self in you, but that conditioning does not describe your essential Nature.

EVOLUTIONARY POINTER: The myriad distinctions of the one ego are dictated according to the forces of individual and collective conditioning. Are you not more striking than that?

MQ: While the essential essence of each person is certainly distinctive and exceptional, whole and complete just as it is, the lesser-self in each of us is most certainly *not*.

P: Therefore, I end up manifesting just from the ego, from the element of humanity that is primarily motivated by self-interest. The impersonal ego in me paints fear, anxiety, goals and plans with the broad stroke of 'my' personal experience.

MQ: Yes. And once you call them 'mine,' the unhealthy-ego has put its hooks in you. Then armed with the limitations of conceptual-free-will, you venture out into the world to make your mark. When the layers of ambiguity so often associated with personal desires are peeled away, you find the ego-mind hiding in the motives, not particularly in the articles of those desires and aversions.

EVOLUTIONARY POINTER: Mere desire does not make a craving personal. Understanding the impersonal nature of desire and aversion greatly advances your quest for peace.

P: As a result, the power of 'my' intention generally has both feet firmly planted in the ego-mind, which explains this tenet of the ego's dharma: *Life is your oyster.*

MQ: And the law of attraction, without objectivity on the ego-mind, is going to attract what?

P: More of the ego's favorite dish of needless suffering!

MQ: Exactly!

P: How can I know if the ego-mind has been fueling my life situations?

MQ: It is best to assume, at least at the beginning of your quest to awaken, that the whole thing has been a manifestation of ego-mind.

P: Everything!

MQ: There is nothing wrong with this. It's just a fact of awakening to new levels of awareness. Starting with that assumption means you won't leave anything out. Accept this news and begin to move beyond the grip of that concealed conditioning. Begin to awaken.

P: That hurts! But, I can see how easily the ego drives me crazy as I attempt to define 'myself' by my career, family, finances, relationships, possessions, philanthropy, knowledge, fame and other endless quests for relief from mortality...

MQ: The core of the universal ego-mind can never be satiated.

P: And what if I say that my engagement with the ego-mind is not that bad.

EVOLUTIONARY POINTER: The ego-mind's favorite den is denial. Be sure you are not dwelling in there as well.

The Relationship with Me

MQ: Why does a dog bark at his reflection in a mirror?

P: Because, mostly he sees another dog?

MQ: Yes, but also because he does not see 'himself'.

P: There is no separate *'me' sense* in a dog?

MQ: Yes, that's the case. Imagine if you looked in the mirror every morning and asked, "Who's that?"

P: Sometimes I do! Also, I'd want to know who put that note on the mirror that says, "I feel good about myself today".

MQ: And if two people look in a mirror at the same time?

P: The physical forms are different.

MQ: Do you think that the *'me'* sense appears the same to each person?

P: Yes, I think so. The structure of the separate sense-of-self is the same in both, while the experiences, talents, and gifts of each individual may be very different indeed.

MQ: The ability to recognize 'me' is the fundamental meaning of self-awareness. Therefore, at the psychotherapeutic level, the idea of accepting and loving yourself is considered to be beneficial.

P: Being wholly obsessed with my own self-image is not the same thing as having a healthy view of my independence and autonomy?

MQ: Not in the least! Therefore, if awakening is your objective, you no longer need to nurture the relationship with 'me'. While a certain level of self-concern is perfectly normal and required, when the ego-mind is in control, all of your attention is diverted into monitoring and manipulating your every thought and feeling about yourself. This is called the struggle with the mind. Awakening frees you from this.

P: This is because the separate sense-of-self exists only on a mental level?

MQ: Yes.

EVOLUTIONARY POINTER: The emergence of the individual 'me' sense is a natural stage of maturity that everyone passes through between four and seven years of age[6]. What took thousands of years to emerge in humanity's awareness, is now completed by about the seventh year of life.

MQ: And since the relationship with 'me' is where you communicate with conditioned limitations and conceptual-free-will, comprehending how the separate 'me' sense is formed in early childhood will greatly aid your progress in shifting perspectives.

P: The point is to help children not be trapped like this?

MQ: In a way. The development of separate 'me' sense is a vital part of growing up. It is unavoidable. It is important, however, to teach children about the development of the separate sense-of-self. Show them that while this notion is essential, the little-self is not entirely who they are. This understanding will help free them from unknowingly developing an exclusive identity with the lesser-self later on. It is important to know, however, that this stage of development takes the child through a three-step process: fusion, differentiation and integration. I think the best moment would be during the level of differentiation, in order that a healthy integration may occur*. Please remember, though, that we all need to go through the process of developing a 'me' sense at the level of thought so that it may eventually be transcended and included.

Me, Myself and I

MQ: Do you notice that sometimes all of your attention is directed inwards in an attempt to influence your thoughts?

P: Yes.

MQ: This commonly reflects the conditioned mind nurturing itself. For example, here are two common exclamations: "I don't like it when I am this way," and "I am not myself today." Notice, that there are two "I's."

P: Yes. The first 'I' is aware of the state of the other 'I'.

MQ: One 'I' sees how the 'other I' is acting and feeling. Again, such inner states may be keys to your shadow, so pay attention to your projections and external stimuli that seem to bring up emotional responses in you. Nonetheless, being obsessed with this inner stance all the time reveals the pathological aspect of the ego-mind.

P: The first 'I' has objectivity on the second 'I'.

MQ: Which begs the question: Which 'I' are you? Are you the 'I' that sees with clarity on the second 'I' or are you the second 'I' that is acting in a particular way or experiencing a particular emotional state?

P: Right now I'm not sure which one is the real me.

MQ: Let's just say you are the former 'I' – the one that has objectivity. Then, when those particular emotions pass, are you not still the same unchanged, undamaged and complete observer who was witnessing these emotions or behaviors all along?

P: Yes. I am just watching them pass by in my awareness.

MQ: On the other hand, let's say you are the second 'I,' the one who is feeling a particular emotion or is acting. Who are you when those behaviors or emotions pass? You are surely more than a litany of those ever-changing states or responses to life.

P: These questions give me great cause to wonder: How do 'I' and 'myself' differ?

MQ: And if indeed they are different, who is telling the difference?

P: Also, if 'I' am not 'myself' then who am I until 'I' am 'myself' again? Can't I be both?

MQ: Great questions. It is important as you figure out these distinctions for yourself not to mix up the schism of the dualistic-mind[7] with the constant witnessing state. Deepak Chopra for instance, has 24/7 awareness. He describes this ever-present witnessing awareness as: *"My body is asleep, but I'm observing the body. My body is dreaming, and I'm observing my body in the dream state. My body is speaking to you; I'm observing my body as it sits with these two people in this room. I might be doing anything, but that witness doesn't leave me; it's here. And it's who I really am, I think."*[8]

P: So, one 'I' is the witness. The second 'I' is the separate sense-of-self.

MQ: The former is timeless. The latter is here, in the stream of time.

P: Having ever-present witnessing awareness and being

obsessed with your thoughts and emotions are entirely different matters.

MQ: Yes. People who struggle with psychological and emotional issues frequently attempt to heal their fascination with the little-self by working with a trained therapist. While therapy most certainly has its benefits, this is somewhat of a futile bid for peace of mind because, in most cases, the therapist is also exclusively identified with the same separate sense-of-self.

EVOLUTIONARY POINTER: The ego's favorite topic of conversation is – *itself* about *itself* to *itself*.

Forming the Separate Sense-of-Self

MQ: A young child will cover his own eyes to play 'hide and seek'. Why do you think this is?

P: He is under the impression that if he can't see me, I can't see him?

MQ: Correct. As modern developmental psychology[9] has revealed, young children are unable to think *about* themselves – so to them, their view of the world is the *only* worldview. Later on the child will go hide behind the couch because he has learned that his worldview is not the only one. But, this is only after a striking development has taken place in the child's awareness.

EVOLUTIONARY POINTER: A separate sense-of-self at the level of a child's thoughts only appears *after* the age of three or four years. This means that when a two-year-old looks in a mirror there appears another child, not yet 'me'.

MQ: This is why very young children don't look forward to events before a certain age. There is still no 'me' and also no concept of a future to put that 'individual' in yet. And similarly, without a concept of the past and a 'me' in that past, there is no reason to regret. Then starting around the age of four, a child's attention will naturally emerge from an unconscious present as he begins to grasp the past and the future as diverse *ideas*. It is at this same time that a 'self' appears at the level of his thoughts. As a child locates that image of 'me' in his new concepts of the past and the future, he is able to project the image of that 'individual' into those concepts.

P: As a result, the child sees a 'me' in the future and learns to imagine, anticipate and worry.

MQ: And he can also see an image of 'me' in the past and hence learn to regret. This is also why, prior to this evolution in his consciousness, a young child is very much at home in the present. This combination makes for a somewhat idyllic, albeit unconscious, 'now'.

P: This is funny because one tenet of the ego's dharma suggests that we should: *Recapture the blissful innocence of childhood.* Who would want to go back to such an *unaware* state?

MQ: Perhaps those who are unwilling to let go of the attachment to the ego-mind in themselves?

The Culturally-Created-Self

MQ: Nonetheless, as a child continues to grow into the familial and societal environment, conditioning solidifies this freshly formed separate sense-of-self. Other egos impact the new one.

P: This brings up an interesting point about Descartes' quote, *"I think, therefore I am."* Since I was born into a fully stabilized ego-mind, maybe it should be: *They think,* therefore I am!

MQ: Indeed. As this self-image becomes more and more solid, the highest part of us — consciousness — gets completely lost in a concept of 'me,' which now appears simultaneously in the past, present and future.

P: Then, the ego-mind speaking through my parents and culture convinces me that the things 'I' want and don't want are of primary importance. They tell me, 'It's all about you', when in fact, it really isn't.

MQ: You are right, it's all about the ego, but your parents or caregivers probably didn't know that. Therefore, you are led to believe that your thoughts and feelings are significant because you're having them. As you mature, the ego-mind condenses originally harmless thoughts into 'my' fears, 'my' desires and 'my' future to strengthen your self-image. You make them 'personal' and mold your 'individuality' based on your exclusive identity with whatever thoughts and feelings you happen to be having.

P: The idea is not to deny the developmental experience?

MQ: No. The point is to question your identity with this internal experience.

P: This is why the struggle to alter my thought patterns is so silly. I am just playing into the tricky hand of the malicious ego-mind as it weakens my attention.

MQ: Yes. When you attempt to do this, the patterns possess you. Thus, the culturally-created-self is fully formed, and despite wonderful diversity in this world, it can be as unique as a rainy day in Ireland.

EVOLUTIONARY POINTER: Uniqueness becomes your way of expressing the ego's way, your articulation of impersonal conditioning, your individual face of the global ego.

MQ: The problem is that most people never grow out of this illusion. Billions unknowingly craft and sustain relationships in this way their entire lives, all on a thought-based self-image.

P: Regardless of the geographical location of my conditioning, my life can become an endless effort to build up, maintain, protect and project this sense-of-self. Then I begin to craft relationships to further enhance and sustain my self-image.

MQ: And this entire process is unconscious. Can you now see why most of us live with the false impression of free will, which of course is also highly tainted by society and culture? In high school, for example, if you think you are slick and hip, then that's the crowd you run with. If you think the whole world is against you, you may have friends who think, act and 'choose' in the same way.

P: In some cultures, if you are groomed to have a self-image as a hero, anything could happen to you before you even have time to finish schooling.

MQ: This is a sad, but it is an extreme example of how self-image can be enforced by cultural conditioning where there is no awareness of this process by the groomer or the indoctrinated.

P: If I was raised in a culture that lives in constant fear of its neighbors, and my family was sufficiently attached to their cultural identity, I might end up taking my last bus ride at a very young age and also the lives of everyone else on that bus.

True Individuality

MQ: With an understanding of how this separate 'me' sense is formed, you can offer yourself the possibility of becoming aware and objective of its existence. Then you can transcend and include the relationship with 'me' into a wholesome new perspective. This is the triumphant emergence of true individuality.

EVOLUTIONARY POINTER: Awakening enfolds me, myself, and I into One.

P: An awakened person has no reason to check his thoughts and feelings about himself before he acts? He has no reason to ask, "How am I doing with myself today?"

MQ: Though he is most certainly aware of what thoughts are present and about how he feels, those objects in his awareness have no affect on the most appropriate response for any situation he uncovers on the uncommon path.

EVOLUTIONARY POINTER: True Individuals have transcended the relationship with 'me' and do not have a concept of themselves as separate from their pure intentions to evolve at the level of consciousness.

MQ: In awakening, your subjective experience no longer exclusively defines who you are. Instead, you are continually discovering who you are by how you respond to life, from response to response, in every new moment.

Brenda's Story: Brenda was interested in spiritual development. Upon her return from a week-long meditation and mindfulness retreat, she greeted each task and person with great reverence and civility. Brenda felt content and confident about her new way of being. She was also pleased with herself since her self-image was that of being spiritual and serene. Nonetheless, as time passed, she noticed that in many of her relevant relationships, especially with close family members, she would respond in ways that seemed perfectly reflective of *their* insensitive and grumpy personalities. Such interactions would destroy her inner serenity; leaving her feeling confused and anxious, until such time passed that she could recover her sense of inner quiet again. But Brenda knew that those who have yet to awaken unknowingly create suffering and that only the lesser-self blames external causes for internal unease.

Therefore, she concluded that by reflecting the ego in her most important relationships, she was supporting everyone else's suffering. Having first determined this was not her shadow, to transcend conditioning in those relationships, Brenda realized that she would have to allow for a different response: one that did *not* mirror the lesser-mind. To achieve this, she would have to let go of this relationship *with herself*. By dropping her self-image as Ms. Internally Serene, she also released the need to nurture her attachment to that idea. Brenda was now able to respond to life free from the need to maintain any particular self-image. She no longer had to recover her inner sense of quiet, because that was always reflected in her outer demeanor and way of being. From this point forward, how she responded was more important than, and unaffected by, how she happened to be feeling in the moment of the response.

After repeated attempts to converse with ease and lightness in situations that were highly imbued with the unhealthy-ego, Brenda noticed that some people vehemently defended their positions and opinions, often citing the strength of their emotional experiences as evidence for their convictions. Several of these relationships were relevant to her own awakening. Brenda realized that if she was unable to evolve the basis of these interactions she would have to choose between the lesser-mind's desire for unneeded conflict and her desire to fully awaken. After many, many genuine attempts to bring light and peace to her interactions, it became obvious to Brenda that some people were clearly expressing a preference of living with the unhealthy-ego over living with her.

P: This means that sometimes a little necessary suffering on the path of awakening is unavoidable?

MQ: Freedom from unneeded ego-based anguish is always a choice. At times, it's a most difficult one to make. But what are you going to do? Grapple with the ego or express your full potential?

EVOLUTIONARY POINTER: The consistent expression of wholeness forms a self-perpetuating cycle of ease of being and confidence in your truest essence. This allows unassailable trust, support and communion to develop as the basis for your most significant relationships.

P: Are you saying that the internal experience of a person who is awakened to the ego-mind may not always be the same as that external expression of wholeness?

MQ: Yes, and notice this is a skill we all share. Our attachment to self-righteousness and the malicious ego's ravenous appetite for anguish, however, prevents us from utilizing this skill consistently.

P: Is this the skill of saying one thing, but feeling another?

MQ: Yes. Except, now you are motivated toward compassion because you care more about the spiritual development of the other person than you do about the way you happen to feel in that particular moment.

Two Forms of Affliction

P: Can I end all ego-based suffering today?

MQ: Yes, of course you can.

EVOLUTIONARY POINTER: *Can you* is a very different proposition from *do you want to.*

MQ: Early awakenings to the infestation of the ego-mind reveal the two forms of affliction: short and long. Affliction, espresso style, is potent, yet finite. The 'full-size' version is not as intense, but is infinite. It is the form of prolonged emotional and psychological strife you can rely on for the rest of your life.

P: The choice is mine: short or long?

MQ: Espresso or full-size?

P: It seems to me that many people choose the longer version. And then they justify their choices with a litany of well-rehearsed excuses as to why they can't let go of all unnecessary suffering.

MQ: Well, not exactly. I think the last two sentences might be more clearly stated like this: It seems that the ego-mind in many people, using only the mechanism of conceptual-free-will, chooses the longer version. And then ego-mind justifies those choices with a litany of well-rehearsed excuses as to why it won't let go of all unnecessary suffering.

P: The unhealthy-ego sees no point in letting go of my unnecessary suffering.

MQ: Certainly. Why bite the hand that feeds you? The sustenance of the unhealthy-ego is strife. Anguish is all it knows. This is because the ego-mind can never see life as a process only as a means to an end for the separate self-sense it is charged to defend.

P: This brings up another tenet of the ego's dharma: *Only exceptional individuals are destined to awaken.*

MQ: In this particular tenet, the ego-mind is almost right, because it, too, knows about karma – a subject we will look at in a subsequent chapter.

EVOLUTIONARY POINTER: The choice is yours: short or long. By choosing finite suffering in the dissolution of exclusive ego-identity, you are liberated.

Death and the Lesser-Self

P: Now I think I'll need some real coffee before we talk about death!

MQ: Do you see that death is all around you at every moment?

P: Yes.

MQ: So does the ego-mind. Do you accept the unpredictability that the awareness of death throws upon you?

P: I have a difficult time accepting this...

MQ: It is by accepting the certainty of death that you come to fully understand what it is to be alive. The ego-mind, therefore, disowns the inevitability of death. In fact, the ego-mind suffers from the delusion that it can outwit death. Even the tradition of burying people in the ground is a reflection of ego-mind trying to hide the evidence of death from itself. Death inspired such despondency in the ego that it created culture and history in a daring bid to suspend impermanence. In so-called advanced societies, death is starved of its place at the dinner table and those who dare mention it are often asked to lighten up.

P: Consequently, the unhealthy-ego motivates in futility to get, to have and to know *more* as the only solution to a sense of existential uncertainty.

MQ: All sorts of distractions are sought by the ego as it attempts to defer the awareness of death. You build your roofs, have your relationships, and make a name for yourself, not knowing that the terror stricken lesser-self is the only guiding hand.

EVOLUTIONARY POINTER: As sanity devolves in panicked delirium, the ego-mind keeps your mind off death by draining your vitality with the presence of personal conflict in relationships.

MQ: And by derailing your full potential for living, it keeps itself safe from death inside your body-mind. The ravages of unneeded conflict start in the home and spread out all over the world.

EVOLUTIONARY POINTER: The ego-mind knows that complex lives leave little time for the awareness of death.

MQ: The point here is never to refute the intimacy of loss and mourning. Nonetheless, when those close to you pass on, you may discover that mixed with your grief is a muted speculation as to the 'point of it all'.

P: Often the tears shed are not so much for the dearly departed, but for the ones who remain.

MQ: Indeed.

P: And sometimes I find it hard to see the point of it all.

MQ: Consider that the point may be as simple as constant evolution.

P: But, it is so hard to hold this focus in my awareness.

MQ: Yes. That's because the unhealthy-ego becomes agitated when you seriously ponder continual development as a possible existence. This is because the malicious ego knows that for you to live from that perspective, its sole responsibility, the separate sense-of-self, has to be transcended to a significant degree.

P: And the ego doesn't want to let that happen.

MQ: And why should it? It only knows its own limits. As a result, the ego dreams up all sorts of ideas to distract your curiosity for ultimate aliveness. At one level of development the ego-mind lets you think you have endless options. Watch how conditioning disorients you with indiscriminate references, and just like a pilot who is flying in zero visibility without instrument training, you, too, can be upside down in less than twenty seconds, without even knowing it. What you think is up is actually down, then like the confused pilot, unnecessary suffering is the unavoidable result of the ego-mind's tactics.

P: Ouch! Can you give me an example of 'indiscriminate reference points'?

MQ: Sure: That there was a yesterday with a you in it; that there is a 'now' that merits your constant attention; and that the universe holds nothing other than its arms open wide with love for you. And granted, it may simply be reassuring to believe that one day you will once again be reunited with your loved ones on the 'other side' but, it is reasonable to assume that those individuals will still have the limitations in that dimension as they exhibited in this world.

EVOLUTIONARY POINTER: Yet, over the tides of eternity the questions linger until death disrupts once again, pausing if only for a while, muted defiance of the mystery of being and becoming.

Oops! I Must be Dead

MQ: Lama Ole Nydahl is a Western Buddhist teacher and the founder of over 500 Diamond Way meditation centers. His concise explanation on the process of dying represents one thousand years of Tibetan research into the nature of mind and his worldwide teachings on conscious death – *Phowa*. It is repeated here with the kind permission of Lama Ole Nydhal himself:

"Though quick or slow deaths may appear to be very different, exactly the same process occurs. First, awareness recedes from the skin and other outer sense organs, into the central inner energy channel or magnetic plus-minus axis in the body. While consciousness diminishes, one loses control of the solid and fluid parts of the body, its heat and breath. Then, gradually, the energies from the crown and bottom centers come together at the heart center, while the mind has strong experiences of clarity and joy.

About twenty to thirty minutes after having breathed out the last time, there is total blackness after which a very clear light appears in the heart center. At that time, people have a unique chance. If they have meditated a lot, have kept their Buddhist bonds, avoided political correctness and have stayed honest to themselves, there is a chance to recognize and hold this light, making them in fact enlightened. Then, there's no separation between space and awareness inside and outside and one is boundless. All personal limitations have fallen away and one can take countless rebirths in countless universes with many amazing powers to help others.

If, however, beings become unconscious because the light is too strong — as is mostly the case — this unconscious condition lasts for about three days and upon reawakening, one usually neither knows nor wants to know that one is dead. For about a week, mind remains in the continuation of one's most recent life. One goes to places and people one knew, but of course they cannot see one. It is also very confusing that due to the lack of a body, one immediately appears at whichever place one thinks of.

Ten days after death, after a week in this situation, one finally recognizes that one is dead. This experience is such a shock that one faints again, and when mind surfaces from this second bout of unconsciousness, the habitual world is gone and one's subconscious comes alive. Deeply stored impressions appear, and within not more than three and a half weeks they mature into a fixed psychological structure, expressing the strongest mental tendency developed during one's last life.

Whether this may be pride or jealousy, attachment or anger, greed or confusion, it colors the mind and at the same time draws it to beings and places, which correspond to its content. Thus good actions produce pleasant rebirths in favorable countries and harmful ones bring about the suffering so prevalent in most of the world today. (The longest time to full maturation of one's subconsciousness and re-birth is seven weeks.)

It has always been like that. Mind moves ceaselessly after death until finding the right slot brings it to a passing but unconscious state of peace. Then it awakens and starts projecting again, as it has since beginningless time."

MQ: Who you are beyond your thoughts is revealed in every new death. Awakening to the ego-mind delivers the same outcome while you are still alive. Then you can relax into the inevitable present with great peace of mind, for you know that in death, not only is *no-one* approaching, but there is *no-thing* to approach.

[1] Francois de La Rochefoucauld (1613 - 1680).

[2/4] See Ken Wilber: *Up From Eden*, Quest Books, 1996.

[3] *Integral Spirituality*, by Ken Wilber: Integral Books, 2006.

[5] In Buddhist teachings, the world of illusion.

[6] A Brief History of Everything by Ken Wilber: Shambhala, 1996.

[7] *Dualism* is to perceive the world as being divided into two categories. For example, when one perceives a tree as a thing separate or when one perceives the "self" as distinct from the rest of the world.

[8] What is Enlightenment Magazine, Issue 40, July, 2008. Deepak Chopra in an interview with Andrew Cohen.

[9] For more on this development, see the work of the Margaret Mahler Psychiatric Research Foundation. * You can find a further article on this topic here:

http://www.mickquinn.com/ucp.article.published.6.htm

Chapter 4

THE GRACE OF RESISTANCE

*"It is often merely for an excuse that
we say things are impossible."*[1]

Change and Changelessness

P: Awakening from the ashes of a wholly conditioned life is an arduous task.

MQ: It can be. Spiritual evolution is challenging, because ultimately we are constantly fighting inertia. This is especially true if you are only now beginning to find out that the separate sense-of-self and the ego-mind have been your lifelong co-producers.

P: Why am I in continuous flight from change?

MQ: Not *you* – only the ego-mind. Is not the surface of the ocean changeless in its relentless alterations? A great oak grows tall, buds and flowers, blossoms, loses its leaves, falls over, sunders and decays. Are all of these movements not graceful, and without labels – only *one*? Is not transformation an endless flourish of creativeness – the lush inventiveness of emptiness?

P: Yet, conditioning calls me to label endless change.

MQ: As endless or beginningless? When you express your thoughts as actions are you not creating that which ultimately has never been? Are you not doing this daily, hourly, or by the minute? Even Buddha said, *"It is with our thoughts that we create the world."*[2] So, are these labels of 'less' or 'more' or 'better' or 'worse' ever the same?

P: Therefore, by acknowledging my interest in ongoing development, I can arrest this flight from change and accept that a discomfort zone is a sign that I am ready to evolve?

MQ: Yes, indeed.

EVOLUTIONARY POINTER: Trust in transformation always transmutes turmoil into Truth.

MQ: And it is also important that we do not condemn the structures that have afforded our evolution thus far. The unformed future rests on the formations of the past, as 'righteous' or 'unjust' as they may appear to the tainted eye of the conditioned mind.

Chaos and Serenity

MQ: Have you noticed that anguish is not really caused by things that happen to you; rather it appears when you knowingly or unknowingly defy the rightness of transformation? You become worried and stressed when you lose a job; you're devastated when a lover leaves you; you're upset even when little things don't go your way. You often have a difficult time accepting change in your life — even 'good' change — and feel the need to manage, re-position, or force everything in an effort to make your world safe and predictable.

P: Do 'I' really feel that need or is that just the ego-mind panicking in the face of the unknowable?

MQ: You only witness change. It's the unhealthy-ego that truly abhors it, or in some cases champions relative change to boost your self-image of detesting the 'status quo'.

EVOLUTIONARY POINTER: If you look closely, you will see that the suffering you experience, as well as the pain and suffering you cause others, is the result of your unwillingness to embrace resistance as an indicator of wholesome direction.

MQ: Resistance is always an invitation to grow to the next level that is being made available to you. Those who have awakened actively pursue development and evolution, thereby seeming to be fearless.

P: But, it's not that they are without the voice of healthy apprehension, right?

MQ: That's right. Unreasonable fear appears only when you resist the process of life. When you let go of the unhealthy-ego, all emotional and psychological struggling is revealed to be the manifestation of mediocrity masquerading as contentment and false bravado. Often it takes more energy to pretend that you are happy than it does to let go of unnecessary suffering.

EVOLUTIONARY POINTER: The awakened person sees chaos as the genius of serenity.

P: Part of awakening, therefore, is to discover that life is constantly in a state of flux.

MQ: And that the expression of harmony recreates itself in spite of prevailing conditions. Out of this knowing emerges the ability to manifest the wildest of dreams without any expectations of success or failure, gain or loss.

P: Do awakened people have preferences?

MQ: Yes. They want things to go well, but a particular outcome cannot fundamentally affect their awakening.

P: Life to an awakened person is a constancy of change, development and growth?

MQ: Awakening is a constancy of *conscious evolution* at the forefront of your awareness. And the forms those changes take are ultimately your responsibility. The future of humanity is dependent upon you.

P: When do I rest?

MQ: Only the ego needs to take a vacation. There is no struggle when out of perfection emerges more perfection.

P: Do all excuses for limitations emanate from the voices of the unhealthy-ego?

MQ: Yes. Now let's change direction a little.

P: Sure.

Change and Clock Time

MQ: Perception, by classical definition, is based on memory. Therefore, the ego-mind regards change as a factor of arbitrary reference points in the historical past. Since a major component in the original emergence of the ego-mind is the concept of the past, you have been trained to perceive the phenomenon of change in terms of clock time.

P: Is change verifiable outside this particular standard?

MQ: The first thing to consider, as you evolve your perspective on change, is that clock time is merely a convenience. Did you know that before the invention of trains, clocks in different parts of the same country were rarely synchronized? There was simply no need for the time to be consistent. The Energy Policy Act of 2005 in the USA extended daylight saving time by one month beginning in 2007. They just moved the time. Relative change can be viewed using clock time, but from an absolute perspective, is there any change that is occurring?

EVOLUTIONARY POINTER: The most dynamic part of your deepest Self champions change when it becomes conscious of itself in your human form. The unhealthy-ego labors against it. Whose side are you on?

P: Change can also be alleged by contrasting current psychological or emotional states with the states that existed during a certain period of time in the past.

MQ: But frequently, as you make such comparisons, the thoughts or feelings you are contrasting can change yet again.

P: We use such words as 'beneficial' and 'useless,' 'minor' and 'profound' to qualify change.

MQ: Since these are all unverifiable ranges of the conceptual-mind, they are also unreliable indicators as to the stage of a particular change.

EVOLUTIONARY POINTER: While random reference points in clock time allow you to view change, they cannot confirm its start or finish. The changes initiated by the big bang are ongoing.

MQ: How do you determine when something is stable, unstable, unchanged, changing or changed?

P: I look at what I have, versus what I had, comparing that to what others have and had and contrast it all to what could be had.

MQ: I'm exhausted already! Do you know that this relentless commotion of comparing and contrasting is a strategy of the unhealthy-ego? Its specific task is to keep your attention on anything other than the flawless perfection of continual evolution and change. The awakened perspective on change reveals it as a graceful flow. Put your trust in the process of life.

Measuring Global Change

P: What about looking at change from a global perspective?

MQ: Spiral Dynamics[3] is a fascinating theory of human development that allows us to view stages of development and the evolution of values at a cultural level. The many levels of development described in this system exist simultaneously in our world, mercilessly entwined, in harmony, in conflict and yet ever evolving. There are communities of people whose meager and strenuous horticultural-based lifestyle — similar to the stage of development predominant thousands of years ago — exists today in an isolated corner of one of the most developed countries in Western Europe. The highest levels and the lowest levels of development co-exist. In between, growth and alteration is harmless relentlessness.

EVOLUTIONARY POINTER: At the collective level, change is a constant movement that must be first anchored at some arbitrary point in the past so we can measure it.

P: This reminds me of a tenet of the ego's dharma that suggests: *If only we could go back to purer times, all our problems would be healed.*

MQ: Indeed. But, the face of humanity is certainly not as it was when 'you' and 'I' were hunter-gathers. And just look at the progress over the past five hundred years. It's been pretty good, don't you think?

P: Yes.

MQ: The average life span is four or five times what it was then. That's great! Who would want to go back? Is not the proclivity of this *unconscious evolution* to progress in a wholesome direction overwhelming?

P: Indeed, it is!

MQ: The fact that more and more people are accessing conscious-free-will by transcending and including conceptual-free-will reveals that this process is waking up to itself. And in wholesome togeth-erness we are learning to *consciously* co-create the future. You and I are becoming conscious agents for change.

P: I find this level of responsibility a little overpowering.

MQ: Then, at least you know you are on the right track. Follow that resistance.

Change and the Present Moment

MQ: Before we look at the precarious nature of the present moment, consider this: If the past can never be altered and a future event has no effect yet, then is all change occurring now?

P: But, if all change is happening now, why is the power of the 'now' such a popular concept?

MQ: Because the ego confuses the timeless ease and presence of those who have let go of their exclusive identity to the lesser-self, with a single moment of clock time.

EVOLUTIONARY POINTER: Pure awareness is *eternal* – clock time cannot measure that.

MQ: As we begin to look for confirmation for the 'now', it is important to note that we are not seeking to disprove the perspectives bestowed through the experience of Oneness.

P: But, we can't ignore the ego's addiction to the promise of the 'present'.

MQ: Yes, which introduces another tenet of the ego's dharma: *Stay in the present moment. All of your problems disappear and you won't have to do anything to be perfectly fulfilled.*

P: Which begs the question, who's trying to get in the 'now'?

MQ: The ego?

P: That's not rational.

MQ: Rationality and the unhealthy-ego are mutually exclusive. But, perhaps as you intuit and taste your original state of Oneness, the ego is picking up on the same source.

P: And I need to distinguish between the two. Okay, thank you. Can we get back to the precarious nature of the present moment?

MQ: Of course. Firstly, it is necessary to ascertain, as best we can, the point at which the present moment becomes the past. This, of course, might be very close to or even the same moment that the future becomes the present. The measurement of the present moment has been found to be somewhat indeterminable. In 2004 the BBC reported that the shortest instance of clock time has been recorded to within 100 attoseconds.

P: How small is one attosecond?

MQ: Tiny actually: one billionth of one billionth of a second. There would be three million year's worth of those in one normal second! Therefore, with the present moment being so infinitesimally small we have to ask: When does the future become the now and the present moment become the past?

P: At what point in clock time does change actually occur?

MQ: So then everything is changing in an infinite now. According to David Chalmers, Professor of Philosophy and Director of the Center for Consciousness at the Australian National University, the farther one goes down the scale of physical objects and reality, the *less material* matter appears to be.

EVOLUTIONARY POINTER: The deepest levels of currently visible reality seem to consist of nonmaterial information, pure potentialities of matter or energy, but not quite either.

P: Okay then. Even the scientists don't have a clue as to what makes up the visible reality!

MQ: Therefore everything that is nothing is evolving in an infinite present. And if you are awakened, you are responsible for how that shows up as your life and your interactions with other people. In awakening, you witness life as perfect in its change-lessness and simultaneously respond to an inherent demand that everything must change. It is at this edge where you will find that consciousness itself is evolving, and you become more aware of who you really are at the dynamic cusp of changeless emptiness and evolving form.

P: So, the past and the future are hardly confirmable beyond concepts located 'before' and 'after' an infinitesimal present. Therefore, how can I conclude that birth and death are not occurring simultaneously?

MQ: You can't. Welcome to the mystery! And note, too, in that immeasurable present, that the process of life is flourishing and all that you will gather and attain will be divided and dispersed. Don't let the ego-mind chase you away from this truth. Allow your future to emerge, not in isolation, but with a myriad of futures. Allow your face to be the future of humanity, together with others at the leading edge of the evolution of consciousness and culture.

Change, Death and Psychotherapy

P: People frequently turn to psychotherapy as a way to deal with change, including the most formidable alteration, which we spoke of in the last chapter – death.

MQ: From the ego's perspective, aging and death are the two greatest changes. It wants to avoid them at all costs. Divorce, starting a new job and changing homes are also at the top of its list. Therefore, the ego-mind keeps you consumed with quantifying, qualifying, sharing, caring and complaining about all the developments and progressions in your life so that its attention is not on its arch-enemies – death! The logic of the ego-mind is: If mortality is not in your awareness, then you have nothing to be concerned about.

P: That's no way to live!

MQ: Indeed.

P: But, I still fear this foreboding event. Is that real?

MQ: Feeling it makes it real. But, are you perhaps paying too much attention to the voice of unreasonable fear? Are you fixated on the fear of this change because everything you currently know yourself to be is limited by those concepts, opinions, thoughts and feelings? *"Maybe you did not have any fear of death until your first death."*[4]

Nonetheless, talking about death to your psychotherapist, while tremendously helpful, may not help you overcome that anguish.

P: Why is this?

MQ: Because it is unlikely the therapist has transcended that particular fear in himself.

P: Therefore, despite the contributions of such Western research to human development, it is good to be clear about this practice.

MQ: Yes. Traditional psychotherapy is not at all about awakening conscious-free-will. As we discussed earlier, a healthy Freudian Ego is necessary for your spiritual development. Therefore, a course of psychotherapy can most certainly take you to the point where you can begin to look at transcending your attachment to the lesser-self and awakening to your full potential.

P: I need to let go of the idea that psychotherapy is ever going to heal that nagging sense of existential lack that really bothers me sometimes.

MQ: Yes. And if a liberated life is your goal, and your time on the couch is not augmented with other practices that will help you identify and transcend the ego, psychotherapy will quickly stall your progress. As Ken Wilber once said, *"Therapists are pimps for samsara."*[5]

EVOLUTIONARY POINTER: Freedom is wearing the "victim" tee-shirt inside out.

P: What might happen if the therapist happened to awaken to his own attachment to the ego-mind? Would he deny his patient's right to pursue further resolution?

MQ: No, not in the least. But, in the vast majority of his cases, it is likely that the root of his clients' disharmony would be plainly evident as their attachment to that same ego-mind. Therefore, an awakened therapist might be unable to relate as he did before to the ego's nauseating gibberish, and its constant need for affirmation and attention.

P: Does this mean that the analyst would become cold, uncaring and incapable of acknowledging and empathizing with the suffering of his patients?

MQ: No. But, he could no longer engage with his clients at that level, because to continue on the same path of treatment would also make him an accomplice to anguish.

P: On the other hand, there is a tenet of the ego's dharma, which states: *Your story is important and needs to be heard no matter how long, laborious and personally suffocating it is.*

MQ: And additionally: *You should also expect a big hug for sharing!*

The Bright Side of the Road

P: What about the role of positive psychology in regard to awakening?

MQ: I like this because it offers an approach away from the focus on that which makes us miserable. But, just look at what happens when this potential falls into the wrong hands.

P: Whose hands?

MQ: You'll see. I once attended an annual European Conference on Positive Psychology, because it was less than an hour from my home in Portugal at the time. There, the researchers revealed their exhaustive efforts to identify the causes and conditions for happiness. What I found even more fascinating than all the research and conclusions, was watching the politically correct viciousness with which the ego in the participants argued whose controls, test bases and results were the best or the most efficient.

P: That was the ego-mind governing the participants' reactions to protect their highly lettered self-images.

MQ: Yes. And who knew what was happening? The unhealthy-ego was running the show.

The Doctor's Story: On the last day of the conference I spoke at length with a leading professor in the field of positive psychology. I asked her to consider the possibility of identifying and transcending all concealed conditioning, toward *complete happiness*. She was quite intrigued and asked me how this might be possible. After a lengthy discussion of this topic, I suggested that she make the pursuit of freedom from concealed conditioning marginally more important than anything else in her life. After a pensive moment she said, in a tone that hardly masked the deep dissatisfaction upon which it rested, "But that would be impossible. I am already trapped in a career and I have a mortgage."

P: That doesn't sound so positive, does it?

MQ: Who do you think was talking? Was that the voice of the full potential of an attractive, forty-something Ph.D., a leader in her field of positive psychology, or was that the unhealthy-ego lashing out in defense of limitation?

P: That was the malicious ego taking a stand for itself!

MQ: And she had no idea what was happening.

Don't Worry, Be Happy

P: Is there anything wrong with seeking happiness?

MQ: Wanting to be happy is perfectly fine. But, do you want complete happiness?

P: I don't think there is such a thing as complete happiness here on earth. I think that anyone who believes that is deceiving themselves. Are you completely happy?

MQ: I am only unhappy when I am reminded of how people are blinded by the evolution of self-awareness. This is not personal unhappiness.

P: I think that you are unrealistic in your view that you are completely happy.

MQ: If the avenue to complete happiness was presented to you as a clear and present possibility, would you opt to explore its potential? Or are you attached to the opinion that complete happiness is unrealistic — which is correct, but only from your current level of development — so that you may defer the consequence of uprooting concealed conditioning. Look not at what makes you happy, but at your intentions for seeking joy in that way. Therein lays the secret to authentic joy.

EVOLUTIONARY POINTER: When you transcend and include the concept of personal happiness, you are liberated from the illusion of personal unhappiness.

Numbing the Voice of God

P: Earlier, we touched on depression as a common symptom of shadow. Is this affliction also related to change?

MQ: Depression often emerges as a consequence of living in a way that is completely counter to your aptitude for intuition and trust. Depression is a common response to a high-volume invitation of consciousness that you are more than ready to let go of a particular life situation.

P: Are you saying that when consciousness recognizes that I am ready to evolve it will bring this joyous news to my attention, but sometimes in the form of depression?

MQ: Yes, in this and many other ways.

P: Therefore, the only reason I am hearing the word of God is because I have already reached a new level of preparedness.

MQ: Yes. What happens then is entirely up to you; invitation issued, grace stands by.

EVOLUTIONARY POINTER: The ego will take whatever steps necessary to numb the voice of God.

MQ: Prescription drugs can often have the affect of stabilizing you in 'hell'. When you *know* you hear the call to evolve, but do your best to avoid it, the degree of your defiance of that which you are already prepared for will determine the harshness of your experiences.

P: How do I evade an invitation from consciousness that I am ready to grow?

MQ: You pay more attention to the counsel of the ego-mind than to your poor soul screaming for release. Emotional and psychological angst then brings you to your knees in harsh defiance. Depression calls you to look not so much at what you do not have in your life, but rather at what you do have — and what you deeply and truly do not want — but are choosing to cling to because of an unwillingness to evolve beyond that level of development.

EVOLUTIONARY POINTER: Hopelessness is a common side effect of denying even the possibility of perfection in the human form.

P: And this tenet of the ego's dharma tries to convince us that: *I am human therefore imperfect by design.*

MQ: When you deny the call for transformation, you often enter the 'dark night of the soul' or more appropriately 'the dark night of the ego'[6]. People medicate so they can deal with life's proclivity to give them what they want. While drugs can have a stabilizing affect on certain destructive behaviors, a common — and naively extolled — side effect of such remedies is that you do not have to hear the invitations of consciousness to your own greatness. Symptoms are merely patched, to reappear at a later time, with more complexity and forcefulness.

EVOLUTIONARY POINTER: God never whispers.

P: This means that the most painful way that I can live is in denial of my discomfort zones, because they are indicating that I am ready for the next step of my evolution.

MQ: Yes, regardless of whether your worldly dreams have succeeded wildly or failed miserably. That simply does not matter. By trying to wiggle around your discomfort zones you become 'piggy in the middle'; dismayed in samsara, but not yet on a direct path of awakening.

P: This remind me of the quote by Krishnamurti from earlier in our conversation: *"In the gap between subject and object lies the entire misery of humankind."* What happens when I intentionally prevent change I'm ready for, or attempt a transformation I am ill prepared for?

MQ: You will find that you are moved directly into a situation of calamity. Be wise, and do not wait until life demands your attention.

The Way of Resistance

MQ: Allow resistance to be your guide to greatness. If you feel that you have reached a discomfort zone then you are set to express that readiness. The path of least resistance quite frequently leads you astray.

EVOLUTIONARY POINTER: You cannot feel opposition to change unless the faculty of success has already emerged within you.

P: Since a discomfort zone always begins as the unfamiliar, resistance to change is therefore the route to and through the next level of your development.

MQ: You can't sense opposition and *be* that opposition as well.

P: This is true! I cannot be aware of resistance and be that exact voice of resistance at the same time. This also means that opposition is not a force, which has an independent existence beyond my ability to observe it.

MQ: No. It's just one of many voices you have guiding you. The voice of resistance is just as legitimate as the voice of surrender. Your role is to harmonize both with wisdom and awakened compassion.

P: And what about physiological alterations in the face of change?

MQ: *"Change and novelty are one of the most potent triggers of the stress response."*[7] This does not mean, however, that you have to identify with the stress response any more than you do with the thrill of change. Remember the resistance you felt to some 'earth-shattering' step in your teens? Where is the might of this opposition now? It no longer appears in your awareness. It only appeared at that time, as a sign from life, that you were ready to transform at that level. You took action. Resistance followed is ended.

EVOLUTIONARY POINTER: Resistance points the way.

P: But, there is no way to predict the future.

MQ: True, beyond planning what you are going to do later today and perhaps this weekend.

P: But, beyond that, is it really possible to see what I will experience or what my life will look like in five or ten minutes, months or years?

MQ: No, unless of course your primary intention for being is the evolution of consciousness and culture. If that is the case, such an outcome will always be your future. Though the details of that future are unknowable, it will nonetheless, be ecstatically rewarding!

Melissa's Story: Melissa had an MBA and a cute dog named Spud. She was single, in her late twenties, and owned her own apartment. Each day she walked to her office through the historic part of her town. Melissa worked in private portfolio management for a major bank. She had high moral and ethical standards and was skilled at gaining the trust of others. Melissa often felt concern for some of her clients' dire financial situations. She was deeply troubled however, because the bank often wanted her to use her natural people skills to direct clients to investments that were more advantageous to the bank. Many mornings when she woke up, her first thought was, 'I hate my job'. She did not know to own this voice and, blaming her work, her shadow of repressed potential just got bigger and bigger. She often cried on her way to work. Nonetheless, right before she entered the bank Melissa was able to switch into the role for her job, which she would drop at the end of the business day.

Melissa's passion in life was literature. When she accepted this job at the bank, she gave herself ten years to earn some money and then she promised herself that she was going to live her life on her terms. With only three years left, Melissa doubted she could make it to her goal. She longed for a day when she no longer had to lie to herself and those around her. She craved to greet a sunrise with enthusiasm and joy. Even her dog Spud, was getting weary of her dim days!

Then, one afternoon while hiking in the mountains, Melissa met an interesting couple. The lady was an author and her husband was a professor of philosophy. When the couple learned of Melissa's predicament, they suggested that the door to release was directly in front of her. But because her attention was so consumed by the ego-mind's fear of change, she was unable to see this option. As the conversation continued, Melissa learned that liberating her free will is a factor of four points, all of which could be learned:

1) Accept resistance as an indication of preparedness.
2) Remain resilient in the face of opposition.
3) Perfectly adhere to a set of higher principles.
4) Trust in one's choices.

Melissa said she was no stranger to opposition, having worked through many difficulties in her college days and in her early career. She admitted that she was not thrilled with the thoughts of a way of life that might not include her safe and predictable job. She also told the couple that her grandfather had been imprisoned by the former dictatorship in her home country. Melissa proudly stated that upon his release, he continued to strive peacefully, to the end, for what he believed. Melissa knew that she had inherited his resilience so it was clear that she was only missing one aspect of the awakened life – trust.

Melissa then asked the couple how she could learn trust. They told her that learning trust is the game of life. Divine Providence, however, only lets you win when two conditions are met: The first is that your intentions are *pure*, meaning that the aim of your actions is not primarily for personal gain, to support a conditioned self-image, or to create any unneeded anguish for others or yourself. The second condition is that you have to make the first move.

EVOLUTIONARY POINTER: Struggling with resistance is the antithesis of trust.

Melissa said her intentions were pure, but admitted that she was intimidated by having to make the first move. She had been thinking about this for years in the hope that she might find a way out, but the hole she was in only seemed to deepen. The couple told Melissa that this fear of change was a product of the age-old ego-mind, it could be safely disregarded, and that because she was sensing such a strong resistance, she was fully prepared for the next step. But Melissa insisted that if she pondered her situation a bit more she may be able to find a way out of her conflict without embracing too much change. After several attempts to convey clarity, the couple realized they were only speaking with the ego, and not the part of

Melissa who could see her full potential. The little-self in Melissa defied all suggestions that Melissa should trust life, so at the end of the day the couple left her, and her dog, to her worrisome world.

> EVOLUTIONARY POINTER: Life already trusts you. By returning that favor it allows you to walk the uncommon path with power and grace. Do you trust life?

P: From this story it is clear that, like Melissa, I control the pace at which I embrace the invitation of opposition and therefore the rate at which my life transforms. This also means I am in charge of the amount of unnecessary suffering I experience.

MQ: Who is guiding your life? You are. Who is guiding your awakened life? You are! Therefore only you determine the rate at which you traverse from *unconscious opposition* to *conscious acceptance* of the constant nature of change. Freedom, as always, is your choice.

Let nothing upset you
Let nothing frighten you
Everything is changing
God alone is changeless
Patience attains the goal
Who has God lacks nothing
God alone fills all your needs.[8]

Change is the Natural State

MQ: Learning to accept change is a matter of remaining conscious when entering a discomfort zone and using resistance as an indication of wholesome direction. When you feel the power and grace of opposition you can:

- Acknowledge your disagreement to the change that you

perceive.

- Acknowledge change as the most natural state in life.
- Acknowledge that consciousness knows when you are ready to change before you do.
- Acknowledge that resistance is a direct invitation from consciousness to evolve.
- Acknowledge that fear of change is dependent on your point of focus, therefore not related to the event or situation.
- Acknowledge that everything is transitory, including thoughts and feelings about change.
- Accept that everything is in a constant state of development or dissolution
- Softly disregard any disparaging thoughts and emotions.
- Accept and be thankful for both the 'pleasant' and 'unpleasant' changes in your life as they are opportunities for you to awaken from the dream of the ego.
- Own the fear of change by saying, "This potential is mine".

EVOLUTIONARY POINTER: Any reservations you may have about your awakening are not yours, but the ego-mind's ultimate self-realization of impotence.

MQ: You can't be averse to a birthright! The ego-mind has taken you this far. Now consciousness is beckoning that you are ready to put down your exclusive attachment to the ego. If you have reached this deeply into this book you are more than ready to transcend and include ego-mind.

"Be the change you want to see in the world."[9]

[1]   Francois de La Rochefoucauld (1613 - 1680).

[2]   The Dhammapada.

[3]   Dr. Don Beck: www.spiraldynamics.net.

[4]   Adi da Samraj, 1988.

[5]   Samsara is also defined as the eternal cycle of birth, suffering, death and rebirth.

[6]   Adapted from the original quote: "the dark night of the ego" in *Transcending the Levels of Consciousness* by David R. Hawkins. Veritas, 2006.

[7]   Esther M. Sternberg is internationally recognized for her discoveries in brain-immune interactions and the effects of the brain's stress response on health.

[8]   St. Teresa of Avila.

[9]   Mahatma Gandhi.

Chapter 5

FREEING YOUR MIND

*"We often do good in order that we may
do evil with impunity."*[1]

The Courtesan of the Lesser-Self

P: Your request that I implicitly trust the process of life seems to induce a nonstop struggle with my thoughts.

MQ: An initial awakening will always include this realization. Remember, the ego-mind is a 4,000-year-old mental construct that thinks its sole purpose is to control your future. Please know that it is not entirely malevolent, yet when you hear the call to *implicitly trust the process of life*, it will always respond to defend itself.

P: What is this constant struggling with my thoughts?

MQ: This is the un-awakened state. Have you also noticed, though, that your thoughts originally appear in your awareness untainted and impartial?

P: I hadn't considered that, originally untainted?

MQ: Yes. Look at what happens immediately after they arise. Concealed conditioning infects them. To survive, the ego-mind takes hold of your thoughts and twists them beyond all recognition of their primary innocence. Consequently, consciousness becomes entangled in restricted modes of thinking. Struggling reflects not so much your unwillingness, but your unknowingness that you don't always have to be qualifying your thoughts.

P: I struggle because I care about the content of thinking?

MQ: That's a nice way of putting it. It is more like you are unconsciously obsessed with that content. Awakening, therefore, is to step aside from the ways in which you have been conditioned to

153

pay attention to thinking. Stepping aside begins by realizing that you and the vital flow of thinking are essentially not one and the same.

EVOLUTIONARY POINTER: While the power to think of, and for, yourself is a sign of a healthy mind, the interpretation of that involuntary flow is the key to freeing your mind.

Who You Are is Not Your Thoughts

MQ: According to the National Science Foundation[2], the average person thinks about 12,000 thoughts per day. A deeper thinker generates about 50,000 thoughts daily. According to Deepak Chopra, 95% percent of our thoughts are exactly the same thoughts that passed through our minds the day before. As my friend, composer Troy Lennerd, once said, *"It's just like a radio station, stuck on the same station, that keeps playing the same stuff every day, over and over!"* Therefore, implicit trust in yourself and in the process of life only emerges when you can interpret random content, free from the chorus of covert conditioning.

P: Simply because a thought is present, even persistently present, in my awareness, does not mean that it has any consequences for me or for the world?

MQ: No, not in the least. A thought may have no implication whatsoever except that it happens to be there in your awareness. And that's not significant at all. Arbitrarily accepting thoughts as factual or noteworthy is quite problematic. But, the ego adores a wild and inventive mind. It is by recognizing its presence in your thinking that you can finally transcend its influence there.

P: *Who I am* is not *what I'm thinking*?

MQ: No, not at all. Who you are is aware of that process.

EVOLUTIONARY POINTER: Rampant thinking becomes the courtesan of the unhealthy-ego when undeserved significance is assigned without due diligence.

Mick's Story: During my own search to resolve the resistance to my mind, I was surprised to hear these words from spiritual teacher Andrew Cohen: *"Who you are is not your thoughts"*[3]. During that period of my life, I was also involved in starting and selling businesses and maintaining an active social life. But, I struggled constantly with the presence or absence of particular thoughts. In other words, I was completely estranged from the process of life. I had yet to realize, like millions of other people, that I had been raised to use thinking as a way to nurture and support a particular self-image: the pictures I held in my mind about myself. At this time my self-image was that of the intelligent male, the spiritual seeker, the risk-taking entrepreneur, the funny and charming date, the good and caring friend and the peacemaking son. And of course, there were many aspects of that self-image I denied: the addict, the control-freak, the obsessive-compulsive, the frantic worrier and so on. Basically, I was honored by the presence of certain thoughts, and abhorred by the presence of others. The latter of course, ended up in my shadow.

P: Sounds a little bit messy.

MQ: To say the least! Not to mention that during this time I also considered myself to be firmly rooted on 'my conscious spiritual path'. Since I was captivated by this teacher's clarity, I studied him, his writings, his organization and his students – mostly to make sure that he walked his talk.

P: Why did you do that?

MQ: Because another 'guru' whom I'd spent countless hours with over the previous seven years turned out to be a bed-hopping sex addict who eventually committed suicide.

P: Wow! That's a big shadow.

MQ: Indeed! My intent observation came to the conclusion that Andrew Cohen walked his talk flawlessly and continues to do so.

Enlightenment – The Way You Relate

MQ: So I continued to *unlearn* a conditioned way of thinking with Andrew Cohen. Then during one of his long-term meditation retreats in the south of France in the summer of 2001, he revealed the following:

> EVOLUTIONARY POINTER: *"Enlightenment is the relationship you have to the experience you are already having."*

MQ: These words had a profound affect on me. I contemplated them full-time for the following three weeks. Eventually, it emerged that the content of my experience, by its very nature, was entirely transient. Therefore, the only stable aspect of this statement was relationship, simply because it could exist within volition. Furthermore, the relationship to the experience I was already having was distinct from both the past and the future. I realized that I was free to choose my relationship to the experience I was already having. By choosing the relationship also meant that I was free to choose the outcome – *enlightenment* and freedom from all unnecessary emotional and psychological suffering.

> EVOLUTIONARY POINTER: Enlightenment is indeed a choice!

P: Sounds good, but... if enlightenment is only a matter of choice, why are there not millions of fully awakened people in the world?

MQ: Well, in my experience, it wasn't that simple...

P: I guess your realization at that time didn't include a distinction between *conceptual-free-will* and *conscious-free-will*?

MQ: No, not in the least. At that time, what I considered to be *my free will* was not really 'mine'.

It was just conceptual-free-will with its standard range of options taken from within the average level of consciousness of the culture from which I emerged. And as you know, conceptual-free-will offers no possibility of liberation. Since I had yet to transcend and include conceptual-free-will as an object in my awareness, the capacity of conscious-free-will was not available to me. At this stage of my development, I was actually not 'free' to choose my responses to the experiences I was already having. I was just under the illusion that those options were available to me.

P: You had no idea that you were stuck in the trap of the ego's conceptual-free-will.

MQ: The folly of arrogance!

P: This is starting to make sense now. I often say, "I want to be happy, so I choose happiness" but, that's generally not my outcome. That's because my choices and subsequent actions are mercilessly bound by the limits of the culturally-created-self. How can I really choose happiness if I am not aware that I only have access to conceptual-free-will?

MQ: You can't. This is old-hat New Age – the 'conscious seeker' who is attached to a *concept* of happiness that doesn't exist, and who at the same time is lost in the false impression of true free will.

P: Funny, but not really. What is the connection between the fact that concealed conditioning distorts my thoughts right after they enter awareness, and my attempts to break free from the ego-mind by only using conceptual-free-will?

MQ: Let's begin with these distinctions.

Paying Attention to Thoughts

MQ: There are basically three ways in which you can pay attention to the content of your mind. They are:

1) Conditioned attention to thoughts
2) No attention to thoughts
3) Awakened attention to thoughts

P: Is conditioned attention to thoughts the most prevalent state in humanity?

MQ: Yes. A significant percentage of the world's population is inadvertently astray at this level. When you pay conditioned attention to thinking, the thoughts that happen to be present in your awareness are taken to mean something about you, when really, they don't mean a thing.

EVOLUTIONARY POINTER: In the un-awakened state, a distinction is rarely drawn between *thoughts* and the *thinker*, between the *content* of the mind and the *context* in which the thinker exists and the thoughts arise.

MQ: It is curious, also, that this percentile includes many people who are absolutely convinced that they have already accessed a path of growth and development that will, sooner or later, lead them beyond their sometimes troubling level of existence.

P: But, isn't conviction admirable?

MQ: Yes. Conviction at all levels is fine. But what if that certainty affords you no possibility of release, and you don't pay attention to the voice of the skeptic, then where are you?

P: Convinced I will awaken, but unhappy in an endless meantime.

MQ: Therefore, conditioned attention to thinking is the pinnacle of the ego-mind's pathological obsession with: *I am predominantly concerned about me and my thoughts about me.* That's where most of the world lives, including hoards of unfortunate 'seekers' who throng to spiritual events in promise of relief, only to deepen their pain.

EVOLUTIONARY POINTER: You can't learn to soar to your full potential from someone who is unknowingly denying those levels of awareness in themselves.

P: Conditioned attention to thinking supports the decision-making structures offered to me by the ego-mind. Conditioned attention to thinking supports conceptual-free-will!

MQ: Yes, they work perfectly well together. After my experience in France, I saw that 'my' free will only reached as far as the walls of individual and collective conditioning. This meant that all of my responses to the experiences I was already having were orchestrated by *conditioned attention* to thinking. Freedom from suffering was nowhere to be found in that scenario. I realized that my entire life up to that point had been carefully constructed by the ego-mind using conceptual-free-will. *I* was nowhere to be found in that plan.

P: Well, not all of your choices were bound by individual and collective conditioning. Despite your deftness for suffering you were on that retreat?

MQ: Okay, but one such choice, while it has the power to get you started, does not crimp the style of the accidental narcissist. I realized that to create and sustain a life beyond the gloom of ignorance, I would have to accept that while some of the signposts on my path may have been authentic, I was not the one who had been choosing which path at the fork in the road to take.

EVOLUTIONARY POINTER: The ego wants you to believe that you are a fully engaged spiritual seeker. As long as you are convinced of this, it can maintain its unchallenged reign over your life.

MQ: In my own case, I spent ten years believing I was an exceptionally passionate spiritual seeker, when all I was really doing was denying the fact that my life was comprised of intense personal disillusionment, self-serving and argumentative personal relationships, and an over-arching desire to become wealthy. My meditation practices were inconsistent, I was reading a chapter or two from the latest bestselling book on spirituality, and spent a few weekends a year on spiritual retreats. The concealed conditioning was controlling me and I had no idea.

P: Okay, so the ego is subtly deceptive.

MQ: My realizations in France left me with no alternative but to decenter the so-called 'successful' life that the lesser-self had helped me build.

P: And not the convenient decentering that is preferred by the little-self?

MQ: No, the awakened decentering that is abhorred by the ego-mind. As I began to apply my realizations, little was left untouched. And because I also moved to another country, the ways in which I earned a living and all of my relationships were radically transformed. Take heart! Your entry to awakening may not require such drastic alterations. In fact, you may not have to change much of what you are doing in order to become free of your conditioned mold.

P: Therefore, thinking and reasoning are great tools so long as they are not wholly interpreted through the lens of the conditioned attention to thinking?

MQ: Of course they are. Concealed conditioning will always insist that the fullest experience of who you are is comprised entirely within your thoughts and feelings. But, when you release your fascination with thinking, another vastly superior experience of who you are majestically unfurls. The fundamental nature of this realization rests beyond the ability of belief.

P: This also brings up another futile tenet of the ego's dharma: *Change your thoughts – change who you are.*

MQ: How silly! Changing your thoughts doesn't change who you are. And your attempts to do so means that the ego-mind has succeeded at keeping you lost in a struggle with your own mind.

P: But, if I am not my thoughts then who am I...?

MQ: Who are you, indeed! You are not your thoughts or your thoughts about your thoughts. Who are you if not that?

P: I just am.

MQ: Therefore, you walk the uncommon path. Now, live from that simplicity.

P: Thank you. What about *no attention to thinking*?

EVOLUTIONARY POINTER: *No attention to thinking* is the art of releasing your focus from all thoughts in awareness, regardless of their nature, persistence, or promise.

MQ: We will look more closely at *no attention* to thinking in great detail in Chapter Eleven.

P: Okay. And *awakened attention* to thoughts?

MQ: This is the way in which an awakened person relates to the content of his mind. Awakened attention to thinking is to be at ease, regardless of what thoughts happen to be present in your awareness. Your mind can be busy and that's okay. Your mind can be quiet and that's okay. Awakened attention to thinking offers true freedom from the constant struggle that is instigated by the ego. In one way or another, every awakened person has passed from paying *conditioned attention* to *no attention* to *awakened attention* to thinking.

As you learn to develop awakened attention, here are a few distinctions that will be of great help to you.

The Harmless Nature of Thought

MQ: Did you know that the random activity of thinking has no inherent power until action is taken or avoided? And, since cultural conditioning does not yet include witnessing the thinking mind, indiscriminate reactions to inherently harmless thoughts cause much unnecessary suffering.

> EVOLUTIONARY POINTER: When you lose objectivity of thinking, you get caught in the illusion that your thoughts are significant. You fall again and again for the fantasies of the little-self.

Tom and Helen's Story: Helen was a motivational coach who struggled with recurring thoughts of unworthiness. She was jealous of the confidence of a male colleague named Tom. Though she learned a great deal from Tom, she always thought of herself as less than his equal. She eventually began meditating in an attempt to ease the pain of constantly having to struggle with her thoughts. While attending a class at her church, she noticed a man sitting quietly in the shadows on the far side of the hall. Though she was unable to make out this newcomer, she immediately recognized the voice when he spoke: it was Tom! He wanted to know how he could overcome the burdensome thoughts he'd struggled with for many years. Tom said that he often questioned his performance as a mentor, primarily because many of his co-workers had put him on a pedestal. Even though he had tried to teach all he knew, they still treated him as being vastly superior. Helen bumped in to Tom a few days later at the office and told him what she heard in the class. They both acknowledged that they had been assigning unmerited worth to obviously insignificant thoughts! They were beginning to discover *awakened attention* to thinking.

P: It sounds like both Helen and Tom were also caught up in their shadows.

MQ: Yes. One symptom of shadow is a mind full of thoughts that just won't leave you alone.

Be Unmindful
P: I have no control over my thoughts.

MQ: No control is needed. You may accept this fact now and never again be bothered by what happens to be crossing — or not — in front of your awareness. For instance, you might be mortified to find that you are having thoughts of a lurid sexual nature. In response to this you might try to cling onto purer thoughts, distract yourself, be detached or beat yourself up even more! Furthermore, the battle with the conditioned mind is lost by your struggling. In the end you lose awareness of the witness of your thought stream and find yourself submerged in a mental hell. Not much of a reward for your efforts, eh?

P: Just as the heart's function is to beat, it is the interior function of the brain to make thoughts. Why struggle against a normal task?

MQ: Are you unmindful of the thoughts that other people might be plagued with?

P: Mostly.

MQ: Be unmindful to your own for a change. Struggling with the presence of otherwise benign thoughts can be evident even in extremely advanced individuals:

"Where I try to raise my thoughts to heaven, there is such convicting emptiness that those very thoughts return like sharp knives and hurt my very soul." – Mother Theresa.

EVOLUTIONARY POINTER: Measuring the splendor of your merit by the presence or absence of specific thoughts discloses the most subtle nature of concealed conditioning.

MQ: This common habit of craving the presence of some thoughts and dreading the absence of others does not stem from the thinking mind itself, but from the ego-mind's need to support your particular self-image. If you want to think of yourself 'this' way and not 'that' way, your attention will continually hunt for thoughts to support the self-image you prefer.

P: Is mindfulness a way I can deal with rampant thinking?

MQ: Mindfulness is the practice of awareness of one's thoughts, motivations and actions or of bringing one's awareness to the present from the past or the future. But, as you can see, if mindfulness is operating inside the boundaries of the ego-mind, it is used to needlessly ascribe value or demerit value to previously harmless thinking. Be sure that you do not have a mind full of ego-motives in regard to the natural rising and falling away of cognition.

EVOLUTIONARY POINTER: Mindfulness can become the ego's chariot of desire.

P: I notice that the ego-mind's version of mindfulness often requires that *affirmations* are kept close at hand and even stuck to the bathroom mirror.

MQ: Again, there is nothing wrong with reminding oneself of the insanity of certain modes of thinking. But, without objectivity on the source of suffering — your innocent devotion to the separate sense-of-self in you — you will only be playing deeper and deeper into the hands of struggle. For instance: Imagine a couple of fire trucks parked outside a building. The firemen are ready, the hoses are plugged in and the buckets are full, but there's no fire. This represents your 'positive' affirmations standing by in your awareness or stuck to the bathroom mirror. The fact that there is *no* fire yet, is what keeps you completely distracted from *what is*. The little-self loves to hold your attention on all the fires that can possibly be, but are not. When your attention is misplaced in this way, the ego-mind is in control of your words and actions. Are you spending your energy in unnecessary preparedness because of the ego's addiction to false alarms?

EVOLUTIONARY POINTER: Such a state of 'just in case' vigilance is a ploy of concealed conditioning to distract you from awakening to conscious-free-will.

MQ: Now, visualize a fireman who has a note on his mirror upon which he has written, 'I create a safe work environment'. Does this seem a little pointless? Consider the influence you might be allowing the ego-mind over your life if your note says something like, 'I am at peace with my life'. But instead of enjoying a peaceful life, you are obsessed with the idea that at any moment something can start burning your peace. This allows the motives of the ego-mind to operate in your relationships, career and maybe even in your spiritual seeking.

P: To be truly mindful is to fully accept the arbitrary nature of thinking?

MQ: Yes, and this means that your attention is no longer being drained by trying to edit, alter, sway, or enforce any of your thoughts. This allows you to use your awareness for other things, such as learning about no attention to thinking and awakened attention to thinking.

P: That sounds like much more fun!

> EVOLUTIONARY POINTER: The ability to be Present is not dependent on being mindful about the content of your mind. Such mental activity simply does not matter to your awakening.

Sir Lancelot's Email

P: Where do my thoughts come from?

MQ: From emptiness as always, but then they are culturally and habitually influenced.

The vast majority of your thoughts are a product of the era of your birth. For example, in Salem, Massachusetts today, the thoughts that your neighbor might be a witch are not so much of a problem for her. The thoughts of a five-hour delay on a trip from London to Sydney can be bothersome for some passengers, yet at the beginning of the 21st century the concern was whether one would ever return from such a trip. Planning the cremation of your late grandmother by the Danube River in Vienna, Austria, could get you in a lot of trouble. Not so by the Ganges River in Varnasai[4], India. In the era of the 'yuppie'[5], there was no need to consider how a law on 'Texting While Driving' might affect your lifestyle. An Israeli woman I once knew thought that the devil was tempting her when she found out that the man she was falling in love with was an Irish Catholic.

To a contemporary *size zero* model, the thoughts of being a Rubenesque from eighteenth-century Europe might be quite different to what a classic Rubenesque would have thought about today's cat-walk participants

The Knights of the Round Table did not think about the advantages of having both audio and video content on their website.

P: So much for the 'personal' significance of my thoughts for today!

MQ: Indeed. They are mostly culturally molded and ultimately only thoughts you observe.

Liz's Story: It had been a year since Phil passed away. His widow, Liz, was thinking that Phil's sister, Natalie would be angry with her for not buying a headstone and completing the work on his grave. Because of these thoughts, Liz purposefully avoided some of her favorite places where she suspected Natalie might be. After not seeing or speaking with Natalie for a long while, there was a knock on Liz's door. When Liz opened the door, she was surprised to see Natalie's oldest daughter, Linda, standing there looking a little disturbed. Liz shuddered, knowing that now she might have to face the fire. Liz immediately asked Linda what was wrong. She replied, "Mom died last night... and she told me to ask you something just before she went." Liz's heart sank, but she was also frantic with what might be coming next. Then Linda said, "Mom wanted to know if it would be okay if she was buried alongside Uncle Phil... she knew you never got around to finishing his grave and thought it must be a sign as to where her final resting place should be."

EVOLUTIONARY POINTER: The kind of attention you most commonly pay to thinking is reflected in your ability to enjoy ease of being and to come together with other people in long-term, committed relationships that are free from all personal conflict.

MQ: What does the evidence of your life suggest?

P: Maybe that I need to let harmless thoughts be for a while and enjoy the beingness.

MQ: Your mind can be agitated and burdened, but don't identify with that. Doing this is a great gift to yourself and everyone else.

Unknowing Experts at Disregarding Thoughts

MQ: Many people assume that the torment that arises with a busy mind is normal. But, they rarely look at *how* they are paying attention – *conditioned, none* or *awakened.*

P: Therefore, my mind can be full, but the way in which I pay attention to it, determines my experience?

MQ: Yes. Have you ever noticed that previously pressing thoughts seem to vanish from your awareness after a time? Focus now and recall a particularly bothersome series of thoughts — that have long since disappeared — but once were strongly present in your attention.

P: Yes. Certain thoughts that once weighed heavily on my mind appear to have diminished significantly or completely disappeared. And I notice, too, that when these thoughts finally let me alone, great relief ensued.

MQ: Indeed, and because this is such a normal occurrence, you sometimes tend to miss it. Let's look at what's going on. When you disregard certain thoughts over an extended period of time their dissolution eventually becomes automatic. Note that if certain thoughts that really bothered you at some other time in your life appear in your awareness today, they don't stay very long and then disappear rather quickly.

P: This is true. They seem to instantly pop in and then just pop out again all by themselves.

MQ: This is because you *discern* their presence, *decide* that they are no longer relevant to your current situations and you *disregard* them. But, often you are doing this so fast that you are not aware that there is a fully functioning underlying process: *Discern, Decide* and *Disregard*. After a while, it just seems to happen on its own. Taking ownership of this process is the key to developing *awakened attention* to thinking. This will free you from the struggle with your mind.

P: I intuitively know that I cannot control my thoughts, and I have become an expert at disregarding some of them without knowing that I am doing this.

MQ: Otherwise, you may have *lost your mind*. This disease is quite obvious in people who still harp on about specific thoughts from years, generations, or ages ago.

P: By losing my mind, I lose objectivity of the benevolent flow of thinking?

MQ: Exactly!

EVOLUTIONARY POINTER: The basis for *awakened attention* to thinking is to make the process of *Discern, Decide* and *Disregard* conscious. You can then pick and choose from the thoughts that are arising in your awareness, selecting only those that you are confident about, will help manifest your intention to evolve.

MQ: Remember I said earlier that in one way or another, every awakened person has passed from paying *conditioned attention* to *no attention* to *awakened attention* to thinking. Buddha, after years of struggling with his mind, learned to meditate, and then he could disregard even the thought 'I am the Enlightened One,' thus liberating true free will beyond the ego. When Jesus spent forty days *alone*, he refused the thoughts that promised the 'riches of the world'.

P: In an earlier chapter I discovered that I create shadow when I deny or repress certain aspects of myself. Now I realize that there can be a very fine line between identifying symptoms of shadow and creating more shadow by disregarding specific thoughts.

MQ: Yes. At the beginning, meticulous attention to your subjective experience will bring up realizations like this. Be steadfast and you will notice that the whole process of knowing which thoughts to disregard, and which thoughts to work with, will become perfectly graceful. You are awakening.

How You Relate to Your Mind

P: Therefore, the degree to which my primary relationships are free from personal conflict and confusion is one indicator of how I relate to and interpret the content of my mind.

MQ: Yes. That logic can sometimes be difficult for the post-modern rational mind to accept. And also, the degree to which you trust in the process of life also reveals much about how you relate to, and interpret, thinking. At some point, as you progress from one stage of development to the next, you have to ask yourself this question: Is my body an extension of a soul driven mad by the misinterpretation of benign thinking?

EVOLUTIONARY POINTER: *"The brain likes to economize on energy wherever possible."*[6]

MQ: In this use-it-or-lose-it sense, the brain of a psychologically stable individual will not waste energy maintaining processes[7] that aren't used. Letting thoughts *be* is more than sufficient cause for the interior of the brain to simply stop regenerating them. Recall, if you will, one of your favorite childhood toys that meant *so* much to you, once upon a time. When was the last time you pondered it in great detail? Maybe it has been years since thoughts of this object crossed your mind. And when did you last talk about it to your friends or write about it in your diary? There was a time, however, when this article may have consumed all of your attention. Then, for whatever reasons, you simply stopped telling anyone about its color, texture, shape, size and what it meant to you. You no longer took action based on those thoughts, such as: searching under the bed for missing pieces or going to the toy store to look for parts or newer models.

P: I have also simply stopped listening to other people speaking about their 'missing toys'.

MQ: And because you have not interacted with all of these thoughts for such a long time, notice how the mind has slowly but surely let them be.

> **EVOLUTIONARY POINTER:** Disregarded thoughts naturally diminish and then completely dissipate.

MQ: Subsequently, an external stimulus or a direct request, such as this conversation, can temporarily restore these thoughts to the forefront of your awareness. But they no longer command your attention in a compelling way. You hardly even notice them anymore. They may be here again, but now devoid of any potency. You, witness them and are *free* of them as they rise and fall away in the field of your attention.

P: But, letting go of past traumas is neither swift nor effortless.

MQ: Naturally so. But, this is because the unhealthy-ego finds solace in useless cognition. Hidden beneath its desire to keep such angst alive are well-fed ego-intentions to prolong your struggle with the mind.

P: This reminds me of a very popular tenet of the ego's dharma: *If I do not fully express my thoughts, emotions and feelings, I will get physically ill.*

MQ: Time mends all wounds, but only if you cooperate with this natural process. Therefore, it is by relentless non-expression that those thoughts, once the root of great attachment, identity and resentment, can again appear in their natural state: *benign and harmless.*

> **EVOLUTIONARY POINTER:** Without your help, the thought-generating interior of the brain has no way of knowing that you do not need such superfluous cognition, so it will keep giving you disturbing thoughts. That's its job.

MQ: As you consciously develop your ability to disregard thinking that is not aligned with your intention to awaken, it is only reasonable to expect that you will have to deal with the sometimes indiscriminate content of the mind.

P: At the same time, I may also have to interact with a world that is still holding onto the belief that thoughts are significant simply because they are present.

MQ: Cooperating with your mind to release the thoughts that may have been causing you pain and suffering for years is a small price to pay for the salvation of humanity.

Discern, Decide and Disregard Consciously

MQ: The Buddha said, *"Look how he abused and beat me, how he threw me down and robbed me. Live with such thoughts, and live in hate."*[8] Observe a series of thoughts now that once bothered you and have since faded to their original innocence. See how those thoughts do not define who you are currently; rather they were just tainted by the ego-mind during particular periods of your life. Who you are now is not the thoughts of the present moment either but, by the time you figure that out, you have already moved on to other ideas and notions.

P: If I don't want to get off that track, my futile identification with thinking just goes on indefinitely?

MQ: It is always so. The Buddha also said, *"Look how he abused me and beat me, how he threw me down and robbed me. Abandon such thoughts, and live in love."*[9]

EVOLUTIONARY POINTER: Disregarding contaminated thoughts begins by accepting their presence without judgment or response.

MQ: To be *unresponsive to cognition* means that you can refrain from the rumination or expression of those thoughts in words. Allowing thoughts just to be in your awareness will free other people from interacting with the malicious aspects of the ego in you. Wouldn't you like to be free from the unhealthy-ego in other people? Wouldn't you like to free the world from needless suffering in you? This is the first step you can take in the salvation of humanity. Here is how the process of *discern, decide* and *disregard* works:

1) *Discern* a thought in your awareness that you suspect is overpowered by the fears or desires of the unhealthy-ego.
2) *Decide* that paying attention to, obsessing over, discussing, or otherwise interacting with that thought may not be conducive to realizing your full potential.
3) *Disregard* that thought as being insufficient in supporting your goal of awakening.

P: How long does it take to make this process conscious?

MQ: Initially, it may take two to three seconds, minutes, or years to discern, decide and disregard thoughts that no longer serve ease of being and authentic joy. Your ability does not depend on your past, future, credentials, or your prevailing emotions.

EVOLUTIONARY POINTER: The time it takes to develop *awakened attention* to thinking depends on how long you wish to hold onto the idea that the thoughts entering your awareness mean something about *who you are*. Disregard all thoughts just for a day and see!

MQ: Now, please consider the wonderful implications of applying this skill to the ideas you may have about the gap between your life, *as it is* today, and the awakened life you may have been envisioning for yourself for years.

P: I think that gap is wide.

MQ: What if you disregard the thoughts of this gap? What if you realize that your thoughts of *not being awake* are just the harmless and undisruptive thoughts of not being awake, that mean nothing at all about you?

P: Oh, the joy!

Accessing Conscious-Free-Will

MQ: *Awakened attention* to thinking is to discern, decide and disregard thoughts that have been tainted and displaced by the fears and desires of the ego-mind. When you do this, *conscious-free-will* begins to awaken. It automatically emerges with awakened attention to thoughts. Conscious-free-will is the power to direct your volition toward a destiny that is free from the limitations of the culturally-created-self. Conscious-free-will is not restricted by your past or your thoughts or feelings about the past. Conscious-free-will is, however, the future un-manifested. When conscious-free-will enters the stream of time, it surpasses, yet includes the power and experience of conceptual-free-will. Conscious-free-will is the medium of creativity beyond the boundaries of concealed conditioning. It links that which is formed and known with all that has yet to be created and is as yet unknown. It is the bond between potential and your actions in the present moment. Conscious-free-will is the bridge between the un-manifested and the already manifested.

EVOLUTIONARY POINTER: Applying conscious-free-will in your life situations ends all unneeded emotional and psychological suffering.

MQ: Conscious-free-will is the conduit of en · thus · iasm[10].

It *will* free your mind.

[1] Francois de La Rochefoucauld (1613 - 1680).

[2] The NSF is the U.S. government agency responsible for promoting science and engineering.

[3] Andrew Cohen, October 1999.

[4] The culture of this city is deeply associated with the Ganges and its religious importance.

[5] *Newsweek* magazine declared 1984 *The year of the yuppie (Young Urban Professional).*

[6] Dr. Antonio R. Damasio, M.D. Ph.D., Head of Neurology, University of Iowa.

[7] According to successive studies published in the *Journal of the American Medical Association.*

[8/9] The Dhammapada.

[10] The root of the word enthusiasm is *God within.*

Chapter 6

KARMA AND THE EGO'S DHARMA

"Our repentance is not so much regret for the ill we have done as fear of the ill that may happen to us in consequence."[1]

The Relevance of Karma

MQ: By applying conscious-free-will you begin to transcend and include the hidden influences of formerly concealed conditioning. Curiously, this is also the beginning of the end of your karma.

P: I've never been clear on the idea or relevance of karma, so here's a question: Do I have to alter my current belief system so that I may fully grasp the idea of karma?

MQ: No, not in the least. For instance, a Buddhist would not have to abandon his faith in order to fully appreciate the Christian rite of First Communion. Therefore, including a distinction on karma in your current understanding will greatly aid your progress to the next level of development. We will be taking a look at karma in a way that is free from the verdicts cast upon it by concealed conditioning.

P: Sounds great!

MQ: And should you find the concept of karma palatable, you will discover how it is created and sustained. Then you can steer clear of important mistakes.

P: What are important mistakes?

MQ: Important mistakes tend to separate you from your full potential.

P: I can see that the unhealthy-ego loves it when I make important mistakes, thus amplifying its favorite pastime: my continual struggle with my mind and emotions.

MQ: That's why it's great to think about karma in a way that can be included in your current understanding. Then, regardless of your background, you can consider the possibility of facing and transcending all of your karma in this lifetime. To help us along, we will begin with a classic definition of karma from Buddhism and look at how this can be applied to contemporary life.

P: But what if comprehending, facing and transcending my karma all seems like too much work?

MQ: You can always take an alternative approach as this tenet of the ego's dharma tells us: *If you don't like the idea of karma, it simply doesn't exist.*

P: Just as denying the nature of gravity would mean I could step off a roof without ramifications...

MQ: Yes, just as the *consequence* of acting unconsciously or on an intention of the unhealthy-ego — or karma by any other name — is also unavoidable. No one walks away unscathed by the outcome of his past *intentions*, not even the non-believers.

EVOLUTIONARY POINTER: Look how the reverberation of a misguided objective from yesterday may be creating an anxiety in your life today. That *momentum* is karma.

The 'X' Factor of Karma

P: This momentum or flow — the karma — has to do with an action I took yesterday?

MQ: Not exactly, but we need to tread lightly here. Since you are inclined to act in particular ways today because of what happened yesterday, it is natural to assume that karma is created by your physical actions.

P: Hindu philosophy says that every time I think or do something, I create a cause, which in time will bear a corresponding effect or karma. In this way, the effect of my past karma determines the nature of my present situation in life.

MQ: I agree that the effects of your past determine the nature of your present.

> EVOLUTIONARY POINTER: It is not just an action that establishes the karma because *doing nothing* also creates karma.

MQ: I am sure that you are familiar with the wonderful — or dire — consequence of a past action of yours. Now think of a situation in which you did *not* act that also created profound results for you or those around you. Those consequences were not the results of an action, but of the objective behind your particular choice to *not act.*

P: Oh, yes, and sometimes those consequences were more intense than if I had chosen to act.

MQ: Doing nothing also has consequences. Consider, too, that different actions that produce the same outcome can have very dissimilar consequences. Here are four different incidents that could create the same outcome, but, a different karma: premeditated murder, self-defense, suicide and a fatal accident. Death is the common outcome for each incident.

> EVOLUTIONARY POINTER: Karma is not particularly a matter of the outcome.

MQ: Also, just *thinking* about doing something is not going to cause much of an effect because your intention is already set to not act. Therefore, thinking about doing something only prolongs an existing consequence and does not necessarily create or resolve any karma.

P: If karma is not specifically a matter of whether I act or not, or the *outcome* of my action or non-action, and is not directly related to thinking about an action, then what creates karma?

MQ: Before we get to where karma begins, let's recall that Buddha told us that *liberation is the end of karma*. Therefore, if you and I are to live an awakened life, it is important that we stop creating new karma. Of course, this would also mean we have to clean up our karma from the past.

P: But this sounds impossible. How can I be in the world without making any new karma? If karma can result from both action and non-action then I can't see how I could live a fully expressive life and *not* create karma?

MQ: To find our way out of suffering, we need to consider the mitigating factor.

P: Which is?

MQ: The *intention* of your action or non-action.

P: It is my intention for an action, or a non-action, that creates the outcome?

MQ: Yes. And not particularly your actions, inactions or thinking about actions or inactions. Note that for the four different incidents described above, the intention surrounding each act would be very different indeed, hence the grand difference in the outcome, consequence, or karma.

EVOLUTIONARY POINTER: Intention is the "X" factor of karma.

P: Let me see if I've gotten this straight. My intentions are the anticipated outcomes of my actions or non-actions, as the case may be. If I do not have clarity on my objectives or if those intentions are unsuspectingly encrusted with the unhealthy-ego and its messy agendas, I will make important mistakes. Important mistakes create more karma. If I keep creating such conditioned consequences, I can never fully awaken.

MQ: That's pretty much it. You may even have consistent access to higher states of consciousness, but you will not be free from unnecessary emotional and psychological suffering.

P: Many great masters have fallen from grace. Is karma the reason why?

MQ: It's one reason why. Karmic consequences remain active until they are resolved. Haven't you noticed that certain destructive patterns seem to repeat over and over again? It is not that your intentions are impure; it's just that those particular objectives are too heavily weighted by the ego-mind to afford release from those cycles. Therefore, you keep making important mistakes.

EVOLUTIONARY POINTER: Karma is created by a response to life that is based solely on an intention of the ego-mind.

MQ: And that's usually some sort of an intention to support a conditioned self-image or to seek safety, affirmation or retribution for the culturally-created-self. Karma is your response to life that specifically demands a further response.

P: I feel the need to contradict the simplicity of this theory that future effects in my life are created by my intentions. I can't believe that this is how I can end my karma.

MQ: You can't believe this or is the ego-mind having a problem? When you accept that your intentions create your future, you also have to accept that if there is any remnant of unhealthy self-interest in those objectives, unnecessary suffering is going to be the result. You alone are responsible for your intentions. Therefore, you alone are responsible for the outcomes. The malicious aspect of the ego despises this because it can no longer blame your past lives or external events for your karma.

Here is a very simple example of individual karma. See if you can notice its flow:

Jill's Story: After months of research and interviewing, Jill found a new job with a much higher salary than her previous position. Jill created this opportunity based on two intentions: her aims were to establish a new career so that she could earn a higher salary and more clearly express her creative abilities. After accepting this offer, she began thinking about the possibility of getting herself a cool new car. She also thought about paying off some serious credit card debt. Jill was aware that this credit liability was the result of her attempts in the past to escalate her standard of living too rapidly. At that time, her actions were based on intentions to boost her self-esteem. Her huge credit card bills were the consequences of those past objectives. Jill was also interested in developing her potential, so she knew that by accepting her new job she could direct her attention to completely clearing the karma of these high-interest loans. This intention stood in stark contrast to another objective that was suggesting to her that by paying the minimum amounts on her loans, she could buy herself a new car. Jill knew the karma of the debt would not disappear by itself, until she set her intention to resolve it. Jill realized that this option would certainly cause inconveniences, but her old intentions to avoid suffering, by using her credit cards to satisfy her desires, were what incurred the debt in the first place. Jill opted to be debt-free and in time, she ended that particular karma.

Back to Basics

MQ: The Buddhist definition[2] of karma, which pre-dates the Esoteric Christian teachings on the *Law of Cause and Consequence and Effect* by about two or three hundred years, is:

> *"The effect of an action is not primarily determined by the act itself, but rather particularly by the intention of the action. It is the intention of actions that cause a karmic effect to arise."*
>
> *"Only a deed that is free from desire, hate and delusion is without karmic effect. In order to liberate oneself from the cycle of rebirth one must refrain from both 'good' and 'bad' deeds".*

P: From this definition it is clear that it is not the act itself that causes the karma but rater it is the intention of actions that causes the outcome. And to what are the intentions of the unhealthy-ego always linked?

MQ: They are always linked to some form of fortification, defense, or affirmation of the separate sense-of-self, or the generation of endless rewards in the 'personal' world. The intentions of the unhealthy-ego also manifest when we deny the healthy aspects of individuality in ourselves or other people.

P: Karma is the antithesis of awakening.

MQ: Well said. And the role of concealed conditioning is to keep you busy making 'good' karma and avoiding 'bad' karma. In this flurry of activity, your attention is on the outcome and not on your intentions. In this way you unknowingly create karma, be it 'good' or 'bad', and it does not really matter – it's all the same sustenance for the unhealthy-ego. Even if you don't believe in karma or ascribe to another theory of karma that does not emphasis intentions, your attention will either be on your opinions or on the outcome, but not on your objectives. Concealed conditioning wins again.

P: So, I sidestep my full potential while thinking I am a hapless victim of circumstance?

MQ: Or worse, always sidestepping your potential while thinking you are a goody-two-shoes!

EVOLUTIONARY POINTER: Liberation from suffering is the result of your intentions, not of your actions.

MQ: What if the intentions of the ego-mind are entirely sourced from within the boundaries of the culturally-created-self and your options for expressing those intentions are completely restricted by conceptual-free-will?

P: Will I end up creating consequences contrary to authentic joy?

MQ: Most likely. Consider also that you may have been doing this since your very first independent choice.

P: Yikes! Now what?

MQ: Awakening is to first become aware of this momentum without judgments.

P: How can I ensure that today is not going to look like yesterday and that tomorrow is not going to replicate today?

MQ: The wonderful news is that because karma is the element of *inborn continuity*, identifying it holds the spark of release for you. The 'you' of today includes all of the consequences of the intentions that the 'you' of yesterday acted upon. The 'you' of the future will include the results of the intentions of the 'you' who is considering which actions to take today.

P: In other words, I can change the outcome for tomorrow, regardless of the past. This sounds great. Now, I am going to attempt a summary here, for the sake of my own sanity.

MQ: Okay, go ahead.

P: It's *not* what I do that causes karma. It is the *intention* behind that action or non-action. My intentions create outcomes that I have to eventually deal with. This cycle never ends unless I bring my awareness to it and distinguish concealed conditioning in my intentions. I am assuming that individual karma can appear as persistent patterns of thoughts, emotions and behaviors that I might prefer to be without. I am also subject to collective karma; those inherited ways of being that emerge from the cultural background into which I was born, that may also be operating habitually without my awareness.

MQ: Now you're getting it! Notice how you are naturally subjected to this momentum from the past. Becoming aware of your individual and collective karma can ensure that who you are in your life and relationships today is not going to mirror the 'you' of yesterday. Do you see that the 'you' who took an action yesterday became the object of the 'you' who must act today?

P: Yes, so karma is a never-ending cycle until I bring awareness to it.

EVOLUTIONARY POINTER: You can resolve your karma by adjusting your intentions today in response to your life conditions as they appear to you.

Karma – A Steady Compulsion

MQ: Karma's presiding quality is *compulsive obligation.*

P: If I am not aware that I am acting on an unhealthy intention of the ego-mind or if I do not include and respect the healthy aspects of individuality in my responses to life, I will regenerate a momentum that I have to eventually resolve.

MQ: Yes, if you wish to ultimately free yourself.

EVOLUTIONARY POINTER: The problem is that you keep creating karma, resolving it, and then creating more. If you continue in this pattern, you can never end it.

MQ: This *independent* force of karma can be compared to what happens when the engines of a ship that has been traveling at full speed are turned off. The ship does not stop immediately, but continues to move forward under its momentum. When something, like you or your loved ones, gets in the way of that momentum , or karma, you are helplessly pushed in the direction of that movement or overwhelmed by its force.

P: Or maybe even destroyed upon impact!

EVOLUTIONARY POINTER: Karma is a constant force that propels you toward the inevitable outcome resulting from your past intentions.

MQ: Notice the key words of this definition: *continuous, force, propels, inevitable, outcome and intentions.* This forms a complete picture of karma – an unrelenting force that drives you toward the unavoidable outcomes of past objectives. Furthermore, karma is directly proportional to the power of the intention that created it, so the consequences of some actions are graver than others.

P: Does this imply that because of the flow of my karma, many of my behaviors today are just attempts to recover from actions that didn't seem to turn out as 'intended' yesterday.

MQ: Yes. A simple example: You are convinced that your intention for being more careful with your next intimate relationship is *to create a more fulfilling partnership.* This is based on the experience that your last few relationships turned out to be rather unsatisfactory. But, if that objective is being exclusively driven by the unhealthy-ego, painful consequences will eventually ensue. Without objectivity on the ego-mind, what you believe your intention to be — *to create a more fulfilling partnership* — is really an ego intention to feel loved, needed, protected and affirmed by another person in the context of this purely personal microcosm. In the absence of objectivity on the ego-mind and its proclivity to produce and sustain its grip on your destiny, unnecessary emotional and psychological conflict will repeat itself. In this case you would just recreate the same set of circumstances because the ego still inhabits your intentions.

P: Is this why people seem to be at the mercy of consequences?

MQ: Yes. We all 'seem' to be until we come to terms with our *attachment to conditioning.* Be open to seeing how the karma of past intentions may be manipulating you. Many lives are like karmic wave pools, where people spend the majority of their time repairing the painful repercussions of their inherited intentions while making more at the same time. If your experience sometimes feels like a mental quagmire, it is likely that you are engaging with intentions based on the dubious logic of the ego's dharma, in a genuine, yet vain maneuver to free yourself from those consequences. You will just go around on the same old cycle.

> EVOLUTIONARY POINTER: The ego's-dharma and the flow of karma are consummate bed-buddies; where you find one, you will surely find the other.

P: Here's a quote from a fellow countryman of yours, Bono, lead singer with the rock band, U2: *"I'd be in big trouble if Karma was going to finally be my judge. I'd be in deep s***. It doesn't excuse my mistakes, but I'm holding out for Grace."*[3]

MQ: This is a common belief of those at the mythic level of development. I hope Grace is holding out for him!

P: But, hoping that karma is going to magically disappear is a little naïve?

MQ: Yes, because you end up deterring yourself from liberation.

P: This is a clever ploy of the conditioned mind.

MQ: Yes. The ego-mind rescues itself by insisting that there are no higher levels of development beyond those you have already mastered. While hope includes such commendable traits as: wishing, expecting and wanting things to turn out for the best, it also can cause you to abandon your greatest ally – your karma. In doing so, you flail at the mercy of unexamined dogma and all the so-called benefits of creating 'good' karma that are touted by the ego's dharma. You can't bargain with Grace. Grace and karma are on parallel tracks, so to speak, and never shall the two meet.

P: But helping other people, like Bono is doing, is a wonderful thing, right?

MQ: Yes of course it is, but by attempting to alleviate the angst of others is one way the unhealthy-ego shrewdly obscures self-serving goals in a cloud of immature purity. Hope will not change your reality until you learn to reinterpret your present, free from the impressions of that ever-meddling concealed conditioning. If you are unaware that you are being disingenuous about delivering a complete resolution to the issues you stand for, you have instead become an unwitting puppet of the ego's dharma. Armed with the best intentions, you are actually doing more harm than good.

P: Bono also said: *"We don't sit around thinking about world peace all day."*[4]

MQ: Indeed.

EVOLUTIONARY POINTER: Without clarity of intention, hope and unhappiness are synonymous.

Acting Without Creating Karma

P: If conceptual-free-will arises with self-awareness, then I am powerless to reach beyond my karma.

MQ: By using only conceptual-free-will, yes. Conceptual-free-will contains all the karma of the past and also, because of its inherent limitations, it is prone to create more karma for you. Only conscious-free-will is beyond the reach of karma.

EVOLUTIONARY POINTER: We have to learn to act, without creating *any* karma.

P: But, my actions always create consequences.

MQ: Yes of course. To act without consequences would be impossible. The key to the liberated life, however, is acting on intentions that do not specifically demand a further response from you.

P: Can you give me a simple example please?

MQ: Let's say you wish to resolve a difficulty you are experiencing in a significant relationship. You could have two intentions. The first would be to create a more *emotionally gratifying interaction.*

Another intention would be to create the conditions for the *development of that relationship beyond the root cause of the suffering.* Now, let's say you can see that the motive for this particular conflict involves the other person's penchant to relentlessly bemoan his lack of enthusiasm for life. Of course, I am assuming you have tried to help this person gain clarity on this matter in the past, but it seems that he is more interested in complaining than changing. You can act on your first intention, to create a more *emotionally gratifying interaction* by continuing to allow him to lament his lot in life as he pleases. Or you can choose an intention that does not specifically demand a further response from you – you can choose an intention that does not create any karma for you. This is conscious-free-will presenting you with an awakened choice. To act on such a pure intention would be to point out, with kind and delicate compassion, that the root of this difficulty is simply a preference of distress over transformation. Regardless of the person's response, there would be no demand for a further response from you.

P: Under normal circumstances I would think that by being a good listener I am creating 'good' karma and that by pointing out the root of suffering I would be causing him to suffer even more, hence creating 'bad' karma for myself.

MQ: But, just look at where your point of focus is.

P: Oops! It's on me, 'good' karma for 'me' and bad karma for 'me'… the trap of the ego's dharma.

EVOLUTIONARY POINTER: Removing yourself as a supporter of the unhealthy-ego in another person is the most compassionate, and karma-free response possible.

P: The ego's dharma always suggests that we make 'good' and avoid 'bad'.

MQ: And this can sound like excellent advice, until you ask

these questions:

Firstly, has acting according to these rules produced the ease of
being you intended?
Secondly, can you be certain that you have not been acting on
conditioned autopilot?
Thirdly, do your intentions for acting allow for the conclusion of all
unnecessary suffering?

MQ: There is nothing wrong with having goals to become healthy,
happy, comfortable and secure. But, if those are *primary* or exclusive
goals, then karma and unnecessary conflict will abound. Only when
you place your interest in awakening marginally beyond your
concern for other matters of life will you be able to identify and
hence manifest your pure intentions.

EVOLUTIONARY POINTER: Actions based on inherited intentions
return as karmic consequences. Therefore, they are future
opportunities to include the *evolution of consciousness* in your
intentions, marginally beyond conditioned fears and desires.
Awakening is to see this cycle.

P: You mentioned *marginally* twice. How much is marginally?
MQ: Fifty-*one* percent is fine.

Karma – The Spark of Release

MQ: When you move your interest from ego-identity towards
awakening to ego-identity, the consequences of your past, experienced in the present moment, offer you the prospect of repentance.
P: Please explain what you mean by that.
MQ: To *repent* is to alter your objectives for forthcoming deeds
where past intentions for actions in similar situations caused pain

and sorrow. In this way, each new moment holds an element of release from the past. Karma has this encouraging effect; it sustains situations in which you are repeatedly offered opportunities to no longer act on the same intentions, thereby resolving those consequences and releasing you from that karma.

P: Hence, it is not until I change my intentions that I can change my karma?

MQ: Exactly!

EVOLUTIONARY POINTER: Karma is the surreptitious 'super-glue' of the manifest world.

P: How do I change my intentions?

MQ: You have to see them first.

P: How might I develop clarity on my intentions so that I may change them?

MQ: You can begin by answering these two questions: "Is my interest in awakening slightly greater than my interests in other things in life?" And, "Is the development of awareness, my primary reason for being?"

P: My life seems to allow only a narrow focus on these intentions. Definitely less that fifty-one percent of attention is there.

MQ: Really? You speak of 'life' as if it is an object that exists beyond who you are. Maybe that's why awakening is still rare. If your intentions are less aligned with awakening and more aligned with the conditioned mind, what does your future hold?

P: More of the same...?

MQ: Yes, more karma – the antithesis of liberation.

Karma and Your Past and Future Lives

P: What about karma from *past lives*?

MQ: While there is overwhelming evidence for past lives, which cannot be ignored, it is refreshing to note that you don't need to be too concerned about how much karma you may have accumulated from past lives, how it might show up, or how long it might take to disengage.

P: Why is that?

EVOLUTIONARY POINTER: The sum total of the consequences of your intentions from the past — your karma — is here for you to encounter today.

P: But, the ego's dharma purports that it takes many lifetimes to resolve my karma.

MQ: And the Buddha said that it is possible to gain enlightenment in this lifetime.

P: *This one?*

MQ: Yes, which other one do you have? Who are you going to listen to – the Buddha or the ego's dharma? And also consider this flaw in the logic of the conceptual-mind: A child who lived for just ten minutes and a person who lived to be 120 years old each had *a life*. If you measure the term of your life according to the life span of the child, you would have about one thousand lives *every* week. However, if you died in your sixtieth year, according to the life span of the older person, you would only have had *half* a life. Which one is true?

P: The ego is frightened that I will accept that this life is sufficient and therefore begin to release my attachment to it?

MQ: The ego is scared of unrestricted joy, so it suggests multiple lifetimes are required to recover from your karma.

P: Because 'I' am special, therefore 'I' must have special karma!

MQ: Of course, this suggestion can be roughly translated as follows: *Because in this life you cannot be free of karma or original sin, you don't have to worry about accepting responsibility for your intentions today*. We even see evidence of this in some of the great traditions that emerged from the conceptual-mind's bid for immortality. For example, someone else has accepted responsibility for your sins so the onus of authenticity, rationality and transparency is not upon you in this life.

EVOLUTIONARY POINTER: Your responsibility to the future is to co-create it with intentions that are free from the attachment to the ego-mind.

Finding Your Karma

MQ: Your responses today to the momentum created by your intentions *yesterday* will determine the consequences of all your *tomorrows*.

P: In the best-selling book, *The Power of Intention*[5], Wayne Dyer writes that *"feeling bad is a choice"*, and offers the affirmation, *"I want to feel good,"* as a remedy. How might we look at this from a karmic perspective?

MQ: Well, first we have to define 'feeling bad'. Let's say it means unwholesome satiation, confusion, unhappiness, unreasonable worry and negative stress. Can you see how all of these can be the consequences of having acted on unwholesome ego intentions in the past?

P: Yes.

MQ: In which case, these circumstances are your cue to identify the conditioned intentions supporting them and change them for subsequent responses. The flow of such consequences can only be quelled by plucking them out at the root. An affirmation, as we have seen, is often like painting over the rust. Therefore, when you encounter these opportunities for growth, in this case, feeling *bad*, please ask yourself these questions:

Firstly, has the intention that created this result a manifestation of my conditioning?

Secondly, was my intention to act an attempt to support a particular self-image?

Thirdly, was the intention that created this situation designed to create or avoid a particular emotional state?

MQ: If you responded with a 'Yes', then you know that if you act on a similar intention again you will get a similar result. If you prefer you could also ask: Is unneeded suffering necessary for my survival?

P: Most likely the answer would be, "Not for me!" But then isn't it possible that this response is coming directly from the unhealthy-ego and not particularly from *me*? After all, if I was absolutely certain that unnecessary conflict was not a requirement, I would already be free from it!

MQ: Indeed. And if you do not uncover the root of the problem, the same situations will arise over and over and over again, so your life will become an endless parade of ineffective affirmations. It is wise, therefore, to review the underlying intentions behind the instances of disharmony in your life, and ask yourself, "Am I just feeding an already inflated ego-mind?"

EVOLUTIONARY POINTER: Awakening reveals that it is *impossible* to have pure intentions and to simultaneously manifest personal disharmony.

Karma and Your Attention

P: It makes perfect sense to me that I have to learn to act on *alternate intentions* to the ones that have taken me to my current level of development. How do I get started with this?

MQ: *Pure intentions* do not create any karma. They create a result, but no further conditioned consequence for you to deal with.

Discovering your pure intentions in all aspects of life begins by finding out where your attention is. *Attention* is defined as the application of the mind to any object of sense or thought.

P: Therefore, if my attention is lost in a struggle with my mind and the 'me' that is suffering, my intentions are born under those circumstances.

MQ: Yes, and you will just recreate those situations over and over again.

P: More karma.

MQ: You got it. There's a lot more that your attention could be focused on: The timeless context in which that experience and 'me' are arising in, for instance. Ponder that for a timeless moment.

EVOLUTIONARY POINTER: Note that the material world elevates what is unimportant and you unquestioningly place your attention on that allowing it to consume all of your awareness, one second at a time, forever.

MQ: The dilemma is that as you strive to transcend conditioning, you are presented with the endless suggestions that arise because you are unknowingly fettered to the ego-mind. These detrimental ego directives, that are based *entirely* on the past, effortlessly grab your attention, goading you into making important mistakes. The state of the world today reveals that the majority of its inhabitants are acting as best they can, yet indiscriminately.

P: I can see how this is related to *conditioned attention to thinking*, which we discussed in the previous chapter.

MQ: Yes, when you assume your thoughts mean something about you, ego intentions shine brightly in your awareness.

P: If my attention is entirely consumed by the ego-mind, then its false intentions show up in my mind's eye. Then as I ponder 'which' intentions to act upon, the trap that I fall into is that the most popular goal is usually the *most* conditioned one.

MQ: Releasing yourself from this cycle begins by shifting your awareness to the part of you that is delicately aware of the ego-mind, but not at all attached to it.

Amy's Story: Amy was a farm girl living in Manhattan. She loved to get away from the city as often as she could to her little place in the countryside. The night before one such escape, she had an argument with her boyfriend, Joe. As she drove out of town the next day, all she could think about was their disagreement and the fact that he wouldn't be with her over the weekend. Then Amy noticed that she had missed her exit for the cabin by several miles. At that same moment, she realized her attention had not been present for a significant portion of the trip.

Eventually, Amy and Joe made amends. A year later, after a little shopping spree, the couple was standing outside of Tiffany Jewelers in the heart of the city. Suddenly a long parade of Secret Service vehicles howled past with lights and sirens ablaze. Amy had never seen such a spectacle, and as she paid attention to this passing event, she missed the fact that Joe had just dropped to one knee to propose!

Locating Your Attention

MQ: Take a moment to discover where your attention is today. Ask yourself if your attention is:

1) Constantly consumed with passing thoughts or prevailing feelings?

2) Constantly consumed with the quality of your subjective states of awareness?

3) Focused on a missed opportunity or pondering regrets or failures?

4) Lingering on wrongs you have suffered or perpetrated?

5) Seeking ways to support conditioned beliefs?

6) Closely monitoring your interactions to protect your particular

self-image?

7) Always seeking out ways to succeed or get ahead?

8) Seeking excuses for not expressing your fullest potential?

9) Anxiously focused on a forthcoming meeting with another person?

10) Anticipating some future event with an over-elevated sense of excitement?

11) Debating the possible effects that the expression of deepest potential may have on a loved one who may not share the same interest as you in that area of life?

12) Wondering about the free time you will have when you finish with this conversation?

MQ: If you responded with 'yes' to any of these questions, there is a fair chance the unhealthy-ego may have a firm grip on your attention. In such a case, it will also have enclosed your intentions.

P: Basically I have to determine if my attention is focused on the development of consciousness or does the ego-mind have my attention spread far and wide on a thousand other 'more important' things. Does my attention have to be on the development of consciousness one hundred percent of the time?

MQ: No, not at all. That's simply unnecessary. Remember fifty-*one* percent of the time is fine.

EVOLUTIONARY POINTER: The sole purpose of endless rumination on the plight of the little-self is to distract your attention so that it is unavailable to the higher aspects of your discrimination.

MQ: The magic in all of this is that an *awakened choice* to shift your attention from the ego-mind always exists in every moment. Your karma is there to remind you that this is possible. Look now to the murmur of thoughts in the background as you are also listening to me. There may be thoughts such as: "I should cut the grass," "It's almost time to pick up the children," "I need to renew my passport" or "I have to take the dog for a walk". All these thoughts are occurring at the same time as you are contently paying attention to my voice. You are choosing where to place your attention while all of this is going on in the background. You are simply witnessing your thoughts.

EVOLUTIONARY POINTER: Being stuck in an endless struggle with the mind pales in comparison to the possibility of being able to freely move between the conceptual-mind and Oneness whenever you want.

MQ: Your ability to direct your attention at will to this very word also enables you to allow all those other thoughts to remain at a manageable volume. You are temporarily discerning, deciding and disregarding other thoughts until you can pay more attention to them later, or until the dog comes over to let you know he really needs to go out!

P: I am capable of consciously directing the placement of my attention because I know how to create a choice at the level of my attention. I do this by distinguishing between the flood of thoughts and the part of me that only observes that flood of thoughts.

MQ: And creating choices at this level grants you direct access to conscious-free-will. If you are differentiating one thought from another, then those thoughts can't comprise the entirety of who you are. This aspect of you is, always has been, and always will be, free from karma. This part of you has never even entered the stream of time. Unfortunately, you more commonly allow your attention to aimlessly wander amongst the desires and aversions of the ego-mind as opposed to just witnessing them as they come and go.

P: Therefore, when Buddha said, *"Life is suffering"* he was pointing to this endless circle.

EVOLUTIONARY POINTER: Karma follows the footsteps of this misguided attention, not from your actions but from ego-based intentions to avoid suffering.

MQ: To reveal the intentions you are going to act upon is a matter of finding out if your attention is on the evolution of consciousness or on the fears and desires of the conditioned mind. Making this distinction delivers the power to alter your destiny. There is no other way out of this loop of "suffering".

And so, a spark of creativity that first begins as a faint idea over the edge of emptiness will slowly form into a loose association of thoughts and eventually emerge in your awareness where you will recognize it as a *pure intention.* Now you, too, can act free from karma.

1   Francois de La Rochefoucauld (1613–1680).

2   Shamabhala dictionary of Buddhism and Zen: Shamabala Publications, Boston, 1991.

3   Bono on Bono: In Conversation with Michka Assayas - Riverhead Books, 2005.

4   Bono in the Dublin-based Sunday Independent newspaper - June 2005.

5   The Power of Intention, by Wayne Dyer: Hay House, USA, 2005.

Chapter 7

AWAKENING CONVERSATIONS

"Few are agreeable in conversation, because each thinks more of what he intends to say than of what others are saying, and listens no more when he himself has a chance to speak."[1]

Concealed Conditioning and Your Fifth-Chakra

P: Paying attention is important when translating my thoughts from intentions to words.

MQ: Yes. Your words are the bridge between formless and form. And they have tremendous power – far beyond that which you may assume. Your words either support or degrade the conditions for awakened living.

P: My destiny is determined from the content of my conversations?

MQ: Yes, and also the fate of humanity.

P: Really?

MQ: If your primary reason for being is the evolution of consciousness and culture, then your words will also reflect that intention. But often, your interpersonal exchanges are entirely consumed by the words and topics of the ego-mind. Inherited ways of conversing greatly inhibit your chances of uncovering and sustaining the next level of your spiritual development. As you awaken, you will realize just how many conversations are comprised of nothing more than the unhealthy-ego at a particular level of development in one person talking with the same unhealthy-ego at a similar or dissimilar stage of development in another person.

> EVOLUTIONARY POINTER: Be sure that individual and collective conditioning is not the sole orator of your *fifth chakra*[2].

P: Is the fine art of small talk in question?

MQ: No, but the proliferation of ego prattle prevents exceptional conversations that can allow everyone to reach beyond such triviality. Little progress is possible in awakening to your full potential if you solely converse with the lesser-self amidst your most important relationships. The awakened life does not preclude harmless banter, but a slight majority of your dialogues are also free of *concealed conditioning*.

P: And, of course fifty-one percent is 'slightly' enough, correct?

MQ: Yes.

P: Therefore, when my goal is to create the conditions for awakening, it is best that the words I use and the topics of conversation I engage in primarily reflect that intention.

> EVOLUTIONARY POINTER: Your intentions — the notions of a future self — may first appear to you in thoughts or dreams, but do not take 'form' until you speak them.

MQ: Primarily, yet not entirely. Wanting to be free, but talking to or about the unhealthy-ego for extended periods of time can only create an outcome beneficial to its agenda.

P: Is it crucial, therefore, to recognize the unhealthy-ego in speech before it is given a voice?

MQ: Yes. It is of no use to dissect such a discourse after the fact. When you know what to listen for, the telltale signs of concealed conditioning in conversations will become obvious and therefore, perfectly avoidable without effort.

P: With practice, spotting the unhealthy-ego's requests to blather will become second nature?

MQ: Yes. It is quite easy.

A Word to the Wise

P: How can I begin to edit the ego-mind from my conversations?

MQ: We are going to look throughout this chapter at many ways you can do this. Let's try this simple exercise first. In response to the following three statements, you will see where a single *word* is a manifestation of conscious-free-will:

1) I am marginally more interested in *awakened living* than I am in anything else, even though the manifestation of that desire may be unknown to me and may also alter many of my current life situations.
2) My awakening is already within my own hands, and though I may not feel fully prepared or know exactly what that may look like, I now accept this responsibility.
3) If my awakening were to be quickly thrust upon me, I would persevere with courage and patience as I learned to interpret that gift.

MQ: The expression of an awakened choice in response to these three statements can be one word. That single word is: *Yes!*

P: It's that simple?

MQ: It is. Did you respond with a 'yes' to all three statements?

P: Yes, I did. This reminds me of the *awakened decentering* phase of the lesser-self, which we spoke about in the "*I am Buddha*" section of Chapter 2. I realize that three positive responses would be the only ones possible here, as evidence of my genuine intentions to awaken.

MQ: This is true. There must always be proof of your intentions. Otherwise, how do you know they are real? Responding with a 'no' or vacillating in non-commitment simply means that your development still rests at the *convenient decentering* phase, which is convenient for the ego-mind, but insufficient to free you from unneeded emotional and psychological suffering.

John's Story: John was a successful businessman in his late forties. His life lacked true meaning and he knew it. After a particular spiritual experience, he was considering the possibility of cashing out of his businesses to dedicate himself to a full-time quest for inner peace and his eternal motives. In response to the three statements above, John replied with a 'yes' to the first and last and with a 'no' to the second statement. He was marginally more interested in awakening than anything else, and willing to patiently interpret an awakening, if thrust upon him. But, John could not accept responsibility for the fact that his awakening was already within his own hands. As he grappled with the possibility of his full potential, he asked a respected friend for advice.

"Now that I am at the first step of awakening," he said, "I find it very difficult to envision the outcome of this path." His friend, who had awakened to the pervasive nature of concealed conditioning some years earlier, replied, "My dear friend John, the reason that you cannot conceptualize your potential is that you have not yet taken the first step. You and the little-self are in a deep hole. Until you admit you are free by crossing from *convenient* to *awakened* decentering, and hence responding with a 'yes' to all three statements, you will remain lost with the ego. Thinking that you have an objective to be free, but speaking and acting to the contrary, drives you in endless circles; never out of them." In that moment John realized that the ego-mind had been leading him to believe that he had already begun to walk a path of conscious evolution, when in fact, all he was doing was pondering the idea of getting started and sounding 'spiritual' along the way.

P: The capacity to liberate my communications from the little-mind does not necessarily result from a spiritual experience?

MQ: Not necessarily. And if it is temporarily so, you eventually come down from such an encounter and reconnect to your preexisting level of conversing. If the ego was the primary custodian of your words before your experience of Big Mind, it will most likely be so afterwards. A spiritual experience can be a great incentive to change the ways in which you communicate with the world. But, all it takes is a little practice to edit out the topics of limitation. Awakened conversations are available to you, even without a flash of satori[3], by simply identifying and removing the favorite words and topics of the conditioned mind.

Kevin's Story: Kevin had just completed his first extended silent meditation retreat on a continent far from home. The participants of this retreat were in silence, except to ask questions of the teacher. At first, Kevin found it surprisingly difficult to sit across a lunch table from others and not be able to talk about who he was, what he did, where he is from, or to share his 'opinions' about the teaching. But, something happened at the end of the second day that was also shocking to Kevin. The silence became pristine, and even in a room with two hundred people; the air seemed to take on a quality he had never experienced before. It seemed to be replete with latent potential.

Fifteen days later, when the event was about to end, the participants were invited to break the silence. The chatter promptly started again, slowly at first and then it rose to a level to be expected of such a large group. Kevin remained silent. He noticed that the refreshing lightness that had permeated the air in the past few weeks had somewhat dissipated. Curiously, he felt no desire to just chat, and in such a setting, his desire for continued silence was respected.

At lunchtime on the final day, Kevin sat close to two energetic women from the United Kingdom. Kevin remembered that they had asked profound questions during the retreat, and that they had sat in silent meditation like little Buddha statues. As he politely craned his neck to eavesdrop, he expected to hear a mixture of talk about the past weeks of evolutionary enlightenment, or conversations related to other aspects of this event. However, Kevin was taken aback by what he heard. Their dialogue had reverted entirely to the domain of ego!

This was to be the first time Kevin objectified the little-mind's need to command conversation. One woman was expressing a complaint about her mother, who was unhappy that her daughter was on this retreat. The other talked about how her cell phone did not work in this country. They also chatted about what their friends might think of them when they are home again, after having been in India on a spiritual quest. From their banter it seemed as though the retreat — on the evolution of consciousness and the identification and transcendence of ego — had not occurred. In that very moment it became clear to Kevin that the ego-mind in these two people had just taken a nap for two weeks and was now, unknowingly to both of them, back in the driver's seat, filling the precious space of potential with unconscious ego banter.

P: When a person who has let go of his attachment to ego-motivated conversations hears those topics of constraint being expressed by another person, he knows that this chatter is not the true essence of the host?

EVOLUTIONARY POINTER: An awakened person instantly recognizes double-talking as the dictates of the ego-mind. He can clearly witness the animation of an individual soul who has yet to differentiate itself from the culturally-created-self.

MQ: And don't be fooled by those who can wax eloquently on matters of great depth. Amma, the renowned 'hugging saint', once said, "The number of scriptures read or satsangs attended is no criterion for gauging the spiritual evolution of an individual. They only indulge in *intellectual acrobatics. There is no difference between them and a tape recorder"*[4].

EVOLUTIONARY POINTER: To an awakened person, a 'great conversationalist' often has absolutely nothing new to say.

MQ: The malicious ego-mind, while it can talk up a storm about spiritual matters, will ultimately want to keep the conversation 'soft'. This means the ego will gladly converse with you about spirituality topics, but mostly so that it can express and defend its existing opinions and its beliefs.

P: Or in the case of the charismatic and intelligent spiritual seeker, the goal is to sound smart and charming enough to hook another soul mate!

MQ: Indeed. But, since the same unhealthy-ego generally supports the self-image of its host as a kind and caring person, please consider what this entity is likely to be saying in the background of a person's awareness as you are engaging with him in conversation:

- My host and I have had some pretty cool spiritual experiences.
- He has interpreted all of his spiritual experiences against the background of his cultural conditioning so he is pretty much lost and looking for love in all the wrong places.
- I keep him busy so that he does not have time for a practice of meditation to reconnect with spirit on a regular basis.
- My host doesn't realize that his true nature is being restricted, because…
- Even though he thinks he is spiritual, he is still completely identified with me.
- My host has no distinction between the Freudian Ego and the two sides of *me*.

- He also has a huge shadow that he knows nothing about.
- My host thinks he makes conscious choices, but only uses my conceptual-will!
- He thinks he relates consciously with other people, but I do all the talking.
- He is a really a great guy, but be very careful that you do not call him to true transformation. I do not want to lose my position as his conscience and if you threaten my dominion I will respond with merciless fury!

The Unhealthy-Ego Snaps

P: Hence, the ego can be a skilled spokesperson in all manner of spiritual development.

MQ: Yes, indeed. The ego's arsenal of lengthy discourses stretches all the way from the hypothesis of healing rocks to Integral Theory.

P: And what happens if such an individual, as one described above, is called to *true* transformation?

MQ: By true transformation, do you mean to awaken for the sake of humanity?

P: Yes, that is the biggest evolutionary call currently available.

MQ: Well, have you ever witnessed a seemingly normal person suddenly become irate or even hostile? Such a 'snap' commonly appears when the malignant ego experiences pressure past its threshold. This can also occur when it feels like it is losing control of the future of its host. This is when the malicious ego rises up to defend what it calls the *boundaries of the self.*

P: But, boundaries are important.

MQ: Yes, of course. We discussed this in an earlier chapter with an example in which an awakened person uses the healthy-ego to secure the rights of personal property. But, this is quite different. This is the malicious ego using expressions of anger or even rage to draw a line around the separate self-sense for defensive purposes.

P: Therefore, this 'snap' is the unhealthy-ego protecting the separate sense-of-self, at all costs!

MQ: Yes, at all costs. The malignant ego is thinking, "I feel you are threatening me and my command of this host, therefore, I am going to respond with great force to protect myself and defend my ward."

P: And the ward of the ego is the separate sense-of-self and all of the cherished ideas of the host?

MQ: Yes. This 'snap' is the switch from consciousness, at the base level of ego-mind, to pure unconsciousness. Man regresses to animal. What looks as if you are becoming consumed by seemingly uncontrollable emotions in verbal battery is simply the unhealthy-ego patting itself on the back for 'taking a stand'. Such emotional suicide attacks cause untold harm to perpetrator, prey, and also to any innocent bystanders.

P: Why are outbursts like this still considered as acceptable behavior?

MQ: Because we usually learn this from watching our parents or other grown-ups. Every child knows the power of a tantrum! The problem is: we don't outgrow this. Now we throw tantrums when called upon to accept responsibility for the paradox of *being* and *becoming.*

The Soccer Captain: In the Federation Internationale de Football Association (FIFA) World Cup final in 2006, the captain of the French team, after exchanging some words with an Italian player, head-butted him in front of millions of people with such vicious force that the Italian was knocked to the ground. A week later, he apologized repeatedly — *"especially to children"* — with these words, *"Above all, I'm human... I tell myself that if things happened this way, it's because somewhere up there it was decided that way."*

P: His attempt at an apology is also a great example of the unhealthy-ego speaking.

MQ: And shadow, too, because he's also trying to project the responsibility outside of himself. As you awaken you will see how many people are at the mercy of such conditioned and unconscious responses. At first it is difficult to believe that talented, cultured and intelligent people are so adrift in the forcefulness of concealed conditioning. "I'm only human," the manipulative ego says, to a swell of nodding heads. The ego likes to agree with itself by nodding in sympathy – the logic is: if you can do it, so can I. Do you see the game it plays with us?

P: Yes, I am beginning to see it more clearly now.

The Threshold in an Awakened Person

P: Does such a threshold exist for an awakened person? The reason I ask is that it seems to me that highly realized people can exhibit great calm in the face of immense adversity from ego-chatter in other people. It seems as if the threshold is completely absent.

MQ: Why might that be?

P: With objectivity on the separate sense-of-self, there is no end to their patience?

MQ: Well, it's not that there is *no* end to their tether. You have to take their perspective for a moment. You can do this by asking yourself this question: Can an awakened person experience great frustration, impatience and annoyance, while in conversation with another person?

P: The ego's dharma would have me believe that they don't. But, is there really no way to know if an awakened person is ready to respond in such a like manner?

MQ: No, there's not.

EVOLUTIONARY POINTER: If an awakened person 'snaps' there isn't any ego present in his motives or intentions for responding that way.

P: Would this be like the Buddhist monks who brawled with Chinese security forces in the Tibetan capital, Lhasa[5]?

MQ: No, not at all. This is a reflection of the culturally-created-self striking out against itself.

P: It is true, though, that an awakened person can use some direct language to point out the manifestation of the malicious ego to its host.

MQ: Yes, this is common. This expression of *awakened compassion* in conversation is often interpreted by the recipient as callous and harsh. The ego frequently mistakes aggression – *to move toward*, as hostility – *to move against*. Therefore, when an awakened person takes steps toward bringing clarity to the ignorance of concealed conditioning, the ego perceives that as a direct threat against itself, and reacts in defensiveness. But, awakened compassion always ensures that when emotions are supercharging words, that transmission is also not a vehicle for the pathological ego, but for the sometimes unpleasant directness of great wisdom. The ego, however, is used to 'idiot' compassion, which is just one unhealthy-ego being subservient to another unhealthy-ego. Therefore, it retorts with cruel vigor when its game is identified.

P: What's idiot compassion?

MQ: Here is a quote from the great Western teacher of Tibetan Buddhism, Pema Chodron:

"Idiot compassion is a great expression, which was actually coined by Trungpa Rinpoche. It refers to something we all do a lot of and call it compassion. In some ways, it's what's called enabling. It's the general tendency to give people what they want because you can't bear to see them suffering. Basically, you're not giving them what they need. You're trying to get away from your feeling of 'I can't bear to see them suffering'. In other words, you're doing it for yourself. You're not really doing it for them."

P: Thank you. So, even in the presence of strong emotions and psychological pressure, an awakened person can communicate with one-pointed severity without generating any karmic repercussions.

MQ: Yes. An awakened person, for example, can choose to express the voice of anger when appropriate.

P: This brings up another popular tenet of the ego's dharma: *The experience of anger is not a part of the awakened life.*

MQ: The unhealthy-ego loves for you to think that the awakened experience is just all bliss and butterflies. An awakened person who does not deny or repress anger, still feels it, of course, but his motives for expressing that voice do not cause unnecessary suffering. As Genpo Roshi's teaching's reveal, if you want to change the world, you have to get really angry, the energy of anger is the gasoline we need to do some good. That's what ultimately matters, right?

P: Right.

MQ: And just as one awakened person who denies or represses anger, and another awakened person who does not, both of these individuals may express the voice of anger; the former at the most inopportune moments and the latter when most precisely appropriate.

P: I feel as if I have much to learn about awakening my conversations.

MQ: Please be gentle with yourself. You may have been using the vocabulary of conditioning since you first said the word *mama* or *papa*. Evolving your listening and your speech, therefore, will take a little practice. We will now look at more specific examples so that you may begin to identify the ego's words in your own.

Choosing Your Words Carefully

MQ: When the unhealthy aspects of the ego are present in your words, many of your daily conversations are counter-productive to awakening.

EVOLUTIONARY POINTER: What are commonly perceived as *meaningful conversations* are very often just the culturally-created-self exchanging its assortment of unreasonable fears, desires, worries and wishes with itself in another person.

P: Can you give me a simple example of how conditioning controls conversations?

MQ: Sure. But, before we do, please be careful not to condemn those at other levels of development. Bring your attention instead to the content of your own daily exchanges.

P: Agreed.

MQ: To get us started, here are three words that are often used by the unhealthy-ego to solicit itself in another person: "How are you?"

P: But, is this not just a simple greeting?

MQ: It most certainly can be and there is nothing wrong with that, but watch what can happen after such a request is issued. This seemingly innocent inquiry is often employed, especially in our most important relationships, by the malevolent aspects of ego-mind to elicit discussions of prevailing thoughts and feelings, the good, the bad and the ugly!

P: This all sounds like a perfectly normal exchange.

MQ: Yes, this is true. Can you see why it's called *concealed* conditioning? Remember the ego-mind has had about 4,000 years to perfect hiding its pathological side!

In order to protect your authentic interest in awakening, you need to tread lightly around this particular clandestine request, because concealed conditioning can also be the gatekeeper to what you accept and reject as 'normal' and 'acceptable'.

EVOLUTIONARY POINTER: *"After all, what goes into your mouth will not defile you; rather, it's what comes out of your mouth that will defile you."*[6]

P: But the idea of removing "How are you?" from my dialogue sounds cold, uncaring and frankly, pointless.

MQ: Does it feel cold and uncaring to you or to the unhealthy aspects of ego-mind in you? What you may be feeling is the shivering ego. When you shine the light of your awareness on the lesser-self, it gets nervous. If you are aware that three words can release the unhealthy-ego into a conversation, it also realizes you are removing a major avenue for its manipulation of your life. The ego will fight hard to retain this outlet in your voice.

P: Does not asking this question mean I do not care about the other person?

MQ: Of course not! And though it may seem totally illogical, editing this request actually creates an expression of awakened compassion toward another human being. Remember, while you may care deeply for another person, the unhealthy-ego does not care for you or the individual to whom it is speaking; it just wants to call itself up in that person.

P: Those people who are close to an awakened person would never ask such a question?

MQ: Let's be clear: It's not that they do not care how he is, but they know he would not want to take his time or theirs, discussing something that is not a real reflection of *who* he is. An awakened person understands that to be *truly* concerned for others and to express genuine empathy for them, is to not allow the pathological-ego to express itself through his voice. This includes not issuing a request for the malicious ego to indulge its self-inflicted misery.

213

EVOLUTIONARY POINTER: To command your conversations free from the binds of concealed conditioning demonstrates that you care more about others than you do about yourself.

P: Now I get it. The pathological-ego knows that the typical answer to "How are you?" can invariably launch a conversation that propagates this illusion: *Who I am is entirely comprised of my thoughts and feelings.*

MQ: Exactly. And when your attention is there, it cannot be focused on creating the conditions for awakening and your liberation from those chains. If this particular greeting is unavoidable, it is certainly wise to be polite, yet vigilant. This way you can divert hidden habituation from emerging – at least in your own words.

P: I can see that bypassing concealed conditioning in conversations can be challenging.

MQ: Sometimes there is not much else you can do.

P: A convenient and effective substitute is to open a conversation with: "Hi there."

MQ: That works for me.

Sarah's Story: Sarah was a northern Californian who could speak with great gusto about the evolution of consciousness, potential, purpose and responsibility. But, she only did this with her 'spiritual' friends whom she frequently accompanied to weekend retreats. By about Tuesday, when the weekend buzz of self-discovery had worn thin, her conversations usually reverted to laments over her comfortable but unfulfilling marriage, complaints about her health, and also how many of her 'real' friends did not like her to talk about awakening. During a subsequent retreat, Sarah mentioned this situation to her teacher, who asked her what might happen if she shared her enthusiasm for potential and authentic joy with her 'real' friends. Sarah declared, "They would think I am crazy!" Then the teacher replied, "Freedom is an *all or nothing* affair. By not sharing your interest in liberation equally in your most important relationships, you are only appeasing the unhealthy-ego – that part of you that is restricting your development to the stages of development that your friends have yet to transcend, thus sustaining the gap between you and awakening. Unfortunately, I cannot create that interest in you. Your fate rests not only in your hands but also in your words."

MQ: This contamination by the malevolent ego-mind of conversations is the same regardless of where you are. In city after city, country after country, the awakened ear hears the same ego talking and witnesses the same ego listening in one exchange after another.

EVOLUTIONARY POINTER: The ego speaks thousands of different languages.

The Lesser-Self's Favorite Topics of Conversation

MQ: A quote from the Buddha points us to the importance of paying attention to our words:

> *"All that we are arises with our thoughts. With our thoughts, we make the world. Speak or act with an impure mind, and trouble will follow you."* [7]

The art of awakening communications, therefore, begins by establishing if an upcoming dialogue is solely a request from the unhealthy little-self for sustenance.

P: And I guess that when I start to move my attention away from a conditioned way of conversing that my significant relationships will respond?

MQ: Of that, there is no doubt.

EVOLUTIONARY POINTER: If awakening reveals that some of your relationships are founded solely on the grounds of gratuitous ego banter, simply removing your attention from such a foundation proves to be a catalyst for profound transformation.

Uncovering Concealed Conditioning in Conversations

MQ: Let's now look at some common incentives for chatting that sustain the unhealthy ego-mind. I will not attempt to describe every possible scenario here, but a sufficient number to reveal how concealed conditioning can command your voice or that of the other person. With a little practice, the influences of this hidden habituation can easily be identified and cast aside.

P: I am going to guess that these suggestions will irk the pathological ego to no end.

MQ: Indeed, poor thing! Therefore, the reluctance you may feel, to the evolution of consciousness, is simply the forcefulness of individual and collective conditioning residing within you. Include that resistance, and you will succeed. Additionally, the lesser-mind may also try to convince you that these suggestions will stifle the basic right of passionate self-expression.

P: Which it doesn't because I know that awakening in *no way* denies my humanity.

MQ: It is also good to note that chatting with your favorite waitperson, commenting on a rainy day with the mailman, or exchanging pleasantries with your neighbors are not the type of conversations that we are concerned about here.

EVOLUTIONARY POINTER: Refusing to share the little-mind in conversation is the greatest gift you can give another human being. This is rare; when you see it, cherish it. Emulate it.

MQ: The purpose of these questions is to allow you to hone your attention to conditioning that is concealed in conversations, therefore, they should be applied only to your *most important relationships*. A positive answer to any of the following questions may point toward the unhealthy-ego's bid to control the conversations that are relevant to your awakening:

• **Do I want to initiate a conversation or respond to another person because**:
- We both enjoy an exchange that is *entirely* composed of gossip and hearsay?
- Small talk is normal in this particular relationship?
- I'm bored and I want to fill the time talking about nothing?
- I know this person loves 'he said, she said' conversations?
- Being with this person in silence would be too uncomfortable for me?
- If I don't engage, they might think something is wrong with me, them or our relationship?
- By chatting as we normally do, we can avoid unresolved issues between us?
- I only speak about matters of depth and consequence in all my *other* relationships?

• **Is what I am about to say**:
- A falsification of the facts as I understand them?
- A gentle twist of the truth to my personal advantage?
- An expression of my truth that is contrary to ways in which I live?
- A defense of a conditioned belief, especially if related to my time and place of birth?
- Weighted with opinions or judgments based on my cultural conditioning?
- A personal expression of limitation?
- Inappropriate for this particular situation or person?

- Emotionally charged because I really feel the need to 'get it off my chest'?

- **In an impending conversation, do I have the intention to**:
- Air grievances about or criticize another person who is not present?
- Make fun of another person who is not present?
- Let this person know how good I am by comparison to other people?
- Distract myself from subjective suffering?
- Make my opinions heard regardless of what the other person's position may be?
- Get something from the other individual to satisfy a personal ambition?
- Give this person the impression that he may get something from me?
- Make the other person believe that I am interested in what he has to say?
- Placate my partner by letting him 'vent'?

P: If these, or similar themes, pervade the dialogues in my *most important* relationships the unhealthy-ego is likely to be controlling my speech.

MQ: Yes. Note that the ego is quick to chime in with comments such as, "Chatting about nothing is perfectly normal" or "I am just being honest when I express my worries" or "I was just being present while he complained about his troubled life". While we can all agree that it is commonplace, there is really nothing normal about supporting the root cause of suffering by entertaining it in your dialogues.

P: That is difficult to accept!

EVOLUTIONARY POINTER: As you grow accustomed to picking up on conditioned banter, it will be one matter to question the content of such exchanges and entirely another matter to look to the motives behind your own desire to repeatedly engage in such ego-based dialogues.

Jennifer's Story: Jennifer did not know the best way to create the conditions for her awakening, especially in relation to her job, which she'd had for ten years. She was aware that she had to disconnect from the mindless chatter and sometimes callous gossip at lunch and during breaks. Jennifer brought a book on meditation to work and instead of joining in the banter, she would sit by herself and read. When she declined repeated requests to rejoin the group, her co-workers started to become suspicious. Because of a series of rumors that were spread about her, she was eventually called to her boss' office. After many meetings about various incidents unrelated to her reading, she was told that she would have to work with a 'minder', someone who would make sure she was still able to do her work well. This response to her desire to not engage in conditioned chatter, but instead focus on her interest in spiritual awakening surprised her, especially since she had always performed her duties impeccably. Nonetheless, Jennifer did as she was told and she continued to read on a daily basis. Shortly after, however, she resigned. Some months later, Jennifer returned to pick up some paperwork and noticed that the malicious chatter continued unabated.

P: I think Jennifer was rather brave to eventually resign.

MQ: Indeed she was. As you recognize the incessant need of the malicious ego to dominate conversations, see also that an opportunity for evolution is being offered to you. Pay attention and you will see that *awakened choices* are always being offered to you.

Stepping up to the plate with actions that verify your interest in finding and accessing your next level of development can sometimes be difficult. At your job, you might be the first to be waking up to the infection of unconscious nattering. Expect your aspirations of greatness to be challenged, from within and without. Be brave, be strong, there are many of us who wish for and work toward realizing a glorious new world.

P: This is great news!

MQ: We will now look at some additional topics of conversation that can be loaded with concealed conditioning. It is important to note that this section may come across as offensive, but only to the malignant aspects of the *ego-mind*. Apply these examples to your *most important relationships* and not just to the interactions you may have with your housekeeper or the staff at your bank. Concealed conditioning is likely to be comfortable and in control when you are speaking or listening to:

- **Conversations about:**
- Past emotional states and the reasons why they are still bothering you.
- Past emotional states and how you struggled at that time to overcome them.
- Your struggle with the voices of unreasonable fear, doubt, insecurity, or skepticism.
- Laying blame for various events and situations in your life.
- A berating you received at the hands of another person.
- Your ill treatment or berating of other people.
- The ills of the world, when personal conflicts co-exist in some/many of your relationships.
- The issues that affect third-world countries while such problems exist to varying degrees in your hometown or homeland.

- **Lengthy dialogues about your most important relationships that:**
- Have long been unsatisfactory.
- Were once wonderful.
- Have long since alternated between these two states.
- Have long since ended.
- You don't have yet.
- You feel you need to have to be complete.
- You have, but wish you didn't.
- You wished you'd handled differently.
- You've missed out on.
- You think other people have or don't have.
- Might improve if only the other person changed.
- Might improve if the other person gave you more independence.
- Might improve if the other person was more open in your relationship.
- Are great as long as the other person doesn't change.

- **In-depth descriptions or lengthy monologues about:**
- Prevailing emotional states.
- Fear or desire for particular future emotional states.
- Your lack of emotional states.
- Your overabundance of emotional states.
- Someone else's lack or abundance of emotional states.
- Comparing your emotional states to those of other people.
- Comparing the emotional states of others to yours.

P: What about when you have such conversations with a skilled professional?

MQ: This is perfectly fine. It is one thing to speak to a therapist or other trained individual in regard to the resolution of specific emotional issues, but it's an entirely different matter when the malevolent ego-mind converses with itself to anyone who will listen. Let's now continue with some more situations in which unhealthy-ego is sustained in conversation:

- **Lengthy diatribes about**:
  - Being powerless in a bad work situation.
  - Being powerless in a good work situation.
  - A work situation that alternates between being satisfying and otherwise.
  - Not having the job you want.
  - Not wanting the job you have.
  - Not knowing whether you want the job you have.
  - Not having a job at all.
  - Comparing your financial worth to others' wealth.
  - Not having enough of something.
  - Having too much of something.
  - Financial worries, especially when this discussion is with someone who is not fully qualified to help you resolve them.

- **Excessive and disproportionate discussions in your relationships of:**
  - Purely personal hopes and dreams for the future.
  - Personal or private business dealings of other people.
  - Suspicions about other people.
  - Suspicions that others may have toward you.
  - Bias, harsh judgments or jealousy.
  - Opinions having to do with race or creed.
  - Personal subjects to the exclusion of other topics.
  - Personal events that have long since passed.
  - Actions you took in the past.
  - Choices you did not make.
  - Choices you could have made.
  - Choices you should not have made.
  - Choices you had no option but to make.
  - Choices you are thinking about making in the future.
  - Choices you have been or will be forced to make.

- **Conversations that involve seeking advice:**
  - Which you have been given before, by that same person or another person.
  - Which you know you are not going to act upon after you receive those suggestions.
  - On the effects of ill-health in the past, present or future, especially when not directed toward a healthcare professional or caregiver. This, of course, would not apply in a situation in which the patient is terminal, when presence and listening are of absolute value.
  - From people whom you know are truly unable to help you. For instance: Do you seek advice about your relationships from someone who has been divorced three times?

- **Conversations that involve giving advice:**
  - You know is ineffective.
  - You know is only partially effective.
  - You do not follow.
  - You have given to this same person several times in the past.

- **Speaking of successes of the past just to show:**
  - That you are not getting any attention for this.
  - That you deserve more or less attention for this.
  - That you can put other people down.

- **Repetitive or motivational discussions that are primarily based upon:**
  - Linking success or failure to a particular feeling state.
  - Looking forward to particular events or rewards.
  - Getting away from situations or challenges.
  - Battling, overcoming or conquering particular habits and patterns.

MQ: Pay attention to the conversations in your significant relationships. Do they include some of the topics we just discussed? Moving your attention from them can bring lightness and ease to those interactions.

EVOLUTIONARY POINTER: Making *awakened choices* in conversations creates the conditions for transformation by replacing the expression of conditioned limitation with the expression of trust.

Ryan's Story: After living in the United States for several years, Ryan decided to move to a small fishing village by the Adriatic Sea, in Croatia. He spoke very little of the local language. When he was in a public place he was unable to understand what people were saying. Gradually, Ryan realized that *not* understanding the content of these conversations was somewhat of a relief. In his former home near San Diego, *not* knowing what other people were saying in public places was mostly impossible. In the U.S., Ryan's experience was that the pervasiveness of ego-chatter could be numbingly narcissistic. He remembered daily conversations that were primarily composed of gossip and rumors, of fears and desires for tomorrow, expressions of envy, self-criticism and criticism of the government and the system.

After settling into this new country, Ryan met a person who spoke both English and Croatian. One day, while at a local café, Ryan asked his new friend to pay attention to what was being said around them. After a minute, his friend described the conversations as "nothing new". He said the content was mostly about personal problems, television, the weather, mobile phones and gossip. Ryan noted that these were very similar to the many space-filling chats he was used to hearing in the U.S. The location, and level of affluence, changed significantly, as had the culture and history, yet the very same ego was still animating the inhabitants' speech, but now it was speaking Croatian!

Ryan realized that these meaningless and banal conversations were only one small part of a grand tragedy. At first, he thought that he was being judgmental, but then he knew that the Americans and the hard-working fishermen from Croatia did not know that the ego-mind was the primary director of the polemic.

MQ: It is good to note that the proclamations of the lesser-self are also plainly evident in the printed word. The unhealthy-ego commonly appears between the pages of many bestsellers in the spiritual marketplace. Frequently the responsibility is unfairly placed on the authors to release their readers from unnecessary suffering.

EVOLUTIONARY POINTER: When the unwholesome ego is directing the writer's pen for a readership in which the *same* ego is the hidden determinant of action, bestsellers are common, but true transformation is unusual.

P: This charade is not new: *"Hypocrite! First remove the plank from your own eye, and then you will see clearly to remove the speck from your brother's eye."*[8]
MQ: Indeed. Such glorious wisdom has been available to us for two thousand years. Have we been paying attention to it?

The Little-Mind Stands Up for Itself
P: Much of what has been said thus far goes directly against the grain of conditioning in regard to conversations. I can hear the unhealthy-ego in me now as it is offering me suggestions, such as: "How uncaring," or "How disparaging," or "How uncompassionate!" "If you take away all of these topics, there will hardly be anything left to discuss!"
MQ: When *Presence* is brought to conversations that have been solely limited to the parameters of the malignant ego-mind, you may

indeed end up with this question: "What *am* I supposed to talk about?"

P: This is a reasonable conclusion considering this chapter thus far.

MQ: Yes, it is. And if you are hearing such internal nonsense, at least now you know the unhealthy-ego is alive and well in you as it always has been. The malicious lesser-self is disturbed by your attempts to identify the influence it has on your words.

EVOLUTIONARY POINTER: Seeing the ego-mind is half the battle. The other half is learning to disregard those thoughts that wish to manifest as conditioned chatter, before that happens.

P: Curiously though, I am also aware of the voice of potential that is saying, "How possible," "How uplifting," and "How unbelievable!" It seems that my conscious renunciation of seemingly normal topics of conversation would bring me a renewed sense of curiosity in the potential of human relationships.

MQ: How refreshing! This is called awakening your relationships. Such an interest often appears in you when you have the ability to respond to it. Often, just hearing the possibility is sufficient to reawaken that curiosity. I wish you the very best!

Selective Silence

P: My interest in removing the ego from conversation is strong. Is there anything else I can do besides editing out the specific topics we just discussed?

MQ: Yes. *Selective silence* is to elect to remain unresponsive to the demands of the unhealthy-ego in the words of another person. As with disregarding thoughts, you will see that you already are an expert at *selective silence*.

P: Why is this?

MQ: Think of how many times you 'bite your tongue' – how

skilled you already are at not jumping in a conversation, because you know that would be a bad move! Now you will just apply this skill when the ego is incessantly speaking through someone you may love dearly.

P: Therefore, being selectively silent in a situation when there is no better option is a great way to disallow the affirmation of the unhealthy-ego?

MQ: Yes, at least your unresponsiveness wins half the battle. The other half is to eventually figure out a way to decrease your listening time.

P: That could be difficult in the case of my mom!

MQ: Judge them not, for often they are lost without their permission. Your awakening reveals to the puppet that not only are strings attached to you, but you also have a puppeteer. On a good day *Miss Piggy*[9] from the Muppets is trying to save the world; the next she is telling her therapist that she feels she has no control over herself. And this cycle just goes on forever. Miss Piggy has no idea that she is being played. "I have free will, I'm an independent thinker", she will shout in that sweet, yet self-righteous voice. And then the unhealthy-ego in her will eventually ask you, "Do you want to hear about my problems?"

P: Advice?

MQ: Run!

P: Seriously?

MQ: There is nothing wrong with being in the presence of the malevolent ego-mind. But, just because it's there, clamoring at you to sustain its meaningless tragedy, does not always imply you have to acquiesce to its every demand.

EVOLUTIONARY POINTER: Be wise in your choices, for this unhealthy-ego would like nothing more than to see the flame of infinite potential go out in you too!

MQ: Remember, every person you know has the opportunity to attain freedom from all unnecessary emotional and psychological suffering. Help them see this potential. That's a great gift to give them, right?

P: That is so true.

MQ: Don't be surprised to find, that as is often the case, the lights are on, but the only person home is the ego-mind. This explains the common phenomenon of the unhealthy-ego offering false affection for the spiritual attainments of others.

P: Why is this?

MQ: In the presence of an awakened teacher, the malicious ego-mind is fearful that its occupation may be pointed out to its host. The unhealthy-ego, therefore, hides behind a shield of fake humility by asking the same old questions, over and over again. This gives the host an excuse that he or she is not yet ready to change, offers the impression of genuineness to other seekers and ensures that control of the host's future never leaves the hands of the ego.

Taking the Truth Home

P: We have covered many ways of renouncing the ego-mind in conversations, from editing specific words and topics, to selective silence, non-judgmental listening and assistance, to removing myself as a source of sustenance to the unhealthy-ego. But, I am still a little bit lost. When I realized that my useless chatter might be shaping my fate, my first response was, yikes! But, when I began to think about the practical application of this wisdom, two people came to mind – my mother and my mother-in-law. Now, my mom is so used to my asking her to stop rambling on about the same old story that she has learned to tread lightly. I am fine with this, especially since I know that she has no interest in awakening. I can really respect the fact that she does not encroach on my desires to live to the fullest of my potential beyond conditioning. I know she understands that the reason we do not see each other so much anymore is that we are very different people in regard to our intentions for *being* and *becoming*.

She likes to suffer unnecessarily, I don't. She's not interested in consciously co-creating the future, I am. It's that simple. And I think she is incredibly strong to allow me the space to grow, because she knows that trying to have me closer would cause me to compromise my aspirations to live in authenticity and transparency. So, we get along whenever we see each other. I know to keep the conversations 'easy' and she knows to keep the ego-dramas out.

MQ: This sounds great, so no problem here at all. Congratulations.

P: With my mother-in-law, however, it's a whole other story. She wails and whines like a three-year-old whenever she's around, but since we don't have the depth of connection as I do with my mom, I don't know quite how to tell her.

MQ: The force is strong in this one.

P: Indeed!

MQ: But, you can't really say this: "You know that I love you dearly. But, did I ever tell you that one of my interests in life is conscious evolution? And because of this, I find it difficult to pay as much attention to the ego-mind in you as it would like me to".

P: No, I can't say that. She already thinks I am peculiar and rude for not wanting to participate in her banter. And because she and I are not close, if I said something like this, she will resent me and maybe even stop talking to me altogether.

MQ: Are you sure?

P: The force *is* strong in this one! And from my years of experience of trying to introduce clarity on concealed conditioning to my own mother I just know she, or at least the malicious ego in her, will likely blow up in my face if I were to pursue the topic.

MQ: But, you really care about her, right?

P: Yes, of course, and this hurts even more because I see the unneeded ego-based suffering she creates for herself.

MQ: That's the beginning of awakened compassion.

> EVOLUTIONARY POINTER: You recognize that meandering monologues are being generated by the independent force of the ego-mind, which is animating an individual soul who has yet to differentiate itself from the culturally-created-self.

MQ: And you understand that to be truly concerned for that person, to express genuine compassion for them, is to not allow the pathological-ego to express itself through your voice. Your mother-in-law, or should we say, the malicious ego in your mother-in-law, has spotted this and labels *awakened compassion* as strange and uncaring. The ego-mind in her can't stand the fact that you are not issuing a request for it to lament its self-imposed misery. You are being wise in your placation because you know that the malevolent ego seeks to disown the flame of truth in you.

P: So what can I do in this situation?

MQ: Well, we know now there is really nothing normal about supporting the root cause of suffering from your lips. Do you want to create more additional anguish for her? Are you willing to suffer so that you are no longer a participant in this charade of the malicious ego in her?

P: But, if I carefully put a little distance between us, I know she has plenty of other friends with whom she can satisfy the ego's need for pointless banter.

MQ: This is very likely; however, that is not the point. Here is the question again: Are you willing to generate additional anguish for her? Are you willing to suffer a little so that you are no longer actively partaking in this game of the unhealthy-ego?

P: Do I want to create more anguish for her? Not in the least. Am I willing to risk a little comfort so that I am no longer a contributor to the indulgence of the pathological ego in her? Yes, if that is what it takes, yes.

MQ: Sometimes a little necessary suffering is required so that we may evolve past the karma of unconscious ways to the glory of conscious living. Whose words are you going to allow through your lips today: Those of just the ego, those that emanate from essential *Presence*, or those of the fully functioning human being, who has clarity on both?

The Bodhisattva vows to save all sentient beings, regardless of the 'personal' costs.

1 Francois de La Rochefoucauld (1613–1680).
2 The fifth chakra, or the throat chakra, is primarily associated with communication.
3 A state of sudden spiritual enlightenment (Zen Buddhism).
4 Satsang is a group meeting with one's guru. Quote from an article: Spirituality is not Intellectual Acrobatics, by Mata Amritanandamayi (The hugging saint). Published by the United News of India in 2007.
5 The New York Times, March 15, 2008.
6 Scholars Version of the Gospel of Thomas by Polebridge Press, 1992.
7 The Dhammapada.
8 New Spirit Filled Life Bible: NKJV – Matt. 7.5
9 A character from the famous children show, 'Sesame Street'.

Chapter 8

AWAKENING RELATIONSHIPS

"We are more interested in making others believe we are happy than in trying to be happy ourselves."[1]

The True Nature of Your Relationships

P: If my conversations have long been driven by inherited habituation, I have to wonder about the true nature of my relationships. Could it be that some of those interactions are primarily based upon concealed conditioning?

MQ: Yes, this is entirely likely. As we delve into the area of human relatedness, it is good to note that not all of your relationships are pertinent to your awakening. Those relationships that are critical to your liberation are referred to as *relevant relationships*. We will be returning to this distinction in just a bit. Become aware also, that the malignant ego will strongly resist the clarity we seek in this chapter on our most important relationships. This is because this aspect of our lives can be one of its favorite feeding grounds.

P: Thank you. I will remain awake to its objections.

MQ: Many people spend their entire lives in relationships motivated by unexamined and conditioned patterns. Such interactions can be fun, loving, challenging, adventurous and full of great moments, but nonetheless, constricted within the limits of conceptual-free-will.

P: Therefore, holding no hope for the release of the participants from suffering?

MQ: Unfortunately, yes.

EVOLUTIONARY POINTER: You will recognize this as you awaken: Mostly it has not been *you* relating with the other person, it's been the ego-mind relating with itself in the other person.

MQ: The good news is that this realization allows the possibility of transforming your existing relationships, and forming new relationships based on authenticity and transparency.

P: This *is* great news! But, might I find that some people are so entangled with their particular stage of development that they feel compelled to oppose the expression of my most authentic nature in our relationships?

MQ: Well, by indicating that you wish to transcend and include the unhealthy-ego in relationships, you are removing yourself as a source of nourishment. You are taking away its number one food supply: an ear for its relentless complaining and unnecessary conflict. Therefore, you can be certain that because of a person's attachment to the ego-mind, they will object to your desire for peace, progress and even rationality.

P: Why would someone who says they truly love me stand in the way of my awakening?

MQ: Look at it this way: the role of the ego-mind is to defend the separate sense-of-self. It primarily does this by supplying that person — its host — with an endless flow of emotional and psychological complexities to 'deal' with. That person becomes attached to this flow as exclusively who they are. In awakening, you wish to transcend and include the separate sense-of-self in your new perspective, and at times, completely drop your exclusive identity with it. To the ego-mind, awakening to authentic joy looks like death. See why the ego gets scared?

P: Yes, I see that now. And this can emerge as irrational behaviors in my experiences.

MQ: This is true.

Your Image in Relationships

MQ: We saw earlier that *conditioned attention to thinking* is the most prevalent state of awareness in the world today. Because of this, you tend to form relationships based on your self-image. Regardless of the geographical location of your upbringing, 'your life' can be an endless effort to nurture and protect the picture of yourself in your mind's-eye, your self-image.

P: Consequently, because of my attachment to the ego-mind, I unwittingly craft relationships to conform to this internal image of 'me'?

MQ: Yes. If you have an ambition to be materially successful, you will surround yourself with those who can affirm and support that self-image. If you see yourself as 'giving' or 'caring', you often have many friends who are 'needy' and 'victimized' and vice versa. Because of concealed conditioning, you learn to manipulate the world around you to match the image you have of your separate sense-of-self.

EVOLUTIONARY POINTER: To paraphrase Andrew Cohen, '*We wear people like jewelry*'.

P: And if everyone is doing this, where is the true relatedness?

MQ: Where indeed? Whose self-image are you unknowingly adorning?

P: But are you not condemning the 'giving' and 'caring' souls amongst us?

MQ: Of course not. Their work in the world is appropriate at that level of development and essential. But you can only truly help your neighbor when the unhealthy ego, as the primary medium of response, has been replaced by awakened compassion that is driven by your higher and deeper Self.

P: Therefore, conditioned relationships can never fully gratify my self-image, no matter how hard I try or how much I wish to give of myself?

MQ: Life-long 'givers' can very often end up being drained; not empowered. Conflict inevitably arises when the self-image of one of the participants is being threatened, is no longer being supported or when too little or too much is being asked for or taken. In such cases, disagreements quickly undermine the 'love' and you get caught in a vicious circle of *defend, attack, apologize, affirm* and so on for the life of the relationship. This is often the point at which 'irreconcilable differences' appear. This is ego-speak for, "You no longer gratify my self-image so I need to find another donor".

P: Therefore, the presence of personal conflict in a long-term relationship implies that I am forgiving unconsciousness in my partner or in myself?

MQ: Naturally. As you attempt to love and accept yourself in an un-awakened relationship you are compelled to condone actions that cause you and others unneeded suffering.

P: Sometimes the bickering goes on in our primary relationships for 50 or 60 years!

MQ: Repeated struggle is only normal at the level of the malevolent ego. This is because the unhealthy-ego does not care for, nor respects you, your partners or your relationships – just itself. Be clear about this.

EVOLUTIONARY POINTER: In an un-awakened relationship, two or more incomplete individuals are seeking completion where it cannot exist – in a relationship with each other.

P: What do you mean by *incomplete*?

MQ: Look to your own experiences. Have you noticed that after years of following promises that the world offers toward finding completion, satisfaction and self-love, you still get the sense that something is missing, that you are as yet incomplete? You naturally seek out other people in an attempt to heal the deepest aspects of yourself. They, by the way, are doing the same thing, and often, neither of you are aware that this is happening.

P: As a result, in un-awakened relationships I am trying to *find myself* in a connection with another person who is wants to find *himself* by interacting with me?

MQ: Yes. You fall in love with your shadow in the other person. You fall in love with the positive qualities of yourself that you have denied, and they fall in love with their shadow in you. You go about this task, convinced by the unhealthy-ego that you are interacting consciously and as completely as possible. There is even a tenet of the ego's dharma that reminds you: *Nobody's perfect, so don't strive for perfection.* The malevolent ego backs up this nonsense with a long list of viable excuses to put up with, or justify, your 'almost' perfect relationships that can be nothing more than emotional minefields.

EVOLUTIONARY POINTER: The gap between your life *as it is* today and the awakened life is often populated and fortified by a network of interactions that have been exclusively structured to maintain the separate self-images of the participants.

MQ: And yet, even though you may be aware of this gap, you will simultaneously be convinced that many of these relationships comprise a significant portion of a conscious spiritual path. This reveals a tenet of the ego's dharma: *Your primary value is 'love', even though your most cherished relationships are plagued with varying levels of divergence and conflict.* True love must glow first within you. Then you do not need confirmation from others, and your reasons for relating become transparent, because you do not enter relationships in search of affirmation, but for the sake of humanity.

EVOLUTIONARY POINTER: The liberated life unfolds when your choices no longer support the malignant ego's objectives to sustain superfluous disagreements amongst your significant relationships.

P: Those are my awakened choices.

MQ: Yes.

Jasmine's Story: As Jasmine worked to awaken, she was developing clarity on the motives for her relationships. She discovered that the basis for many of her interactions was a fertile ground for the unhealthy-ego. For example, a number of her relationships were comprised only of gossiping or the relentless sharing of personal problems. She also discovered that other than a connection to an individual as a result of her place of birth, there was really no conscious basis for the relationship at all. Even Jasmine's most cherished relationships, with her boyfriend, parents and her siblings, seemed to oscillate through varying degrees of loyalty and disappointment, caring and discord, trust and deceit. Jasmine was beginning to realize that only the unhealthy-ego would condone such behaviors. As her awareness continued to expand, Jasmine also noticed that repetitive conflict in some of these relationships was commonly driven by motives exclusively related to unwholesome ambition and control. In order to transcend and include this conditioning as part of her new perspective, Jasmine saw that she could continue to sustain relationships that were prone to repeated disagreements. Or she could let go of the appearance of the unhealthy-ego in her. This she could do by a simple expression of her intention to be free more than anything else. Jasmine continued to disregard the thoughts and ideas of the unhealthy-ego that prodded her to engage with conditioned limitations in others. Her subsequent attempts to not instigate, invite or sustain personal conflict were wholeheartedly welcomed, strongly rejected or completely ignored. When her efforts were met with curiosity and openness those relationships immediately began to awaken. With consistent effort, Jasmine redeveloped the basis for all of those interactions to a point she had only dreamed was possible.

P: Jasmine realized that freedom and personal conflict are mutually exclusive. Her story also exposes one of the most ridiculous tenets of the ego's dharma: *Repetitive conflict in personal relationships is unavoidable, normal and healthy.*

MQ: This is only true when you do not realize that there is a higher and move evolved alternative.

Uncovering the Unhealthy-Ego

P: What could I expect to happen as I identify possible aspects of concealed conditioning in my relationships?

MQ: There are generally three outcomes:

1) Those with whom you are interacting will follow your glorious lead and those relationships will awaken to a degree of purpose, passion and peace that was formerly unimaginable.
2) Your efforts to edit the unhealthy ego-mind will go completely unnoticed.
3) The lesser-self in the other person will show subtle, severe, or brutal opposition to your desire to evolve the basis for that relationship.

P: Is there any way that I can know what might happen before I introduce my genuine interest in awakening to my relationships?

MQ: There's no way to predict what's going to happen. And what if you decide to introduce this possibility, regardless?

P: That reflects my interest in letting go of ego-generated anguish.

MQ: That's correct. And if you don't introduce this possibility, it is easy to predict what is going to happen. Stabilizing a new basis for your interactions that is not exclusively based on conditioning is the most challenging aspect of the uncommon path. When those with whom you are interacting follow your glorious lead to identify and transcend the attachment to the ego, *awakened relationships* emerge.

EVOLUTIONARY POINTER: Awakened relationships are *free from all personal conflict.*

MQ: They reveal the possibility of perfection in the human relatedness right in your own living room.

P: Many relationship therapists will refute the idea that relationships can be free from personal conflict. They seem to be more concerned with the management of personal conflict than with its complete resolution. This kind of therapy reminds me of a movie in which the arsonist was also the fire chief!

MQ: This is often the focus when you do not know to look to the root cause: attachment to the ego-mind.

EVOLUTIONARY POINTER: Though we can all learn from each other, accepting directions on coherency from those who are still floundering in the backwash of the little-self is futile.

MQ: The key to awakening is not to abandon the wisdom of current therapeutic or coaching practices, but to combine them with teachings that have been successfully proven to uncover and release conditioned ways of being. Integral Psychotherapy, Integral Coaching, and The Big Mind/Big Heart Process are noteworthy examples.

P: And what about the other two possible responses you mentioned earlier?

MQ: After years of seeing the hidden agendas and ulterior motives of other so-called 'caring' souls, some people may find it hard to trust your awakening. It is good to be aware of this so that you can respond to them with the utmost compassion.

P: Okay, duly noted.

MQ: Therefore, even a small request from you to curb the expression of the malevolent ego may reveal a depth of denial and cynicism that you didn't know existed. Unfortunately, there are many emotionally intelligent people who are not only circum-venting their full potential, but who have yet to reach a stage of development that allows their responses to such a request to be comprehended as rational.

EVOLUTIONARY POINTER: Remember, you have to see the ego-mind in yourself first, before you can identify and transcend its malevolent aspects in your relationships. Judging the ego-mind and shadow in others, because of their presence in you, only deepens everyone's suffering.

Shaking the Ground

P: Is this why, when I gently point out the ego-mind in relatedness, the common ground beneath long-standing relationships seems to shake?

MQ: Yes. By using conscious-free-will, you create this awakened choice: to sustain conditioning as it appears in your relationships; or invite the harmony of your new perspective to emerge.

P: So, the 'shaking ground' is the unhealthy-ego realizing it has been discovered?

MQ: Yes.

> EVOLUTIONARY POINTER: It is simply beyond the compre-
> hension of the unhealthy-ego that long-term, committed and
> intimate relationships can also be conflict-free.

MQ: Consciousness has often been derailed for so long that purely personal anguish is considered to be part and parcel of human relationships. Nothing, however, can be further from the truth. The malicious ego doesn't want anything to change, let alone a relationship that is a rich source of emotional and psychological conflict.

P: And what if my interest to redevelop the basis for a relationship is met with opposition over long periods of time?

MQ: Often, your gentle suggestions, compassionate requests, heart-felt pleas, rational insistence and even direct ultimatums are to no avail. But, don't dismay! It is possible to maintain a relationship, so that it is irrelevant to your awakening.

P: And if my suggestions to edit concealed conditioning from my relationships go unnoticed?

MQ: This frequently occurs with those at lower levels of consciousness. The option, however, to continue nurturing that part of the ego-mind in those interactions will still be yours. As always, be tender in your approach with those who are suffering unknowingly, yet at the same time are unwilling to consider the possibility of embracing the full potential of their humanness.

Defining a Relevant Relationship

P: You mentioned earlier that not every relationship is pertinent to my awakening.

MQ: Isn't that a relief?

P: Yes. But, how can I tell which ones are and which ones are not?

MQ: Those interactions that are pertinent to your desire to create the conditions for awakening are called *relevant relationships*. For the sake of our conversation a *relevant relationship* is defined as one in which you spend *more than 48 hours per year in direct, conscious interactions.*

P: You have to forgive me for saying this, but that number sounds a little bit cut and dried. Is the formula of 48 hours per year arbitrary? Can you tell me how you came to this definition?

MQ: This amount of time is not arbitrary. It is based on fifteen years of observations of highly evolved individuals and awakened teachers and the ways in which they conduct themselves in relationships with people who clearly have no desire to uproot concealed conditioning. Without contradicting or confining their own genuine aspirations, this amount of time allows an awakened person to continue to have relationships with special people who have absolutely no interest in awakening. In this way, important relationships, such as those with family members who have no interest in awakening, are not denied in any way.

EVOLUTIONARY POINTER: Running away from personal conflict is not an aspect of awakening, but neither is dealing with it just because you don't want to bruise the other person's self-image. The key is finding a ground that is marginally beneficial to evolution in these complex situations.

P: The bottom line is that if my mom wants to remain attached to the ego-mind, that's fine?

MQ: Perfectly fine.

P: That's great to know.

MQ: Please understand; my goal is to help you clearly distinguish your *relevant relationships* from those that have little or no impact on your quest to express your full potential. And in a further explanation, note that *conscious interactions* do not include time you spend sleeping under the same roof with other people.

EVOLUTIONARY POINTER: The time spent in the *unconscious presence* of another person is not even relevant to that particular relationship, let alone to your awakening – not unless you and your partner are co-creating realities by lucid dreaming while asleep at night!

MQ: When you aspire to live in authenticity, you will find that with clarity of awareness, even the most challenging interactions can be adjusted so that they are no longer hindering your desire to awaken.

P: As a result, I can appease the conditioned mind in certain relationships, but in a way that has no affect whatsoever on my quest to realize and express my capacity for conscious evolution?

MQ: Yes, absolutely.

Identifying Relevant Relationships

There are 168 hours in a week. After sleep and other necessities, we are left with about 100 hours of free time for work, family, socializing, entertainment, meditation and other pursuits. To identify your relevant relationships, follow this exercise:

1) Make a list of all the people with whom you have an important relationship. For the sake of this exercise, start with the first 20 to 30 people who come to mind.

2) Estimate how much time you spend in the *conscious presence* of each person? Count how many hours you spend interacting with those on your list by week, month, or by year.

3) Sort your list according to time spent in conscious relatedness. Put the person you interact with the most at the top of this list.

MQ: The first person on your list has the privilege of having the relationship that is most relevant to your awakening. This particular relationship influences your ability to participate in the co-creation of a new world in a most profound manner.

Awakening Your Relationships

MQ: Now that you have a list of your relevant relationships we will look at how you can begin to awaken them. *Awakened relationships* contain all of the most familiar aspects of normal relatedness, and they are also completely free from personal conflict. Awakened relationships exist primarily for the development of consciousness and culture. They are the vehicles for the expression of creativity by which we can co-create a conscious future.

P: Passing interactions with my mail delivery person or the drycleaner are not relevant to my awakening, assuming, of course, that I am appropriately pleasant and courteous.

MQ: This is true. For instance, you cannot have a relevant relationship with the person who works at the coffee shop, whom you see every morning for a few minutes. This is simply because this small amount of relatedness cannot deliver an outcome beyond pleasantries and a nice latte. Nonetheless, such relationships always have the *potential* of relevance.

MQ: Of course, it is not out of the question that you could meet a new person with whom you can immediately create a relationship whose basis is beyond the unhealthy-ego. But, it is only with extended periods of time spent in conscious relatedness with this person that you can see the true depth of their perspectives and understanding. Because the basis for this relationship is more advanced than simply ego-bonding or sharing concepts and beliefs of conditioned perspectives, a little more effort is usually required, especially when beginning a new relationship. This is a topic for my next book.

P: Okay. I see now why it is good to divide my relationships into those that are relevant and those that are not, because the ego-mind likes to jumble all of them together in one big heap.

MQ: Exactly! Because, that's the way it's always been done. And if you can't tell which relationships are relevant to your awakening and which ones are not, the ego-mind is always going to be able to hide in that unknowingness.

EVOLUTIONARY POINTER: You can only engage *consciously* when you are clear that your intentions for interacting are not completely embedded in individual and collective conditioning.

P: Therefore, if I am not certain about the basis for a particular relationship, then it is likely the unhealthy part of the ego is certain.

MQ: Yes. And the implication of this unconsciousness eventually leads to conflict.

P: But the ego-mind likes to have me think that every interaction I have is important.

MQ: Every interaction is important, but that's not really the point. Awakening to your full potential and being perceived as a nice person are two completely different matters.

> EVOLUTIONARY POINTER: It is only by bringing the clarity of your purest intentions to all your relevant relationships that together we can forge the evolution of consciousness and culture.

P: The point is: to awaken all of my relevant interactions. This is very different, and certainly more challenging, than being nice to the checkout person or the people at the yoga center. Having a goal of expressing myself beyond attachment to ego-mind in all of my relevant relationships is an ultimate call to responsibility.

MQ: That's it!

P: What about group interactions?

MQ: Group relationships, such as: playing in an orchestra, singing in a choir, having an involvement with a spiritual group, or as a student of other kinds of learning, can all be relevant to your awakening. If you are spending more than four hours every month; eight hours, six times per year; or about one hour per week in direct, fully focused, interpersonal exchanges in such situations then please consider the relevance of these relationships in regard to your awakening. The key, of course, is not to distance yourself from such activities, but to bring your awareness to the possible presence of concealed conditioning in your interactions.

P: And what about adventure sports?

MQ: Extreme sports are very often a response to a lack of meaning and purpose in other areas of your life; therefore, relevant relationships that revolve around such activities need to be examined carefully.

P: Then, there is nothing wrong with bungee jumping off a bridge once in a while?

MQ: Not in the least, but if your life is completely consumed with the next adrenaline-charged event, it is safe to say that the dark side of the ego has you handcuffed to a high that is detrimental not only to your immune system, but to your awakening as well.

P: Then it's okay to have fun with my friends in social settings that I know are based entirely on the ego?

MQ: Yes, of course. Everyone's life situations are different. Remember the distinction between *relevant* versus *irrelevant* relationships and you'll do just fine. We will further explore awakened relationships in the last chapter.

An Authentic Stand

P: But, to stay in a *relevant* relationship in which the other person is unwilling or unable to let go of needless ego-motivated suffering is to include myself as part of the cause of their unnecessary anguish?

MQ: Yes. You can always allow for an exception, but then you will have to choose conditioning over awakening, suffering over resolution and mediocrity over potential. Why might you do that?

P: Because I want to put compromise ahead of evolution in that particular interaction?

MQ: Yes. The unhealthy-ego would like that karma, but I am sure you don't. Do you?

P: Not particularly!

EVOLUTIONARY POINTER: *Awakened compassion* is to figure out a way to show someone that they are much more than just the conditioned fears and desires of the culturally-created-self.

P: Now I know where to focus my efforts in identifying concealed conditioning in my relationships. I will start with the person at the top of the list, which I generated earlier, and work all the way down to the last person.

MQ: Yes. The unhealthy-ego's intentions to perpetuate anguish and your intentions to end suffering meet on the frontiers of your volition. This is your private 'front line' where you will find awakened choices awaiting your attention. The second and conspicuously more public battleground reveals itself in those who, for whatever reason, wish to challenge your interest in awakened living. Frequently, the unhealthy-ego in those who love you the most, proves to be your worthiest adversary. Remember to dearly embrace them with great care, and always forgive them, for they may not know what they are doing.

EVOLUTIONARY POINTER: People will often oppose your efforts toward authentic joy because the malicious ego-mind in them is having an adverse reaction to your awakening to the same ego-mind in you.

Eric's Story: Eric led a destructive lifestyle. He worked as little as possible, slept all day and preferred to go out after nightfall. In all his darkness, however, he sensed that a better way was possible, but he was oblivious to what it might be. By the grace of coincidence, Eric met a wise and wonderful woman. Clara immediately recognized an authentic spark of interest in him. She introduced Eric to the concepts of awakened living through stillness meditation, selective silence, awakened choices, attentive action and trust. Clara's way of being, however, defied what Eric had pictured as the philosopher's lifestyle. But, it quickly became clear that Clara was free from most, if not all, unnecessary emotional and psychological suffering, so Eric followed her lead impeccably.

Soon Eric noticed that he was changing in subtle and profound ways. He began to identify conditioning and the ways in which the 'ego' had restricted him within culturally accepted boundaries. Then he began to let go of some old relationships that primarily revolved around the motives of the unhealthy-ego.

As a result, a new light was beginning to emerge from the ruins of the old Eric and he eventually wished to introduce Clara to his parents. In this first meeting, Eric's mother was quite cold toward Clara. This behavior was most unusual for his mother, especially since she knew Clara was prodding him to live in a new and enlivened way. When Eric asked his mother about her behavior, she said, "In this house I make the rules. This woman is not good for you. She is no longer welcome here." Eric was shocked, yet respected his mother's wishes.

As the holidays approached, Eric was expected, as was customary, to attend a number of family events. In light of his obligations, he asked his mother for an update on her position on Clara. She told him that he was most welcome but added, "*She* has to stay in the car." In Eric's mind, he pictured Clara sitting outside with Nuwa, his Husky pup. That year Eric made the painful decision not to go to the family dinners. After several visits home alone in the subsequent months, Eric's mother unashamedly berated him about his recent choices. It was now clear to him that she was not interested in hearing about a way of living that had profoundly transformed him. After several more attempts, Eric finally gave up. Though it hurt, it seemed he was left with no other option.

Eric and Clara wed and are now working full-time on projects related to the potential of awakening. He misses his family sometimes and wonders why his mother was so afraid to let him change and be happy. He was certain that having a son who was overjoyed to be alive was much better than one who had to leave the holiday dinner tables three or four times just to feed his cocaine habit. A pitiful solace for Eric was that he knew that the berating he received whenever he tried to have a discussion about Clara with his mother, was not her but the pathological ego-mind in her. Unfortunately, she was not aware of this, and for Eric to continue to battle with this aspect of his mom would have only exacerbated the suffering all around.

P: Okay. Eric's story reveals that sometimes our relationships can be extremely distressful, yet even with an offer of release, there is little interest in changing anything.

MQ: Who do you think might be hiding behind that logic?

P: The malignant side of the ego. Therefore, there may be some cases in which I am left with no option other than to detach for a while from those who continually try to sabotage my intent to be free?

MQ: Yes. And later on, of course, as your new perspective stabilizes, you can re-enter those former life situations, if you wish. As always, though, be gentle and empathetic.

The Greatest Expression of Love

MQ: As your awareness expands, note that the quantity, quality and intensity of the love you feel for those special people in your life is not at the heart of this discussion. What is most important are the ways in which you express that love. Eric's story brings us back to an earlier tenet of the ego's dharma, which tries to convince us that: *Repetitive conflict in personal relationships is unavoidable, normal and healthy.* This is true, but only when you are involved in relationships in which the malevolent aspects of the ego-mind are at the foundation.

P: What then is the greatest expression of love toward another person?

EVOLUTIONARY POINTER: *Awakened love* is to care about the spiritual development of another person more than you care about any other aspect of the relationship itself.

MQ: This can be achieved by replacing the lesser-self's relentless need to be right — in the exact moment of conflict — with compassion for the evolution of that individual. You are ultimately compassionate because your partner may not be aware that the unwholesome part of the ego is moving in them to sustain emotional and psychological conflict in that relationship.

P: Okay. But, what if I think that I already relate to others consciously?

MQ: The ego's dharma tells us that part of *conscious relatedness* is to be open and aware of the suffering of the other person. Fundamentally, this is correct. The ego's dharma, however, ignores the fact that if we are interacting without any requirement of resolution with the root of that anguish — the lesser-self — we are also the cause of that person's suffering. All too often, the ego's opinion about what is conscious rings loudest in your ears, so much so that those judgments are all you can hear. Therefore, your relationships are conscious, but only at the level of inherited habituation.

P: How can I be sure that my current interactions are not being influenced by concealed conditioning?

MQ: Review these four statements from the Introduction of this book. Did you answer 'Yes'?

	YES	NO
1) I have implicit trust in myself and in the process of life.	___	___
2) I do not create unnecessary suffering for others or myself.	___	___
3) All of my important relationships are free from personal conflict.	___	___
4) I interact with other people in relationships free from unhealthy-ego.	___	___

EVOLUTIONARY POINTER: The evolution of the basis of your relationships beyond personal conflict is impossible when your attention is trapped by concealed conditioning, yet, at the same time, you may be convinced that you are already maintaining conscious interactions.

Carla's Story: Carla was a single mom with a twelve-year-old daughter. Since her declaration of freedom, her intention to awaken was unfolding as complete self-reliance, autonomy, peace and harmony. As part of her ongoing efforts to bring her awakening to all of her relevant relationships, Carla began to screen her cousin Jenna's intrusive, and sometimes caustic, phone calls. She did this in spite of a gnawing desire to not offend Jenna and to just put up with more years of such treatment for her cousin's sake. As Carla removed herself from Jenna's irrational demands, the relationship with her own daughter opened up tremendously. Together they were able to face the challenges of life in unison. Carla discovered a direct correlation between her willingness to not interact with the unhealthy-ego in Jenna, and her ability to identify and transcend the manifestations of that same ego in herself, and therefore also in her relationship with her daughter. By letting go of a long-standing self-image of being a 'good cousin/friend', she was awakening the relationship with her own daughter by *truly being* a good mother. Carla realized that only the unhealthy-ego would enforce a self-image as a 'good cousin/friend' in order to sustain intentional or unconscious mistreatment from other people. In time, Carla condensed her interactions with her cousin so that they were no longer relevant to her awakening. Simultaneously, she and her own daughter enjoyed an awakened relationship that was free from personal conflict. In time, Carla's daughter passed on these skills of peace, gratitude and awakened compassion in relationships with her friends and eventually to her own family.

EVOLUTIONARY POINTER: Because truly awakened people care more about the spiritual development of others than they do about their own personal comfort, they are simply unable to consistently sustain the malevolent aspects of the ego-mind in any of their relevant relationships.

A New Way of Interacting

MQ: Practice awakened observation in the next interaction you have with a person with whom you share a relevant relationship. Observe who you are being in the exchange. Observe, also, who the other person is being in their interaction with you. Can you see if the unhealthy ego-mind has that person locked into specific personas that he or she is using to support a particular self-image? Are you perhaps watching yourself or a part of yourself that overlaps with one of his or her personas for mutual benefit?

EVOLUTIONARY POINTER: The more awareness you bring to the little-self in you, the more its reflection will show up in your relevant relationships.

MQ: Are you shocked, surprised, humbled or overjoyed? Is the little-mind goading you into denial, defense, or self-righteousness? Have you also been building and sustaining relationships at the ego's bidding to support your self-image? Acknowledge any tension or opposition you may be feeling now for what it is: a manifestation of malevolent ego in resistance to your awakening.

P: But, this doesn't mean that *all* interactions with that person will cease?

MQ: No, not at all. You can still maintain a relationship with this person, but in such a way that it is no longer relevant to your awakening.

P: I understand. And, what if they begin to show interest in awakening also?

MQ: That would be wonderful. After all, to consciously co-create a new world, you are going to need all the help you can get!

Nefesh or Ruach[2] – Animal or Spirit?

MQ: In this acknowledgement, know too, that many emotionally potent relationships are a reflection of a force that is simply not *who you are.*

EVOLUTIONARY POINTER: Your choice to be free from your attachment to the ego-mind also frees the world from the ego *in you*. This is an awesome achievement!

Devora's Story: Devora was a passionate and caring woman, well loved for her calm, ease and compassionate directness. Because of her passionate interest in awakening from concealed conditioning, she worked diligently for many years to build a retreat center in an opulent suburb of Tel Aviv for residential courses on a wide variety of spiritual disciplines. Devora's only son, however, with whom she had a relevant relationship, ridiculed her on a weekly basis because she was unwilling to listen to him bemoaning his seemingly pointless life, gossiping about his friends, and complaining about his lack of joy and contentment. He also criticized her about her life's work of providing a venue for spiritual development.

Over the course of many years, Devora had tried to explain her passion to her son, but he refused to listen. He always insisted that she was being unrealistic and demanded that she live in the 'real' world, like other mothers he knew. Though she felt great compassion for her son, his relentless critique of her desire for authenticity and responsibility caused great anguish and disharmony between them. Then Devora realized that her awakening to the ego-mind also called for her to interact as the *same* unified person with *every* person with whom she had a relevant relationship. She saw that the malicious ego in her had been swapping masks to suit the relationship with her own son. In her own case, Devora had to become the 'verbally abused mother' so that she could sustain a relationship with her son whose primary interest in his relationship with his mother, by the evidence of his years and years of ridicule, was to sabotage her interest in sharing the glorious possibilities of an awakened life with other people. Devora realized that the continual emergence of her full potential was presenting her with an awakened choice: to support a repetitively conflictive interaction with her son or to continue to pursue her dream, as free as possible from all defiant and derogatory commentary, by making this relationship irrelevant to her own awakening.

P: What are you trying to get across here? Did Devora give up the relationship with her beloved son because he chided her for wanting to be free from conditioning?

MQ: No, she did not completely abandon the relationship with her son, but she made her son's commentary irrelevant to her own awakening by significantly reducing the amount of time she spent with him. Devora was choosing between *nefesh* and *ruach*, between animal and spirit.

P: But is not variety in our personalities the spice of life?

MQ: Yes, and that's the wonder of diversity. But an unconscious switch of personas driven by your attachment to the ego-mind is not the same thing as consciously changing how you express yourself according to the level of consciousness of the individual with whom you are interacting.

P: Such a conscious shift is often misinterpreted by those at lower levels of consciousness. For example, an awakened person can be a pure joy to a peer, but to a person still stuck in the ego, sometimes such an individual can come across as quite rude and insensitive.

MQ: This is true. We will talk more about this distinction between 'idiot' compassion and 'awakened' compassion in the last chapter.

Philanthropy as the Expression of Awakening

MQ: As you learn to awaken your most important relationships, there will arise many ways in which you can express this potential for the sake of humanity.

P: Philanthropy is just one area of life in which I can come together with others in service of our fellow man. Can you tell me a little about the possible presence of concealed conditioning here?

MQ: Yes. Magnificent gifts of time, money, and resources abound in philanthropy and it seems these efforts are providing love, light, and hope for millions who have little else. Any effort you make to alleviate the suffering of those less privileged is most certainly praiseworthy.

EVOLUTIONARY POINTER: Be sure that the insidious aspects of the ego are not influencing your humanitarian endeavors. Is your 'generosity' also consistent throughout your relevant relationships and not exclusively reserved for your charitable roles?

P: Therefore, my efforts to rescue those who struggle to survive while I am still a hapless victim of the ego-mind, albeit at a different level, is like *putting out fire with gasoline*[3].

MQ: Yes. A true benefactor first gains objectivity on the culturally-created-self. Only then are their selfless acts — at home or across the world — free from the consequences that will sustain the suffering they seek to alleviate.

EVOLUTIONARY POINTER: To 'give' in your personal relationships means that your attention is primarily donated to supporting those who are not unwitting guardians of the ego-mind.

MQ: In your efforts to support the needy, the unhealthy-ego also regularly suggests intentions by which you can give 'quietly' or 'privately'. While anonymity is admirable, this type of generosity can also be carefully structured so as to not interfere with a busy 'personal' life.

P: Are you saying that such secret activities allow me to separate my personal life from the full burden of responsibility for my favorite causes?

MQ: This is very often the case. Such 'giving' frequently arises after other great attainments have perhaps failed to deliver contentment. Unfortunately, all the philanthropy in the world won't appease your unease when your intentions are in any way persuaded by the little-self. *"It's actually, I think, more honest to say we're rock stars, we're havin' it large, we're havin' a great time and don't focus on charity too much – that's private; justice is public."*[4]

EVOLUTIONARY POINTER: The ego-mind merely pretends to care about humanitarian issues.

MQ: The fleeting motives of conditioned kindness compound dire consequences because there is rarely sufficient follow-through to provide permanent resolutions. Charity will remain conclusively impotent until the ego is removed as its director, both privately and publicly.

Peony's Story: Peony was a famous Hollywood movie star. She fell in love with an English actor while shooting a movie with him in India. Together they decided to start a charity to care for orphans there. The couple enrolled dozens of other celebrities to add their voices and funds to this project. The results were magnificent and even the gossip press was enamored at their selfless acts. However, when this couple broke up a few years later and moved on to other partners, neither one wanted to assume sole responsibility for the organization they had started together. The fund-raising dinners came to an end and the support dwindled. Soon, all traces of this once thriving organization had all but disappeared. The ones who were affected by this the most were the children in India who wondered why their care packages stopped coming.

MQ: While at the outset of this project, the actors' intentions appeared to be pure, their subsequent breakup revealed that sustaining their promise to the orphans was less important than their personal goals. In the un-awakened state, the intentions of the malevolent little-mind always overtake what was once considered to be a really wonderful idea.

P: Even though the ego says it wants to save the world, it really can't.

MQ: Not in the least. The ego feigns worldcentric empathy, but can't ever follow through because its intentions are all based on its cravings for 'personal' recognition, affirmation and even immortality. An awakened person's perspective on the challenges facing this world has transcended the ego's need to remain separate. Such an individual is now fully available, willing and able to respond to the plight of those who are suffering so unnecessarily.

EVOLUTIONARY POINTER: To save the world, you have to first do a much harder thing: *save yourself* from a sole identification with the ego-mind.

P: But aren't charities feeding millions today.

MQ: Yes, of course, and this reflects a glorious truth indeed. But, many millions more will starve tomorrow. According to a former director[5] of the U.N. World Food Program — the world's largest charitable organization — the percentage of people who are hungry has decreased while the actual number of hungry people is increasing by about five million people per year. The World Bank estimates that with the current growth trends in the world population, by 2050, there will be a 50 percent increase in the numbers of those living in poverty over that same statistic for the year 2000.

P: That's two billion more starving people than the world is contending with today!

MQ: The generosity of the lesser-self can cure an injustice today, but a thousand new ones will appear tomorrow. One of the goals of this work is to allow you to come together, temporarily beyond ego, with five or 500,000 individuals who are now awakening to the realization of how the ego-mind has been driving our planet for thousands of years. Let's now begin to form, deliver and sustain effective solutions.

P: So many of these organizations flaunt altruistic agendas that are primarily driven — unfortunately for those they profess to serve — not by the release of the many, but by the preservation of the *one* – the ego.

MQ: Indeed. The ego-mind has turned the 'poor', the 'homeless' and the 'starving' into objects that it uses to make its hosts feel good about themselves. Interactions at this level of development are based on a limited perspective and reveal that the *many* are still *one* with the malignant ego-mind at a collective level. A new world begins when you and I can come together beyond ego-mind.

If you can truly *be* with me, there will never be a problem that we can't tackle and transcend.

EVOLUTIONARY POINTER: What is your universe of relevant relationships like today? Are they open, complete, passionate, replete with purpose and awakened potential; or are you best friends with the ego-mind? Be careful that you, too, do not get lost in the waiting room of life.

---

1   Francois de La Rochefoucauld (1613 - 1680)

2   *Nefresh* is ego, *ruach* is spirit. *Nefesh* is the Hebrew word that literally means "animal" though it is usually used in the sense of "living being". *Ruach* is the spirit that supports the life in Nefesh.

3   From the album – Cat People by David Bowie, 1983.

4   Bono in the Dublin-based Sunday Independent newspaper - June 2005.

5   James Morris - December, 2006.

Chapter 9

THE FIRST INSIGHT

RENOUNCE CONDITIONED MOTIVES

*"We should often be ashamed of our finest actions if the world under-
stood our motives."*[1]

Unconsciousness Before Coffee

P: Why is the discipline of waking up sometimes challenging?

MQ: Because your brand of coffee is not strong enough. Seriously, by the time you get out of bed in the morning, the conditioned mind has already consumed the majority of your attention. Your daily rebirth to inherited limitation occurs without you even knowing it and before your feet hit the floor. Notice how your attention is immediately spread across thousands of thoughts, feelings, impressions and scenarios. You are beset with habituated beliefs, judgments, opinions and legions of fears and desires. This seemingly 'normal' movement of the mind, which is often accompanied by the appearance of thousands of *voices*, depletes the lion's share of your attention. This leaves only a tiny sliver of your attention at the command of your willpower.

P: Sometimes I even wake up in a particular mood.

MQ: And by now you know this most likely a shadow. Own that draining occurrence, so as not to identify with its inauthentic emotion. Then, become clear about the particular are feeling and follow the instruction to neutralize your shadow, which we discussed in the third chapter.

EVOLUTIONARY POINTER: Watch the act of waking up tomorrow morning. See how your awareness is flooded. A vast majority of this invasion is a result of accidental ego-identity.

MQ: As we discussed in the chapter on karma, your awakening in each and every tomorrow depends solely upon every yesterday. Do you know if you unwittingly engaged with a malicious ego-motive yesterday? If so, there will eventually be consequences.

P: Do you mean consequences like my agitated mind that seems to be out of my control?

MQ: Unfortunately, yes.

Identifying the concealed motives of the unhealthy-ego brings to mind this wonderful quote: *"Whoever desires to come after me, let him deny himself... and follow me."*[2]

To *come after me* is to live as this awakened one did, beyond the binds of concealed conditioning. Denying yourself does not require that you abandon your car payments or give up your current career. It does imply, however, that you relinquish your constant attention to the voices of individual and collective conditioning as your primary motivators.

P: *Whoever...* does not exclude anyone.

MQ: No one is excluded, yet note how the purity of these words have since been assimilated by the ego-mind.

EVOLUTIONARY POINTER: The awakened life is founded upon eternal motives that only appear after those of the little-self have been relinquished and then included in your new perspective.

MQ: Releasing the conditioned drives of the lesser-self also brings up these words from Buddha: *"He cuts all ties. He gives up all his desires. He resists all temptations. And he rises."*[3]

To cut all ties and *rise* — to an awakened life — implies you have to identify those ties first.

Imagine for a moment that one of your relevant relationships contains a significant amount of gossiping or the sharing of personal problems. In order to rise beyond this situation, you would first have to realize that these topics are the favorite topics of the unhealthy-ego. It is only after you identify that there are conditioned motives at work in those conversations that you will be in a position to transcend and include those ties as part of awakening that relationship.

EVOLUTIONARY POINTER: Letting go of the conditioned and the already known part of *you*, allows the awakened and unknowable *you* to manifest here and now.

Identifying Conditioning in Everyday Life

MQ: Because our lives are naturally incited by desires, physiological needs and emotions, these also become our motives. Are you aware, however, that concealed conditioning may also be compelling 'your' reasons for being, based exclusively on *its* motives? The First Insight is the art of uncovering evidence for conditioning that is concealed in the motives behind ideas, beliefs, relationships and everyday situations. The short-term motives of the ego-mind are limited to the term of this lifetime. While they are essential for day-to-day living, if you focus entirely on them, they become counter-productive to your ability to live an awakened life as a fully functional human being.

P: Does my attachment to the short-term motives of the ego prevent me from going beyond the illusion of separation?

MQ: For any significant period of time, yes. When you consciously face the forceful yet benign nature of the ego-mind, you will ultimately replace its temporal motives with eternal or awakened motives. The First Insight creates the conditions for eternal motives to emerge as the leading and creative edge of your life.

EVOLUTIONARY POINTER: *Eternal motives* unfold as the uncommon path of your life unimpeded by inherited restrictions.

The Object of Your Desire

MQ: Here is a question for you: Is your primary reason for *being* the evolution of consciousness and culture?

P: Right now, I cannot say that it is.

MQ: Self-honesty is a beautiful place to start. If you are not in touch, to a significant degree with the part of yourself that is already perfect, *One* and complete as it is, it is likely that your motives are influenced by the ego-mind. Concealed conditioning naturally commands your noblest dreams, your worst nightmares and most everything in between. If, on the other hand, you are blessed with the prevailing presence of your Higher Self, then the First Insight will enhance your capacity to fully express that completion.

P: But, if concealed conditioning is compelling my reasons for being, I will also seem to be locked in to the never-ending pursuit of enlightenment.

MQ: Yes.

EVOLUTIONARY POINTER: When concealed conditioning is stimulating your creativity with *its* wants and needs, you will repeatedly question your *raison d'etre*.

MQ: It is often difficult to be objective about your reasons for *being* because conditioning creates experiences for you that are comfortable and familiar, albeit illusory in the promise of perfection they offer. Waking up can be challenging at first because you are becoming aware of the fact that you were previously afflicted, but ignorant of the symptoms.

P: So what I want, or don't want, is not nearly as significant as *why*: my reasons for wanting.

MQ: This is true. Strewn amongst your motives you will also find those of the unhealthy-ego.

P: This means that there is absolutely no problem with my desire to be wealthy or to have lots of love in my life?

MQ: Not in the least. The objects of your desires are not an issue.

P: I notice, too, that when I attain what I want, there is a part of me that always wants more. Sometimes a new craving appears in the same moment that I reach the object of my current desire. It's endless.

MQ: Have you also noticed that the unhealthy-ego does not want your possessions or attainments to change or be undermined in any way. It tells you, 'Hang on to what you have,' 'Don't let anything go,' 'What's next?' or 'This is not it, keep seeking'. This causes great anguish as you attempt to cling to all that has passed and to manipulate that which has not yet appeared. The secret to misery is: not seeing the malignant ego cowering in your motives. Renouncing those drives becomes possible when you discover the pervasiveness of this habituated state.

EVOLUTIONARY POINTER: Freedom from conditioned commonality begins when you realize that you may be an integral yet unwitting aspect of the confusion.

Motives of the Malicious Ego-Mind

P: How might I know that conditioned motives have been manipulating my experiences?

MQ: With the help of these statements you can paint purely ego-based motives with a broad brush. Please read each one and then apply it to your own experience:

1) You are certain that you are living your life with purpose, but every now and then you get the distinct sense that some part of that mission may be absent.

2) You honestly admit that you have yet to discover your eternal purpose.

3) Life has no real purpose, other than enjoying yourself, being safe, and being happy.

4) You long to change many aspects of your life, but do not know where to start, or sometimes why you should even bother.

5) There is one major part of your life, which, if altered, would endow you with greater contentment, purpose or potential.

6) You would like one particular person — with whom you have a relevant relationship — to treat you with greater reverence and civility.

7) You have an active or hectic lifestyle, yet are unsure that all this busyness is the best use of your time and resources.

8) You are good at manifesting, but when the goals are reached, you find that the rewards you were expecting are somehow still lacking.

9) You couldn't manifest your way out of a paper bag, even if your life depended on that outcome!

10) You have big plans and great intentions that frequently fizzle due to lack of interest.

11) The secret to success, as far as you know, is watching other people live lives of great passion and completion.

12) You are perplexed by the actions of some, disgusted by the actions of many, confused and surprised by some actions of your own.

P: If I concur with any of these statements there is a likelihood of conditioned motives existing in my life situations without my even noticing. And, now I feel some resistance to self-honesty is arising.

MQ: Because this realization can be hard to accept?

P: Yes.

MQ: Awakening always reveals that your True Self and the universal ego-mind were seamlessly entangled right up to the point of that realization. The discovery of previously concealed conditioning is nothing to be ashamed of, as long as you remain aware of its presence. After all, those who instilled self-interested drives in you did so because they loved you dearly and only wanted the best for you. In most cases, parents, caregivers, therapists and training gurus were unaware that those same conditioned ego-directives were guiding their lives.

EVOLUTIONARY POINTER: There is no gain in finding fault with the sincere, yet misguided, intentions of other people. Their level of development does not absolve you of responsibility. Asking for forgiveness, however, for your own erroneous actions, may at times be most appropriate.

P: Should I ask for forgiveness immediately and also for long-past actions?

MQ: Yes. The ability to ask, however, does not release you from paying intimate attention to your responses to life. You do this so that you do not keep creating unnecessary suffering, then apologizing, then creating more unneeded anguish and apologizing again.

Uncovering Concealed Conditioning

"Voluntary Simplicity means singleness of purpose, sincerity and honesty within, as well as avoidance of exterior clutter, of many possessions irrelevant to the chief purpose of life. It is a partial restraint in some directions in order to secure greater abundance of life in other directions. It involves a

deliberate organization of life or a purpose. Because purposes vary, the degree of simplification is a matter for each individual to settle for himself."[4]

MQ: The following four-part exercise takes you on a journey of *voluntary simplicity.* You will go from identification, to renunciation and finally, to objectivity. Identification of previously concealed conditioning presents you with opportunities to reinvestigate and evolve your interactions with it as it appears. Renunciation frees the world from the weight of hidden habituation in you. Objectivity on previously hidden habituation allows that which you have transcended and included to arise in your awareness without impelling any further actions. When the once concealed motives are neutralized in awakened compassion, you will have access to the awakened motives upon which you can base your new responses.

P: But, objectivity on conditioned ways of being, thinking and acting that were formerly concealed only takes me half way home.

MQ: Yes. The remainder of the journey unfolds when you accept responsibility for your actions.

Let's look now at concealed conditioning arranged according to Wilber's Four Quadrants[5]. They are:

Quadrant 1   – Subjective: *Thoughts, Emotions, Meditation and Introspection.*

Quadrant 2   – Inter-Subjective: *Relationships, Belief Systems and Culture.*

Quadrant 3   – Objective: *Body, Energy, Health, Medicine and the Sciences.*

Quadrant 4   – Inter-Objective: *Economics, Environment, and Social Systems.*

MQ: Each one of these four aspects of the exercise is divided in to individual statements. Your responses to each will help you uncover where conditioned ideas, beliefs and opinions are concealed as inherited motives for your ways of being in the world. The connection between many of these statements and awakening may not be clear at first.

P: Let me guess: The malevolent aspect of the ego generates this vagueness in its attempt to remain in charge of my motives.

MQ: Yes. The ideas you have about 'who you are' have entirely emerged from the cultural background into which you were born. As you begin to witness how this concealed conditioning may have been directing major aspects of your ways of being, the subtler instances of its influence will also become clear.

P: Eventually, my task is to redirect my awareness away from all of these motives?

MQ: Yes, so that you can transcend and include them in your new perspective. This comes as evidence of a deep aspiration to live an awakened life. Please note that these exercises are not intended to be comprehensive, but sufficiently inclusive so that you will recognize how your unwitting attachment to the *impersonal ego* may have been masquerading exclusively as your *personal* world.

P: And then what happens?

MQ: By recognizing the matrix of concealed conditioning you are given the opportunity of recognizing those *preexisting structures in consciousness* upon which you can confidently step up to the next level of your development.

EVOLUTIONARY POINTER: As the anesthetic of distraction and the making of meaning wears off, the pain of awakening to the affliction of samsara is ushered to the forefront of your awareness.

Instructions for the Exercise

MQ: Each individual statement points to the possibility of concealed conditioning across various levels of development. The statements are not meant to be comprehensive, but sufficient enough to open your awareness to the veiled motives of the malignant ego. You are asked to rate your responses to each of the statements individually based on a scale of 0-10. The keys to evaluate each of your responses will be revealed at the end of the exercises.

- A rating of 0 represents a negative response; that you *strongly disagree with* and/or *rarely adhere to* the situation being described in a statement as you honestly apply it in your life.

- To indicate that you strongly agree with or completely adhere to a statement, you can apply a rating of 10. A rating of 10, however, must be accompanied by overwhelming evidence to support your response. For instance, if a statement reads: "*Smoking is dangerous to your health,*" you might reply with a 10, but only if you are a non-smoker.

P: A rating of 10 reveals that I *strongly agree with* and/or *wholeheartedly adhere to* a statement because of the fact that there is abundant evidence to back up this level of total agreement.

MQ: Yes, for complete and wholehearted accord, a rating of 10 would naturally have to be accompanied by consistent evidence in your life to support that particular response.

P: Responding with a 10, but lacking proof to verify its existence, reveals a mistruth.

MQ: This implies that the ego-mind is supporting a specific self-image, for which, beyond your agreement in theory, has no foundation in reality.

- Lesser levels of disagreement can be rated with a scoring of 1, 2, 3 or 4.

- A rating of 5 indicates that you are unsure or undecided about the circumstance under consideration. In other words, sometimes you agree with the statement or sometimes you adhere to applying this statement in your life and sometimes you don't.

P: This middle rating of 5 implies that sometimes there is evidence to prove my agreement, while at other times there is proof that refutes my accord with that particular life situation?

MQ: Yes. For instance, if a statement reads: '*The purpose of life is clear*,' you might reply with a rating of 5 if you seem to fluctuate between periods of great certainty and other times of deep uncertainty during which the expression of that purpose is more or less absent.

P: I understand.

MQ: A rating of 5 means that your position on that point is constantly fluctuating.

-   Ratings of 6, 7, 8 or 9 indicate *lesser degrees of vacillation*. In other words, you agree with the statement or you adhere to applying this statement in your life more often than you don't.

P: Can I disregard any statements that are not applicable to my life situations?

MQ: Of course you can. And just so that ego-mind does not turn this exercise into a 'to do' list, it is best to apply these instructions to all of the individual statements first. Then you can trust that the emergence of a new level of awareness will dictate the most appropriate responses after you have completed the exercise. Good luck!

EVOLUTIONARY POINTER: The First Insight helps you to verify that you are not unsuspectingly dancing to the tune of the ego's dharma.

Quadrant 1 – Subjective: *Thoughts, Emotions, Meditation and Introspection*

MQ: The *subjective* encompasses your internal awareness and experience. This includes sensations, perceptions, perspectives, impulses, emotions, images, symbols, concepts, values and intentions. It is also the compelling sense of being 'you', which you experience in the present moment. For the sake of this description, we will say that the *subjective* is primarily experienced in three different states of consciousness.

First is the waking state — also called the *gross state* — which is the condition of awareness you are in right now – holding this book and reading this line. Subjective experiences also occur while dreaming at night – this is known as the *subtle state*. In addition, subjective experiences are available to you during meditation, chanting and prayer – known as the *causal state*, which allows you, amongst other things, to experience consciousness directly.

Note to the reader: Because of the purely subjective nature of the first part of this process, you may find it quite a demanding and intense exercise. Please take your time with the instructions and also be gentle with yourself as you allow for the arising of new structures in your consciousness. Remember, there are no right or wrong answers, just the perfect answer for you at your present level of development.

Summary of Ratings:

Rating – 0: You *strongly disagree with* or *do not adhere to* the statement.

Rating – 1, 2, 3 and 4: Indicates lesser degrees of disagreement.

Rating – 5: You are unsure, undecided, or your position is constantly wavering.

Rating – 6, 7, 8 and 9: Indicates lesser degrees of vacillation.

Rating – 10: You *completely adhere to* and *strongly agree with* the statement. This level of rating must be accompanied by significant evidence to support your response.

_____ *Who you are* is not your thoughts.

_____ *Who you are* is not only your emotions.

_____ Your current beliefs and knowledge do not define your *true essence*.

_____ *Who you are* transcends and includes your current beliefs and intellect.

_____ Rampant thinking is a natural process and is no indication as to whether your awakening has occurred or not.

_____ Awakening includes freedom from all unnecessary emotional and psychological suffering.

_____ A fully awakened person feels anger in the same way as an un-awakened person.

_____ An awakened person experiences joy just as much as, if not more than, an un-awakened person.

_____ You are consciously disregarding thoughts all the time.

_____ You do not struggle with the arising of thoughts and emotions.

_____ Your fears and desires are relatively the same as everyone else's.

_____ The structure of the Freudian Ego, the self-organizing principle of the psyche, is fundamentally the same in you as it is in every other person.

_____ The level of development of the Freudian Ego can vary greatly from one person to the next.

_____ The essential structure of the ego-mind and the separate sense-of-self is basically the same in all of humanity – albeit at different levels of development.

_____ The separate sense-of-self or the conceptual sense of 'me' begins to emerge at the level of a child's thoughts around the age of four years.

_____ Fascination with conditioned fears and desires varies according to the level of consciousness of the individual.

_____ The evolution of your awareness, beyond the average of the culture into which you were born, is a matter of choice and does not occur by itself.

_____ There is a direct relationship between your values, your intentions and your destiny.

_____ You can never see beyond the choices you don't fully understand.

_____ You are aware of your primary value in a single hierarchy of values.

_____ Freedom is a choice when you have access to conscious-free-will.

_____ You co-create the reality you perceive.

_____ Psychotic individuals are the only people who create their own realities.

_____ You are aware of the single most important value sustaining each of your existing relevant relationships – this may or not be the same value in all your relevant relationships

_____ The intentions sustaining some of your most important relationships demonstrate shared values to effect transformations at a global level.

_____ Wisdom emerges from paying attention to the outcome of your actions.

_____ All of your karma — the consequences of your past actions — is here now for you to deal with and resolve.

_____ Who you were in your past lives, or might be in your future lives, is not as important as your intentions for your actions today.

_____ To surrender is to consistently accept responsibility for your actions.

_____ You are comfortable spending long periods of time alone.

_____ With your eyes closed, you can count from one to ten repeatedly for an hour without losing count.

_____ Meditation alone cannot heal your shadow.

_____ You can meditate for one to two hours without moving your body.

_____ You have had at least one direct experience with the Oneness, Emptiness or Fullness in which all phenomena appear.

_____ You know not to interpret spiritual experiences solely against the cultural background into which you were born.

_____ Spiritual experiences are generally insufficient to free your choices from the grip of concealed conditioning.

_____ Telepathy, extrasensory perception and psychokinesis are valid practices.

_____ Lucid dreaming (while sleeping) is a good skill to develop as part of your path to the discovery and expression of your full potential.

_____ Many 'power spots' exist on our planet where, if attuned, you can notice dramatic shifts in your subjective experience.

_____ When you wake up in the morning, you are eager to grapple with the potential of each new day. You 'bounce' out of bed.

_____ Emotions only _prepare_ the body for action.

_____ The repression of emotions does not necessarily cause illnesses.

_____ You rarely make major life decisions based solely on how you feel.

_____ The expression of emotions is, without exception, within volition. In other words, you can choose whether or not to express those emotions.

_____ Nine out of ten emotional responses to external stimuli are a reflection of your shadow.

_____ It is possible to completely cure your shadow.

_____ You respectfully edit the conscious expression of your awakened potential so as to minimize the impact on other people's feelings.

_____ You strive to attain freedom from conditioning, in all aspects of your life, even without knowing what that outcome is actually going to look like.

_____ You are aware of at least eight divergent interpretations of the causes of illnesses and diseases.

_____ A woman has the right to an abortion. The randomness of gender does not detract or enhance your capacity to express yourself to the fullest of your abilities physically, emotionally, intellectually, or spiritually.

_____ Cultural conditioning significantly influences the predominant acceptance of heterosexual relationships.

_____ Being a homosexual or heterosexual is irrelevant to the ability to awaken.

_____ You fully accept people and situations just as they are.

_____ You consciously pass judgment on other people on a regular basis.

_____ You judge others by the level of awareness as evidenced in their choice of words and actions, yet do not condemn those at lower stages of development.

_____ From an eternal point of view, we are all equal.

_____ In the relative world, all human beings have equal rights, yet we are not all equal.

_____ The opinion that hierarchies are 'bad' or 'wrong' is in itself a hierarchical statement.

_____ You have clearly decided for yourself whether you consider the process of life to be fundamentally *good, bad,* or *neutral.*

_____ You trust in your own ability to make great decisions.

_____ You are fully trustworthy.

_____ Your personal interpretation of God is not exclusive to a particular image, gender, or epoch and was not assigned by the culture into which you were born.

_____ *Eternity* points to the fact of *timelessness* and not that clock time continues on forever.

_____ The existence of clock time is a meager guarantee of immortality.

_____ The evidence that you have accepted your death is revealed by the fact that you are living to the fullest of your potential (except in cases of terminal illnesses).

_____ Your individual transformation is a prerequisite to world peace.

Quadrant 2 – Inter-Subjective: *Relationships, Belief Systems and Culture*

MQ: The second quadrant refers to the interior meanings and values we share in community with those around us. If you were not raised in a culture that told you the evolution of consciousness and culture is of primary importance, you may be experienced in building and sustaining relationships that are unknowingly based upon concealed conditioning.

Therefore, many of the statements in this section reveal the basis for your relevant relationships. Please be open to the possibility that the motives for many of your relevant relationships belong to the part of you that has no interest in awakening.

P: Because malicious ego-motives may be concealed in the foundations of my relevant relationships, great difficulties can arise as I move toward truly conscious interactions and awakened relationships with my friends, co-workers, parents, siblings and my children.

MQ: Yes. Because it is very likely that such conditioning is also in charge of what they truly believe to be their motives. As we have seen, those nearest and dearest to you are often less than thrilled with your willingness to stop generating or prolonging unnecessary conflict. Therefore, those who commonly commend your efforts to be a 'nicer' person frequently fight your desire to completely transcend all ego-motivated strife.

EVOLUTIONARY POINTER: Finding the malignant ego-mind concealed in your motives doesn't always imply that it is also present in another's motives.

MQ: It is important to maintain a broad stance of compassion toward those who, through no fault of their own, have yet to transcend the desire to sustain unnecessary conflict in their relationships as a way of augmenting aliveness.

EVOLUTIONARY POINTER: Awakened relationships do not coexist with personal conflict.

MQ: It is also good to note that the unhealthy aspect of the ego is going to want to emerge from this part of the exercise looking like a saint. Radical changes in how you interact with others might sound like the end of the world. It *is*, but only for the unhealthy-ego, and not for *you*. For you, it can be a process of great celebration. Allow this exercise to be the beginning of an enlivening adventure with those you truly love. By awakening your deepest compassion for all of humanity, you also set them free.

———— You would prefer to be alone rather than be involved in a long-term relationship with a person whose primary interest in life is not letting go of individual and collective conditioning.

———— You do not have cause to question your love for someone, or doubt another's love for you.

_____ Your relevant relationships are free from repeated personal conflict.

_____ You are involved in at least one long-term committed relationship, intimate — or otherwise — with which you are fully content.

_____ Separate sleeping arrangements between spouses or significant others are entirely acceptable to you.

_____ It is possible to co-create reality together with other people.

_____ When disagreement arises in a relevant relationship, it is usually about the most efficient way to express your full potential or to direct the *endeavor* or *creation* of the relationship for the sake of humanity.

_____ Misunderstandings do not linger and matters are directly addressed until they are brought to a point of mutually acceptable resolution.

_____ You do not listen to expressions of complaints, jealousy or limitation except when you have requested that the other person intentionally speak from that particular voice.

_____ You accept each member of your family exactly the way they are.

_____ You do not receive unsolicited input concerning your life from your family.

_____ You, likewise, do not offer any unsolicited advice to family members.

_____ Your family members do not know how to 'push your buttons'. (Note that when someone 'pushes your buttons', they have control over your emotional state.)

_____ The expression of your feelings such as impatience, confusion, frustration or anger, are always delivered to the appropriate person at the appropriate time and in the appropriate degree.

_____ The ideal basis for each relevant relationship within your family is to allow for the awakening of that individual and of that relationship.

_____ You have forgiven all those who have harmed you, regardless of who seemed to be at fault at the time.

_____ Forgiving does not necessarily imply forgetting.

_____ Unforgiveness is just as legitimate as forgiveness.

_____ There is no one you purposely avoid, or whom you would not like to randomly 'bump into' on the street or at your local market.

_____ You consciously treat every person with impeccable reverence and civility regardless of *your* or *their* prevailing emotional state.

_____ In regard to the previous statement, you do not want to learn more about impeccable reverence and civility before you can apply it in all your interactions.

_____ Those who cannot trust themselves are inherently untrustworthy.

_____ You do not purposefully lie, but you also know that the obvious truth can sometimes be unnecessarily painful.

_____ You frequently deliver responses that are a perfect blend of the voices of *male* and *female* compassion.

_____ You are accountable for every possible outcome and consequence of your responses to life.

_____ Parental mistakes or shortcomings are no longer a topic of discussion.

_____ Your childhood and upbringing were perfect, exactly the way they were.

_____ You have made peace with your parents – living or not.

_____ The desire to create a new human life is driven by the *same* impersonal biological force moving in both you and your spouse, or partner.

_____ When or if you make a choice to create a new life, you do so conscious of your ability and the earth's ability to support an additional human being.

_____ When or if you make a choice to create a new life, you do so knowing that your role as the creator of that life and of parent is the most significant contribution to humanity available to you at that time.

_____ Since *relationship* implies a connection between two or more subjects with *self-awareness*, a relationship with an infant is not possible at the conceptual level. Without a 'self' at the level of the infant's thoughts there is no subject with which a relationship can be sustained.

_____ You and/or your spouse spend more time consciously interacting with your children outside of school than do any other individuals such as nannies, day care staff, or babysitters.

_____ Together, you and your spouse spend more time consciously interacting with your growing children than one or both of you does in your career.

_____ You accept full responsibility for your growing child's education, health, eating habits, behavior, socialization skills, grades, tutors, and access to TV, video gaming and the Internet.

_____ Beyond the exchange of pleasantries and other useful information, the conversations in your relevant relationships do not exclusively revolve around topics of a purely personal nature.

_____ Social events are not a primary component of your interactions with other people.

_____ You are comfortable with large crowds when necessary.

_____ You can converse openly and freely about your physical death and the passing of those you love.

_____ The conversations you have about death are often focused on accepting responsibility for your life and the potential of self-awareness.

———— You have interactions and relevant relationships with those who vary in ethnicity, as well as spiritual and religious affiliations.

———— Multi-ethnic, inter-religious and gay marriages are completely acceptable to you.

———— You make no distinction between relationships in your 'spiritual' life and those of your 'real' life relationships.

———— Superstition is a reflection of a lower level of development.

———— Individuals such as Buddha, Jesus and Mother Theresa were born mere mortals, just like you.

———— Your rating in the previous statement indicates how you view your full potential as a human being.

———— It is evident from your actions that the discovery and expression of your awakening is marginally more significant than your interest in other important matters, such as the earning and spending of money.

———— You prefer to be engaged in activities that are a direct expression of higher principles rather than mere socializing.

———— There is no doubt that some people are more evolved than others.

———— The evolution of values in cultures can be mapped into a vertical hierarchy (such as Spiral Dynamics, for example).

_____ The inclusion of everyone's opinion is not necessarily the best way to find lasting resolutions to challenging issues.

_____ Organized religions symbolize only one of the many possibilities for the evolution of consciousness in the individual.

_____ Petitionary prayer, commonly used to bargain for favors with a mythic God, is also effective when transitioning beyond that level of development.

_____ The 'law of attraction' is an evolution of the petitionary prayer; however, in this case, it is even more narcissistic in that it is no longer _God_ who grants your wishes, but your own thoughts that fulfill your personal requests.

_____ Contemplative prayer is a form of authentic spiritual practice.

_____ The time period and location of your birth/childhood is not the sole determinant of your current religion.

_____ Your religious/spiritual practices are not complex or exclusive with elaborate barriers to entry or contain 'secret' levels or practices.

_____ Choice with regard to religious beliefs often reflects cultural conditioning and not necessarily individual volition. For example, a child born in Spain is as likely to be Catholic as a child born in Algeria is likely to be Muslim. Your current beliefs/practices transcend such conditioning.

_____ The beliefs of the mythic traditions are eventually transcended and included as evidence that you accessing higher stages of development.

_____ Beyond the requirements of specific lineage practices and rituals, you do not identify your religious/spiritual affiliations by your clothing.

_____ Spiritual practice can be defined as *fighting the inertia of both individual and collective conditioning.*

_____ Culture and history, while fascinating, useful and enjoyable, both reflect the ego's flight from the inevitability of physical death.

Quadrant 3 – The Objective: *Body, Energy, Health, Medicine and the Sciences:*

MQ: The third quadrant is the study of the objective organism. This is the aspect of life that we are most familiar with which also includes key areas of health, energy, diet, medicine, and the sciences. The ways in which you respond to these aspects of your own life can be influenced by the hidden motives of the unhealthy-ego. The statements in the third part of this exercise draw your attention to these objective aspects of life, or the 'outside' of the 'I'.

P: Does this quadrant also include physical objects and artifacts, such as my possessions and other inanimate objects and artifacts?

MQ: According to Wilber's Integral Theory only sentient beings and organisms possess four quadrants. I have, however, chosen to include statements in this part of the exercise that are related only to the objects of life – all the things you can see and touch. Such artifacts can be looked at from four quadrants, while not possessing them, so this exercise is just one view.

The reason I do this is because the hoarding of belongings, and all the work it entails also consumes your attention with maintenance and can be heavily laden with conditioned motives. The range of ego-trophies can include countries, islands, yachts, multiple homes, exotic cars, an overflowing basement, the junk in your kitchen drawers and unopened mail.

Note to the reader: If the connection between any of these statements and the discovery and expression of your full potential is unclear, remember, that the attachment to the malignant aspects of the ego creates this ambiguity in an attempt to stay in charge of your motives. Please disregard any statements that are not applicable to you.

_____ You have more than enough energy to get through the day.

_____ You allow for short naps during the day when needed.

_____ You are free of pains and aches from unverifiable injuries or disease.

_____ Western orthodox medicine is only one of _many_ approaches to the prevention and treatment of physical diseases.

_____ The cyclical phases of your body never create unneeded disharmony in your relationships.

_____ You seem to avoid getting the flu and other common ailments.

_____ You are not dependant on controlled substances and/or prescription medications.

_____ You are not dependant on alcohol, nicotine, caffeine, sugar, et cetera.

_____ You do not have any 'personal' habits that you consider to be objectionable.

_____ You have regular medical, dental and eye exams.

_____ Your blood pressure, cholesterol levels and T-cell counts are normal.

_____ You participate in habitual strength training exercises, even if this is as light as 10 minutes of weight training a few times per week.

_____ You do not regularly engage in dangerous sports.

_____ You make time for recreational activities on a regular basis.

_____ You are within the recommended weight for your height/body type.

_____ Your diet is based on observation. Starting with an ideal body weight, you observe your psychological and emotional states and physical energy levels throughout the day, and regulate your food and drink intake to maximize your capacity to operate at a peak level of efficiency.

_____ You choose the content of your diet consciously, avoiding foods that have been genetically modified, opting for organic and local sustainably produced foods.

_____ You avoid consuming animals that are subject to undue suffering and deplorable living conditions.

_____ The physical placement of objects by shape or color, while aesthetically pleasing, does not necessarily promote changes in your life without the application of your volition to those particular situations.

_____ Weather patterns, such as rain or overcast skies, leave no lasting impressions on your feelings of well being or energy levels.

_____ Your ability to act with great accountability is rarely affected by the possibility that your seven, eight, or ten chakras[6] might be out of balance.

_____ Full moons and solstices generally pass unnoticed.

_____ The magical powers often assigned to certain stones and crystals are valid at that particular level of development.

_____ The representation of a person, as in a _Voodoo_ doll, originates from an epoch when human consciousness was fused with objects in nature.

_____ The presence of _Siddhi_[7] or other magical powers does not necessarily imply that the person has awakened to individual or collective conditioning.

_____ One role of a genuine healer is to teach you how to heal yourself.

_____ The proof offered by the sciences can help us determine meaning, yet does not create nor deny it instead.

_____ The males of our species, as a whole, are incapable of suppressing themselves, therefore wholly incapable of subduing the females of our species.

_____ Your books, magazines, personal files and papers are neat and orderly.

_____ You are free from a backlog of emails, telephone calls and letters to return.

_____ Your clothes and shoe closets are organized.

_____ You have nothing in storage in your home or at other locations that you do not use on a regular basis.

_____ You recycle, not because you are required to do so, but because not doing so is tantamount to suicide – killing the planet is killing the self.

_____ You live in an apartment/home/area/country of your choice.

_____ Your bedroom and your bed itself allows you plenty of restful sleep.

_____ You rarely use an alarm for waking, except when you have to get up at an unusually early hour.

_____ You make your bed before you begin the day.

_____ You do not own firearms as weapons of self-defense.

_____ There is nothing missing from your life that you would expect to be there if you were to awaken today.

Q 4 – Inter-Objective: *Economics, Environment and Social Structures*

MQ: Human beings are social creatures. Hence, this section concerns your interactions with the structures and organizations that nurture this need. Concealed conditioning, however, has often managed to wiggle its way in as the leading character in such affiliations. To awaken, it is important to be clear that you are not participating in muted or bitter battles for the preservation of your self-image without your knowledge.

EVOLUTIONARY POINTER: The accumulation of people, possessions, accolades and experiences only briefly anesthetizes the ego-mind and the prospect of its temporary control of your life.

MQ: To facilitate the ravenous appetite of the culturally-created-self to consume, produce, distribute and recycle, financial institutions and the credit they provide have become the backbone of developed nations. There is nothing at all wrong with the earning and spending of money. In the process of awakening, however, it is essential that you become clear about the real reasons for this aspect of your life. As you move to higher and wider perspectives you may realize that the motives claimed for the earning and spending of money are fully loaded with the voices of the little-self.

EVOLUTIONARY POINTER: The ability to be financially independent is the gift of the global ego, but so are fiscal entrapment, encasement and addiction to borrowing, earning and spending.

MQ: Please remember that the statements in this exercise are not meant to be comprehensive, but sufficient enough to open your awareness to the veiled motives of the malignant ego.

_____ You have a good idea of your current net worth, even if it is a negative amount.

_____ You are free from cash flow problems.

_____ You have a foreseeable source of income for at least one year.

_____ The potential exists for you to earn a greater income this year than you did last year.

_____ You know approximately how much will be in your bank accounts over the next six to twelve months, even if it is a negative amount.

_____ You always pay your bills when or before they are due.

_____ You are carrying minor or no unsecured debt.

_____ You spend less than you earn, and you are comfortable with this fact.

_____ Your spouse's or partner's spending habits are acceptable to you.

_____ Provisions are in place for your own passing.

_____ The ways in which your parents and in-laws handle their money is not a severe burden on your ability to sustain yourself.

_____ The arrangements for the passing of your parents, in regard to titles, deeds, wills and trusts, are in order.

_____ Shopping is not a leisure pastime or a group activity in which you participate.

_____ All of your tax returns are filed or are currently in process.

_____ You have adequate insurance policies.

_____ You do not have any legal issues consuming your attention.

_____ There is little or no difference between who you are in your 'spiritual life' and in your 'work' life.

_____ Your position at work is clear and it enables wholesome growth and development.

_____ You are able to relate with your teammates at work in a context that is beyond ego.

_____ Your salary is an important, but not the primary motive for your work or career. (To frame your response, think for a moment what you would do if your current job compelled you to give up half of your salary.)

_____ If you were financially independent, you would work without monetary compensation in the exact same job or career that you are in now.

_____ Your current work/job/career is a clear expression of your full creative abilities. (A job that is an expression of your full creative abilities means that you cannot imagine, even in your highest moment that another 'job' exists that you would prefer to have, other than the exact one you currently hold.)

_____ Financial independence would give you more time to *work*.

_____ If your current career is similar to the career or profession of either of your parents, your *conscious* choice to pursue that mode of employment is reflected in a high rating to the previous few statements.

_____ If you work solely for support, you also spend a portion of your non-earning time engaging with activities or organizations that allow you to express your deepest creativity.

_____ If you support family or friends financially, you do so without any emotional or psychological strings attached.

_____ If you do not have a job in the traditional sense, your means of support flows to you without any emotional or psychological strings attached.

_____ Having weekends or public holidays off is not so important to you.

_____ The purely social aspect of your job is of little relevance to you.

_____ You rarely, if ever, participate in family power struggles and squabbles.

_____ Family history and ancestry is of minor importance to you.

_____ You have a structured network of contacts to leverage when in need of a particular expertise which you do not possess.

_____ You do not consider yourself to be under-educated or over-educated.

_____ The relevant relationships that you maintain with high school or college alumni include an *endeavor* or *creation* of those interactions that is of primary benefit to humanity.

_____ You enjoy the company of others without knowing or discussing their credentials.

_____ Your primary role in life could easily be transferred to, or is likely already performed by another person.

_____ The alleviation of inequality is often less prevalent where/when it is more obvious.

_____ World peace begins in your own living room.

_____ Your volunteer work is not entirely relegated to your 'spare' time.

_____ Your generosity in philanthropic projects includes a promise to follow through on finding lasting solutions to the causes that you support.

_____ The fully functioning human being places his interest in the evolution of consciousness and culture just one step ahead of personal desires.

_____ True charity is giving the world the gift of the ego-less you.

_____ If you discovered that the future of the organization to which you donate the most funds or time to depended solely upon you, you would be willing to sacrifice a significant portion of your lifestyle to ensure its continuation.

_____ You acquiesce when necessary to unnatural hierarchies.

_____ You can adhere to natural hierarchies as a leader or as a follower. It is clear to you that extreme feminism perpetuates the inequalities it purports to abhor.

_____ Current taxation laws and social security systems do not inhibit your personal career growth or retirement plans.

_____ The vast array of social institutions are bastions of the ego-mind's attempts to overcome physical death.

_____ The opportunity for success, at all levels of life, is available to everyone.

_____ Regional and national insignias, emblems and flags are of no real significance to you beyond the convenience of identity.

_____ Borders between countries are historically tribal, sometimes necessary, yet ultimately imaginary, lines.

_____ You do not make a determination of a person's merit by the dialect or languages they can or cannot speak.

_____ You have a current passport. When you travel, you do not only seek the company of your own nationals.

_____ You have spent extended periods of time in more than six countries.

_____ The collective thought patterns prevalent in your homeland are no longer primary to your individual insights.

_____ Your homeland is as important as any other country in the world.

_____ Your homeland is not regularly threatened by another country.

_____ Your homeland is not regularly threatening to another country.

_____ A significant number of the multi-national organizations currently charged with global peacekeeping, disarmament, terrorism and humanitarian efforts are fundamentally incapable of delivering on those mandates.

_____ Police and armies are essential to the preservation of social order in highly developed countries.

_____ You are open to the possibility of a new social order that may differ greatly from the existing structure, which would transcend and include the 'positive' and 'negative' aspects of the current system.

_____ The use of force to 'resolve' conflict is sometimes an essential and necessary response.

Analyzing Your Ratings

MQ: Are conditioned ideas, notions, concepts and beliefs concealed as the motives for your ways of being, thinking, acting and interacting? Is the authentic joy of your essential essence bound by inherited habituation? To determine the degree of your unsuspecting entanglement with concealed conditioning, please review your ratings of all applicable statements in each part of the preceding four-part exercise alongside ranges offered below.

P: Are the ranges presented here only general guidelines by which I can analyze my ratings?

MQ: Yes. One size could not, and should not, fit all. These parameters are designed to help you highlight where inherited limitations may be trapping your attention without your knowledge. Only you can see into the intimate intricacies of your own life.

EVOLUTIONARY POINTER: To let go of the root cause of unnecessary suffering — the attachment to the ego-mind — you must first identify how it is manifesting in your life.

Rating of 0 – 3: This rating reveals the *significant* involvement of a hidden ego-motive underlying this particular position or perspective. This concealed motive is propelling actions that sustain the malevolent ego in that life circumstance. This conditioned motive has most likely existed outside of your awareness or it has been denied or repressed within awareness. In either case the consequences of habituation have been operating beyond *conscious-free-will* and may be creating painful symptoms for you. Now that this particular motive has been revealed, you can begin to fully uncover how it has been manifesting in your words and/or actions by bringing more and more awareness to this particular situation. This renewed attention gives you access to awakened choices and to the possibility of letting go — or renouncing — your attachment to the ego-mind in this way of being.

P: We discussed earlier that the specific origins of these motives and their possible meanings are irrelevant to the intention of awakening.

MQ: Yes. This is not to deny their importance, but awakening to your full potential requires that you let go of the fascination with the baggage, including any reasons why that baggage appeared in the first place. Having recognized concealed conditioning, it is much simpler to apply yourself to putting it down, rather than continuing to dig around in that past.

Rating of 4 – 7: This rating indicates a *partial awareness to important awareness* of a conditioned motive supporting this aspect of your life. Resistance to change at this level, however, can be strong. Despite your best efforts, you may find that you are unable to successfully transcend this motive and its associated habits and patterns. The reason for this is that the lesser-mind has also corralled your values. This creates great difficulty at the time of major decisions. We will look at this in greater detail in the next chapter. Note, also, that a rating of 5 indicates that you are frequently indecisive or unsure about your position on this particular aspect of life. Vacillation reveals there may be great evidence to prove your agreement, and sometimes proof that clearly supports your disagreement. In such a situation, it is wise to reconsider your attachment to vacillation. In doing so, you may begin to increase your rating by no longer identifying with the manifestation of these partially concealed motives.

Rating of 8 – 9: This rating indicates *a more conscious awareness* of a conditioned motive, than is available to you in the previous ranges. It also reveals that there may be even stronger opposition to the complete renunciation of this particular perspective than experienced in previous ranges. Remember, opposition to transformation indicates a direct invitation of consciousness that you are already prepared to develop at that level. You can't feel resistance to a change that you are not ready to undertake. So, there can be much unnecessary suffering here, simply because you are simultaneously *close* to awakening, but also so insistent on keeping this circumstance alive. Transcending and including this particular aspect of yourself completely will greatly weaken the unhealthy-ego's influence on the direction of your life. In doing so, you become the one who freely chooses, rather than the one who is stuck in the middle — between unconsciousness and superconsciousness — holding onto the last vestiges of the ego-mind.

Rating of 10: A rating of 10 indicates *an evolved perspective* on the particular life circumstance. This means that you have *transcended and included* this aspect of your originally conditioned perspective as an integral part of how you express yourself. Be careful not to bury the past, but instead harness its wisdom, thus allowing yourself to move on to the next level of development. Should you sense strong opposition that 10 is not the optimal response to each of these statements, you have succeeded in bringing your attention directly to concealed conditioning and its overwhelming desire to remain in charge of your life. Its tenure is now within conscious-free-will.

P: And what if many of my ratings to these statements seem to constantly vacillate between the three ratings of 8, 9 and 10?

MQ: The implication would be that your attachment to the ego-motives supporting those situations has not yet been fully renounced and they are still very much in control of your life.

Transcending Conditioned Motives

MQ: Now that you have discovered the possible presence of ego-motives concealed in your life situations, you can set about doing something regarding their influence as further evidence of your interest in awakening. To help you include these formerly concealed conditioned motives as part of a new perspective, review the statements in each of the four parts of the previous exercise and divide those attitudes, perceptions and life situations in to these two broad, yet distinct groups:

1) Those situations that you believe have the potential to be *radically transformed*.
2) Those situations that you believe you have to accept as fundamentally *unchangeable*.

P: Please give me an example of the first case scenario.

MQ: Sure. The discovery of a motive of the unhealthy-ego does not automatically compel an additional response from you to its presence in you or in another person or situation. *Selective silence* or *non-action* is in most cases sufficient to release you from its tether. You may discover that *no response* is all that is needed to detach your attention from this situation. For example, a family member or friend requests that you engage in a gossiping session about another acquaintance. Selective silence is the perfect response.

You can also surpass the motives of the malignant ego in this way: Accept the resistance you are experiencing as an arms-wide-open invitation of consciousness that you are ready to grow into this new level of awareness. Even the most forceful opposition to change will dissipate when you follow that resistance all the way with awakened choices. See resistance as an invitation of consciousness for your preparedness to evolve.

P: And what about the second group, those that I view as being unchangeable?

MQ: This is where an expression of awakened compassion is most important. If someone you love dearly does not have the same interest in awakening as you do, the single greatest expression of caring for that kindred soul is to be sure that you are not also a cause of unnecessary suffering for them. Perfection takes constant practice and beyond the weight of past conditioning, you have realized we *already are* perfect! Strive for that instead. Oh the joy!

EVOLUTIONARY POINTER: Is your primary reason for *being* the evolution of consciousness and culture? When your attachment to unhealthy motives of the ego-mind is released, you will find that this eternal motive will assume a primary position as your reason for being!

---

[1]   Francois de La Rochefoucauld (1613 - 1680).

[2]   New Spirit Filled Life Bible: NKJV – Matt 16.24.

[3]   The Dhammapada.

[4]   Author, Duane Elgin quotes a student of Gandhi on his definition of "Voluntary Simplicity."

[5]   These are based on the four quadrants developed by Integral philosopher Ken Wilber. For more, see: *A Brief History of Everything*, Shambhala Publications, Inc., 1996.

[6]   Energy centers in and out of the body.

[7]   *Siddhi* powers are healing powers often attributed to highly realized beings.

Chapter 10

THE SECOND INSIGHT

RECLAIM YOUR CONSCIOUSNESS

"Your beliefs become your thoughts,
Your thoughts become your words,
Your words become your actions,
Your actions become your habits,
Your habits become your values,
Your values become your destiny."[1]

Knowing Your Values

MQ: By uncovering concealed conditioning in your motives, you are now in a position to ask this question: Would you like to consciously co-create the future for the sake of humanity?

P: Yes. I would.

MQ: Then your values can be arranged to allow that intention to manifest. The Second Insight is a ten-part exercise, which liberates the arrangement of your values from the influences of the individual and collective conditioning. With the Second Insight as your guide, your choices will *reclaim* consciousness that otherwise would have been consumed in a continuous struggle with conditioned outcomes.

P: So, I don't need to exchange my existing values, just modify their arrangement?

MQ: That's correct. From an early childhood the ego-mind plays a leading role in the selection and arrangement of your values. This is often why your best efforts to let go of emotional and psychological suffering can be trying.

P: What I value is what I consider to be important to me?

MQ: Yes. The more essential something is to you, the more that *value* is evidenced in your life. For example, it is likely that Hollywood actors value *fame*, Kuwait values sobriety, airlines value security, and reclusive monks value privacy.

P: Those values are clear because we can see them in action. By the same logic, it is unlikely that the most intimate value of a Wall Street banker is compassion for humanity.

MQ: Yes. What you claim to value the most in your life should be strikingly obvious. The actions of the following individuals will reveal different primary values guiding their lives: The President of a war-torn central African country, an Olympic equestrian gold medalist, a bestselling author of 'get rich quick' books, the leader of an international human rights organization, a four-time winner of the Tour de France, a stockbroker in New York and an artist in Paris. While they may share similar values, the arrangement of their values will differ greatly.

P: Why is that?

MQ: Because, what is of *primary* importance to each of them will be quite dissimilar in order to achieve their aims and goals in life.

EVOLUTIONARY POINTER: Your primary value in life is consistently proven by your actions.

MQ: What do you value more than anything else?

P: Well, I know what I think it is, but by the evidence of my actions, it might not be that at all!

MQ: This is a common discovery on the uncommon path. Let's start with the definition of what we call a value.

Defining Your Values

MQ: Values are the core psychological structures by which you make all major decisions. This is true whether or not you are aware of this or conscious of this process. Therefore, you already possess the qualities necessary for your awakening. The formations in awareness by which you will manifest that realization are also in existence.

EVOLUTIONARY POINTER: The arrangement of your current values is the key to accessing those preexisting structures in collective consciousness that will allow for the discovery and expression of your full potential.

P: To create the conditions for an awakened life, I can shift the current arrangement of my values from a primary emphasis on the fears and desires of the separate sense-of-self?

MQ: Yes. When you alter your decision-making structures to a primary but not exclusive focus on such values as *development, evolution* and *liberation,* a life of joyful expression enters the realm of possibility.

P: I do this as part of giving up my attachment to the ego-mind?

MQ: Yes. Remember the values you held in your college days? Where have they gone?

P: Nowhere, really.

MQ: But, the positions of those guiding principles have certainly shifted.

P: This is true. Perhaps they've taken a back seat or I don't focus on them so much anymore, I'm not really sure. Is that vagueness a matter of conditioning?

MQ: In regards to your values, yes it is.

P: So, if I want my awareness to continue to grow and expand from my current level of development, a conscious reorganization of my existing values is going to be necessary.

MQ: Yes. It's fairly straightforward.

P: I often feel the need to look for direction in life, but when I look to what's most important to me, my internal compass seems to spin wildly, pointing in different directions at different times, and rarely settling on a stable bearing.

MQ: Can you see now why that might be?

P: Yes, because the ego has significantly infiltrated the composition of my values.

MQ: Exactly.

EVOLUTIONARY POINTER: At the time of decision-making, the ego-mind presents your values, but according to *its* arrangements. This is how the ego controls your future.

P: Therefore, these arrangements are designed to support conceptual-free-will, which of course I cannot use to liberate myself from all unneeded emotional and psychological conflict. Before realigning my internal compass — the values I use to make choices — I have to first gain clarity on those values and their arrangements.

MQ: That's it! Such conscious decision-making is not a new concept. The following paragraph is a reference to conscious decision-making, in a bestselling spiritual book by Deepak Chopra *The Seven Spiritual Laws of Success*:

> *"When you make any choice...ask yourself two things: First of all, what are the consequences of this choice that I'm making? In your heart you will immediately know what these are. Secondly, will this choice that I'm making now bring happiness to me and to those around me? If the answer is yes, then go ahead with that choice. If the answer is no, if that choice will bring distress either to you or to those around you, then don't make that choice. It's as simple as that."*[2]

P: But, it can't be that simple! Isn't a little distress an integral part of making important life-changing decisions? I've made several significant choices that have caused a wave or two, but simultaneously opened up a whole new world of potential. Does the Second Insight offer an alternative to the wisdom you quoted here?

MQ: Yes, it does. Conscious decision-making calls you to delve deeply into the mechanics of choice and into the formation and configuration of the guiding principles that will direct your intentions for transformation. Feathers will always be ruffled, whether you choose to hold tight or spread your wings and soar to infinite possibilities.

EVOLUTIONARY POINTER: In honing your clarity of intention to live an awakened life, please note that you may incur and inflict little necessary anguish.

MQ: There is, however, a big difference between this finite quantity of *necessary* suffering and a lifetime of so-called 'unavoidable' personal conflict.

Understanding Your Choices

MQ: The Second Insight is a behind-the-scenes look at the way you make choices. It frees you from the anguish that so often accompanies major decisions and the complicated outcomes that can result from making 'incorrect' choices.

P: And if I am making decisions without a clear understanding of the underlying processes, I will eventually crash?

MQ: Exactly. It's impossible to see beyond the choice you don't understand, so sooner or later you will 'crash'. I will share this story as an illustration. I once had the opportunity to visit a flight simulator that is normally used to train commercial airline pilots. While at this facility I asked my friend, who was the chief-trainer, if we could simulate an emergency situation. The scenario was that both the captain and first officer were unable to fly the plane and I, as the only willing passenger, had to land the plane by listening to instructions from the ground.

Sitting at the controls of this jetliner was overwhelming! Slowly but surely, my friend guided my attention around the cockpit, through a dizzying array of switches, dials, knobs and levers. Every time I made an adjustment, based on his request, the plane immediately responded. After a series of about fifteen-or-so separate instructions, the runway finally came into sight. Then I was instructed to put the wheels down and make an additional adjustment to the flaps. It was a great relief to hear the familiar sounds of wind rushing through the landing gear and to be able to finally make out details of the ground in front of us. Now we were on our final approach. I asked him if I needed to take the main control — the joystick — in my hands. He said that would *not* be necessary, which really surprised me. We were fast approaching the runway, when my friend guided my attention back to the control panel and instructed me to set the brakes on 'max'. Then he said, with a big smile on his face, "Now, put your belt on and enjoy the ride."

The plane landed perfectly and shuddered to a stop. I could only imagine the emergency vehicle rushing out to meet us on the runway. "Well done!" my friend said, "you just landed a jet with 300 passengers on board!" Then he added, "This particular simulator is based on the most technologically advanced jet in our company. As you can see, the plane flies itself." As I recalled the many steps needed to bring the airplane safely to the ground, I realized that while I was making all of the adjustments, I had *no idea* about the process he had taken me through. I asked my friend about this and he said, "You managed to land the plane, but without knowing *what* you were doing or *why*. One wrong turn and it would have been over, for you and all of the people who were in your care!"

P: Therefore, as I approach important choices, I want to be sure that I am not running on conditioned autopilot.

MQ: Exactly! You want to understand the choices you are making so that you do not cause a whole lot of damage, too!

The Choices You Make

MQ: Mihaly Csikszentmihalyi, the author of the bestselling book *Flow*[3], said, *"Through the choices you make, you create the future."*[4] Your future, therefore, is a reflection of the values upon which you base those choices. Whenever an important decision is required, you order your values according to your priorities and the options at hand. This means that every time you make major life decisions based on a conditioned arrangement of values, you recreate that conditioning in the future.

P: If I am unclear about the composition of my values, I will always be unclear about my destiny.

MQ: Well, other than the fact that the future will be a replica of the past. But, the opposite is also true. If you are clear about the composition of your values, you will always be clear about your destiny.

P: But, I believe that because of the way I was raised, my values and their arrangement are sufficient to create and sustain my awakening to authentic joy.

MQ: Such conviction is great, but it is also good to test that belief. If you have confidence in the purity of the values bestowed upon you as a youngster, then you will also find the following five statements to be true for you:

1) Your parents or primary caregivers are, or were, exemplary models of autonomy, selfless compassion and insightful creativity.
2) Your parents understood the relationship between the values of their culture and their own capacities to express themselves at higher levels of development.
3) Their actions revealed a profound sense of trust in themselves and in the process of life.

4) They instilled in you every possible confidence, inspiration and encouragement.
5) They raised you to believe that the evolution of consciousness and culture are some of the most important aspects of life.

MQ: If you answered 'no', or 'maybe not' to any one of these statements, then it is likely that the unhealthy-ego is influencing your values and their arrangements. This means that the options from which you are choosing and the possible outcomes of those decisions are also restricted.

EVOLUTIONARY POINTER: The ego-mind perfectly augments conceptual-free-will by its arrangement of your values.

P: And what if I answered 'yes' to these five statements? Would that mean that the ego *doesn't* have an influence over my values?

MQ: This is likely and sustaining the effects of such an upbringing on your values would imply that you have adhered to this wisdom ever since your childhood. Do you have overwhelming evidence for your 'yes' responses in your life today?

P: There is some evidence, but it is not all significant.

MQ: To be free of the ego-mind's influence, therefore, your first task is to accept the pervasive nature of conditioning that is concealed in your values. The next step is to become clear about the ways in which your direction has been misguided because of this manipulation.

P: To awaken, I must be sure that the arrangement of my values permits me to make awakened choices.

MQ: Yes. Conceptual-free-will does not allow for choices that transcend the ego. You have to be sure that the way in which your values are structured allows you access to conscious-free-will.

Alex's Story: Alex valued *security* and *hard work*. He was married and was employed as a shipbuilder. Alex also had a deep interest in spiritual seeking, which eventually evolved into a desire to be free from the attachment to the ego. One day, Alex was injured on the job. After his recovery, he decided to find a safer job. Five years later, after having tripled his salary as a manager of a small engineering design company, he was laid off because of a downturn in the market. Alex returned to college, to follow another dream of becoming an interior designer. Three years later he was a much-in-demand consultant for a prestigious company in the same city where he was once a shipyard worker. Alex valued *persistence* and *follow through*. He noticed that his intentions — *to increase his earning potential and have a safer and more fulfilling career* — always became his future when his values were arranged to direct those objectives. Alex wondered if the same could be applied to liberation from the unhealthy aspects of the ego-mind? Which values could he rely upon to manifest that intention as his reality? Perhaps a primary value of *development* or *evolution* would suffice. But, Alex was also comfortable with his current lifestyle, so he decided to keep his first value as *security*, his second value as *family* and relegate *evolution* to third place. Despite this arrangement, Alex still believed that one day he would free himself from conditioning.

MQ: *"He who loves his life will lose it; and he who has no concern for his life in this world will keep it to life eternal."*[5] Did Jesus value *security*, *family* and then *Truth*?

P: The Buddha also left the safety of his father's palace, placing his value of *seeking* over and above that of *security*.

> **EVOLUTIONARY POINTER**: Awakening is synonymous with the trust to allow that outcome.

MQ: Is the existing arrangement of your values capable of creating and sustaining the conditions for your awakening to ego-mind? Look at these five statements:

1) Once a major life decision is made, I rarely, if ever, change my mind.
2) I can easily recall my top five most important values.
3) Major life decisions are not the cause of personal conflict in my relevant relationships.
4) I fully express my full potential in important aspects of my life.
5) I interact on the basis of shared values with other people for the sake of humanity.

MQ: Each 'no' provides you with a small amount of evidence that the ego-mind has a stake in the structure of your values, hence securing its place in your future. And it is curious to note that one negative and four positive responses does not necessarily mean you are any closer to release from that bind than if you responded with four negative and one positive.

P: This brings to mind the movie, *Matrix II*[6], in which the 'architect' admitted that the first matrix failed because the inhabitants discovered that they had no choices. In the revised matrix, the population was given the ability to choose, but at such a low level that it did not matter.

MQ: The 'architect' is talking about the original emergence of choice, which we discussed in the first section of Chapter Three. This is what you know as *conceptual-free-will*.

EVOLUTIONARY POINTER: Awakening calls you to question your decision-making structures, to see if the choices you think actually 'matter' are actually corralled within such a narrow range that unnecessary suffering is unavoidable.

Liberating Your Value Structures

MQ: The Second Insight liberates your awareness and radically revitalizes your interactions with the new world in which you are expressing yourself. It allows you to transcend and include conceptual-free-will as part of a newly emerging conscious-free-will. Awakened clarity eventually permeates every area of your life – nothing is left out. Freedom from all unnecessary suffering unfolds and the ability to come together with other people in relationships of nonviolent communication is also possible.

EVOLUTIONARY POINTER: Reclamation frees you from the consequences of attachment to the ego-mind in the future.

P: The Second Insight brings the evolution of consciousness within my volition.

MQ: Yes. You rearrange your values so that you can directly access conscious-free-will. This reveals a fascinating relationship between your *intentions*, your *values* and your *destiny*. Awakened choices produce awakened results. To achieve this, the Second Insight helps you select a primary value, which places your interest in awakening marginally ahead of other important values. By placing a value such as *development, evolution,* or *freedom* over and above all other values on a single hierarchy, you can perfectly guide your intention to awaken.

EVOLUTIONARY POINTER: The Second Insight demonstrates how a conscious realignment of your existing values guarantees your awakening. In this specific context, values aligned with intentions cause those objectives to manifest.

MQ: You will, of course, freely select this primary value to be assigned within a unified life domain – the *awakened life*. This new arrangement fully supports other aspects of your life, since subsequent values will include *money, security, family, hobbies, learning* and so on. There is no limit to the number of other values you can have.

P: Variety is also the spice of the awakened life.

MQ: It certainly is. As you enter the domain of awakened choices, it is important to note that not all choices are relevant to your awakening, just, as not all of your relationships are relevant.

P: This is great to know. An example, please?

MQ: Sure. Going to yoga class once or twice this week, having a cheeseburger instead of vegetables, sipping white wine or red, are choices that simply don't matter to your awakening. Don't let the ego get you lost in every choice or preference. It's simply unnecessary.

Complexity and Transformation

P: Decisions that are relevant to my awakening are those that will consume significant portions of my time and attention?

MQ: Yes. And when you need to make such choices, you may ask yourself, 'What are my priorities here?' 'What are the best options for me?' or 'What's important to me in this situation?' By doing this, you are calling up your values for consideration.

P: I am seeking my most important values in that situation so that I may make a choice.

MQ: Yes. You generally rely upon several values to make key decisions. Do you know what they are?

P: I could list them, but there seems to be so many values to pick from.

MQ: Do you know which one, if any, of these guiding principles is the most important one?

P: I never thought of having a single most important value!

MQ: *You* didn't think of it or is it that the ego-mind prefers you to have a whole legion of most important values?

P: But how can I have a whole slew of most important values?

That would make major life decisions very…

MQ: Stressful and complicated? That's exactly what the unhealthy-ego wants. Are you beginning to see the game it has been playing for the past 4,000 years or so?

P: Yes… please continue.

EVOLUTIONARY POINTER: It is considered normal to have separate groups or spheres of values representing various components of your life. For example, values related to your career may not be the same as those used in major decisions about your hobbies or your relationships.

Life Domains / Value Spheres

MQ: We will refer to these various value spheres as *Life Domains*. Each one of these life domains or value spheres play a distinct role in your life.

P: My life domains represent different aspects of 'me' as the parent, boss, employee, spouse, lover, best friend, spiritual seeker, sportsman, adventurer and so on.

MQ: Yes. And here is where you first see the influence of concealed conditioning. Through no fault of your own, you create multiple groups of values, one to suit each of your life domains. These value spheres guide your decisions within each role and across your life in general.

P: It is obvious to me that the life domains of *Source of Income*, *Shelter* and *Company* are widespread and the application of the values that are grouped together within each of these areas is advanced.

MQ: You are correct. There is much evidence to prove this.

P: It is also clear, however, that even my good job, my fine home and my comfortable relationships have yet to complete me. Even though I might think I have all the right values, something is strangely amiss – evidence of ease and contentment.

MQ: Yes. And you do already have all the 'right' values. As we discussed earlier, it's just the way that they are arranged for you that's at the root of the distress. Thus, in your finest attempts to find fulfillment and your honest endeavors to avoid reproducing the suffering of the past, you achieve an unfulfilling present.

P: Therefore, to co-create a conscious future, it is critical that the arrangement of my values is capable of directing just that – my pure intention *to co-create a conscious future.*

MQ: Exactly! Inherited arrangements of your values do not allow for, or create, the space for awakening; therefore, they are incapable of delivering anything other than another mess for you to untangle. The ego-mind although it tries, can never bring you all the way.

EVOLUTIONARY POINTER: The key to freedom is to learn to navigate with *one* core group of values. This has always been the way of the awakened person.

Josh and Diane's Story: Josh had recently become engaged and at the same time received an offer for his dream job in Chicago. He and his fiancée, Diane, loved being close to their families and the apartment they shared in Boston. They were naturally torn between the fulfillment of Josh's carefully planned career goals, and what was best for their relationship. After much discussion with Diane and their families, Josh accepted the job offer. Shortly after he started his new job, however, Josh realized that this choice clearly demonstrated that his most important value was *career*. Up to this point, he had believed that his primary value was *love*. After a year or so of flying back and forth between the two cities, both his work and love life were straining. In another six months, the couple acknowledged that things were not working, and decided to separate.

Before long, Josh realized he was lonely in Chicago, and that maybe his primary value was indeed *love*. Now he was thinking about permanently returning to Boston. He mentioned this idea during a phone conversation with Diane, who had also been doing some soul-searching. Though enamored by the possibility of his return, she lovingly explained to Josh that she was no longer able to trust him. She also suggested that perhaps he could not trust himself. By the evidence of his decisions, he was obviously confused about his primary value. Was it *love* or *career*? Diane knew that until he could gain clarity on what was of primary importance to him, his actions would reflect that he was untrustworthy, and perhaps unknowingly to him, his actions and choices suggested that he wished to remain untrustworthy.

Josh thought long and hard about his values. He came to the conclusion that to be completely trustworthy he would have to arrange his values in such a way that *one* value would become marginally more important than his other values. This primary value could then be used to direct all of his most important choices, the consequences of which he would have to stand by regardless of the personal inconvenience of acting in that way. While considering this level of commitment to himself and to those around him, Josh realized this would also mean becoming fully accountable for his actions. Since he was more interested in the ability to change his mind, Josh began to seek a new relationship in which 'flexibility' was more important than responsibility.

Aligning Your Values with the Awakened Life – A Ten-Part Exercise

PART 1 – Life Domains in The Four Quadrants[7]:

MQ: The purpose of this ten-part exercise is to unravel concealed conditioning in your decision-making processes. Since values and value structures are continually developing we are not going to try to pigeonhole a magical, multifaceted and truly unknowable life experience. Nonetheless, developing clarity and objectivity of your values generally implies a humble examination of your life situations. Remember, simplicity is the hallmark of the awakened perspective; complexity is the calling card of inherited habituation.

P: I'm ready to go!

MQ: Start by taking an integral view of your life domains as they appear across the four major aspects of life, which are: subjective, inter-subjective, objective and inter-objective. While one value sphere/life domain may support, augment and overlap with others, you will also find that certain values appear within each life domain that are distinct to that particular area of life. For instance, it is not uncommon to have a 'spiritual life', 'home life', 'work life' and a 'social life' with values in each that are rarely intermingled. For example, to support yourself financially — this is the life domain of *Source of Income* — you may use values such *ambition, power and leadership*. These values are usually kept separate from other life domains and are rarely considered for decisions in such life domains as *Hobbies* or *Religion*.

EVOLUTIONARY POINTER: *"Once your ego's values have become objectified in your awareness, then you are in a position to begin to freely choose: Is that who I want to be or not?"*[8]

MQ: Notice in Table 1, which follows, how most of the life domains are described as one or *two* words. It will be important for you to describe your own life domains in a similar fashion.

Table 1 – Examples of Life Domains in the Four Quadrants:

Quadrant 1	Quadrant 3
Subjective – (Thoughts/Emotions/Learning)	Objective – (Body/Health/Fitness)*
Life Domains:	Life Domains:
Cognitive Development	Health
Emotional Intelligence	Hobbies
Self-Development	Creative Expression
Spiritual Seeking	Home Environment
Quadrant 2	**Quadrant 4**
Inter-Subjective – (Relationships/Culture)	Inter-Objective – (Finances/Social Structures)
Life Domains:	Life Domains:
Family	Source of Income
Conscious Service	Philanthropy
Relationships	Politics
Religion	Volunteering/Charity

* Artifacts and inanimate objects do not possess four quadrants, but are placed here for the sake of the exercise.

P: Some of these life domains sound like individual values.

MQ: Yes, but for the sake of this exercise, please consider your life domains as the broad categories that compose your life.

Note to the reader: For the sake of clarity, from this point on in this chapter, life domains are indicated with an uppercase letter and values are indicated with lowercase letters, except for the sample values in Table 4 that are capitalized for presentation.

Values Within Your Life Domains

P: Can identical values exist simultaneously within multiple life domains?

MQ: Yes. For example, decisions in the life domain of *Source of Income* are often based on a value of *money*, whereas in the life domain of *Family*, you may also make decisions based on the value of *money*. Questions such as, 'Is this job worth this cut in pay?' (life domain of *Source of Income*) and, 'Can I afford to take the family on vacation?' (life domain of *Family*), call up the same value of *money*, but in two distinct life domains and in two quadrants (2 and 4)

P: Some decisions will affect several life domains simultaneously, even though the values I have within each of those life domains can be quite contrary.

MQ: Yes, this is true. For example, a decision about your job — in the life domain of *Source of Income* — might be made using a value such as *ambition*; whereas the outcome of that decision may have an impact on the life domain of *Relationships*, where a value such as *relaxation* is the most important value.

P: I can see how I might switch between life domains and also switch values within those life domains when I am making decisions.

MQ: Yes, this is quite normal. For example, during a day of charity work, you can take a phone call from your mother without significantly disturbing your flow. If a client calls you on the same day, you can easily switch into a work-mode, and then revert back to your volunteering. But, if you receive a call about a child who is unwell, you may replace your value of *service* in your life domain of *Charity*, with a value of *responsibility* in your life domain of *Family*, so that you may respond to this urgent situation by leaving your volunteering position right away.

P: My values help me to prioritize between my life domains, based on what I feel is most *essential* to me at any given time?

MQ: Yes. Assuming that value does not already exist in a life domain, you use your values to switch between value spheres. And you will also prioritize values *within* your life domains.

322

Amanda and Katie's Story: The most important value in Amanda's life domain of Relationships was *fun*! Amanda had many friends, but she had been very close with Katie for over twenty years. They had done many things together and they had so many great memories. Life then became a little harder on Katie. Amanda became concerned that Katie's alcohol drinking was becoming a problem. Amanda mentioned her concern to Katie a few times, but usually when they were out partying together. Soon, however, it become clear that the effects of Katie's drinking were getting out of control, to the point where Amanda was considering an intervention to show Katie that she had many people around her who cared about her and who were concerned about her problem. In order to make the final choice and arrange the intervention, Amanda had to switch her primary value of *fun*, for the value of *responsibility*. Katie eventually got sober and now the fun continues, but without the altered states of consciousness.

P: Why am I getting the feeling that this is all hair-splitting psychobabble?

MQ: It is perfectly normal to be feeling a little overwhelmed or even intimidated by the prospects of having to figure out which values you have assigned to each of your life domains. If you are envisioning a big chart on your kitchen wall, that might not be such a bad idea!

EVOLUTIONARY POINTER: Although it is sometimes frowned upon as unspiritual, the development of your cognitive function is essential for spiritual progress. Strange as it may seem, the ability to think clearly and take different perspectives is most essential if you are to transcend the struggle with constant thinking.

MQ: Without clarity on your values, and how they are arranged, the ego is going to still be the boss of those indoctrinated ideas called the *human mind*.

P: I understand, thank you.

MQ: Here, then, is a brief description of some of the more popular life domains as outlined in Table 1, and a sampling of individual values common to each one. Please note that the names of these life domains are only samples. You can use whatever names you like best.

Table 2 – Common Life Domains With Some Sample Values

Family: Includes such values as *integrity, love (feeling), love (selfless), trust, caring, company and responsibility; money* is also a value here because of the expenses incurred in this life domain. The nurturing and support of your own children and grandchildren, to the exclusivity of other children, can be best represented in this life domain.

Source of Income: This life domain represents your primary means of financial support. The primary value in this life domain is *money*. Other values may include, *ambition, learning, power* and *security*. There are five basic ways you can generate financial support:

1) You earn money by means of your career or occupation.
2) You are fully supported by a spouse/life partner.
3) You have independent means – such as trust funds, investments or retirement income.
4) You live on government welfare.
5) You live on charitable donations.

Extortion, robbing banks and begging are also options, but for the sake of the majority audience, they are not included here. We will look also at several distinctions between earning money in the life domain of *Source of Income* and in the life domain of *Conscious Service* (see below) as we progress through this chapter.

Marriage: This life domain represents primary emotional and psychological support structures with your spouse or life partner. They can contain many wonderful values including *love (feeling), love (selfless), sex, money, security, company, growth, sharing, support, sense of humor, trust, honesty, health,* and *happiness.*

Relationships: This life domain represents emotional and psychological support structures within a wide range of friends and acquaintances. Values can include; *sharing, love (feeling), love (selfless), compassion, community, fun,* and *responsibility.* As you incur expenses in your relationships, *money* as a value, can also appear in this life domain.

Volunteering/Charity: This life domain represents the giving of your time, funds and/or resources. Common values are; *compassion (feeling), compassion (selfless), sacrifice, learning, service, love (feeling) and love (selfless).* Part-time charitable work, such as on weekends or after you have done your work for your career, family, or other personal relationship obligations, may be represented in this life domain.

Spiritual Seeking: Values common in this life domain are *truth, self-development, growth, personal enlightenment, salvation, repentance, learning, love (selfless & feeling)* and *honesty.* The value of *money* is also found here since you might use it for donations, retreats, books, courses, travel and so on. Other values associated with your search for inner peace or your quest for purpose and meaning may be more appropriately allocated to this life domain of *Spiritual Seeking* than the life domain of *Conscious Service*. The life domain of *Spiritual Seeking* represents you in pursuit of awakening, whereas the life domain of *Conscious Service* represents you in expression of your awakening. The life domain of *Spiritual Seeking* is that of the 'spiritual seeker' in which the evolution of consciousness and culture has yet to stabilize as one of your primary reasons for being.

Conscious Service: The life domain of *Conscious Service* is that of the 'spiritual finder' in which the evolution of consciousness has stabilized as your primary reason for being.

This life domain emerges as a profound expression of your own awakening. It is here that you express your interest in the evolution of consciousness for the sake of humanity. The life domain of *Conscious Service* reveals itself when your shadow is healed, all of your relevant relationships are free from personal conflict, and you have completely transcended and included the life domain of *Spiritual Seeking* at the personal level of development. Now your reasons for growth and development are no longer personal but, for the sake of others. When the life domain of *Conscious Service* is active, the consistent expression of values such as *development, evolution, community* and *potential* become of great importance in your life work or full-time career. Therefore, the emergence of the life domain of *Conscious Service* transcends and includes the life domain of *Source of Income*.

The life domain of *Conscious Service* commonly unfolds as a career of full-time philanthropic works, awakened parenting, the development and implementation of awakened business practices, or the facilitation of the evolution of consciousness in individuals and/or groups. Therefore, you can earn an income and also incur expenses in the life domain of *Conscious Service*. This simply means that *money* is a value here, but is not a primary value in this life domain. The primary value here is usually *development* or *evolution*. Frequently, as a demonstration of the depth of your awakening and as proof of your genuine aspiration to live an awakened life, you have already taken the necessary steps to provide the funds so that you can dedicate yourself to the life domain of *Conscious Service* on a full-time basis. When this life domain is active in your life, 'working for a living' in the traditional sense is quite rare.

As part of the emergence of the life domain of *Conscious Service*, the interactions in your relevant relationships are based on the discovery and expression of the full potential of each individual and of the relationship itself. Such interactions, though they include many of the same values as the life domains of *Marriage* and *Family*, reach far beyond that personal microcosm and are not associated with ego's agenda of sharing emotions, history, and personal stories.

PART 2 – Identify Your Life Domains:

MQ: Let's begin by identifying your life domains. If you have a means of financial support or if you make purchases of any kind, please be sure to include the life domain of *Source of Income* at least once in this table. As much as possible, please title your life domains with one or two words only.

INSTRUCTIONS FOR TABLE 3: Select at least eight life domains that you feel best represent your prevailing life situations. Write one life domain on each line to a maximum of 12 in Table 3. The order of your life domains is unimportant. Refer to Table 1 for some examples if you wish. Be sure to pick at least one or two life domains from each of the four quadrants (Table 1).

Table 3 – Your Major Life Domains:

PART 3 – Identify Your Values:

MQ: Below you will see a list of about 120 sample values. Before you begin to make your own list of values, it may be helpful to circle in the table below as many values as you feel represent you. Notice how these principles are usually single words:

Table 4 – Sample Values:

Accountability (self)	Creativity	Justice
Accountability (whole)	Curiosity	Knowledge
Accumulation	Depth	Leadership
Achievement	Development	Learning
Adventure	Discipline	Leisure
Ambivalence	Environment	Logic
Assertiveness	Evolution	Love (feeling)
Authority	Excitement	Love (selfless)
Autonomy	Experience	Manipulation
Authenticity	Family	Meaning
Beauty	Free will	Money
Being	Freedom (personal)	Peace
Being caring	Freedom (from ego)	Perseverance
Being loving	Friendship	Potential
Being nice	Fulfillment	Power
Bonding	Fun	Providing
Civility	Gratitude	Purity
Challenges	Growth	Purpose
Clarity	Happiness	Reason
Cleanliness	Harmony	Relaxation
Change	Healing (self)	Responsibility (self)
Compassion (feeling)	Healing (humanity)	Responsibility (for the Whole)
Compassion (selfless)	Health	Romance
	History	Salvation
	Humility	Sacrifice Security
Complexity	Humor	Self-confidence
Community	Independence	Self-esteem
Conflict	Integration	Self-expression
Consciousness	Integrity	Self–security
Control	Intelligence	Self–worth
Courage	Intimacy	Service
	Joy	

Sharing (emotions)	Status	Truth
Sharing	Stillness	Understanding
(self–as–One)	Success	Unity
Simplicity	Tradition	Wisdom
Sincerity	Transparency	Willpower
Socializing	Travel	
Spirit	Trust	

Please note that as you begin to identify your own values in Table 5 below, if you incur personal expenses or have an income, regardless of its source, the value *money* is somehow of importance in your life. Therefore, please be sure to include the value *money* at least once in Table 5. If you do not earn an income or have any expenses, there would be no need for you to include the value *money* in Table 5. Distill your value to *single words; 'Always there when needed by my friends'* could be succinctly described as a value of *dependable*.

INSTRUCTIONS FOR TABLE 5: Complete the table below using your own values or by drawing from the samples in *Table 4*. Please enter at least 16 of what you consider to be your most important and cherished values. Write one value on each line to a maximum of 24 in Table 5. It is not necessary to place your values in any particular order in this table:

Table 5 – Identify Your Values:

PART 4 – Allocating Your Values into Your Life Domains:

MQ: Now you will place some of your values into your life domains. The goal here is to allow you to view the arrangement of your values as they appear across various life domains. The order of your life domains and the arrangement of your values are inconsequential in this part of the exercise. Because life domains can often overlap, you can repeat values in different life domains if you wish in this exercise. For instance; *responsibility* and *money* are values that exist in more than one life domain, therefore, you can repeat them as often as necessary.

INSTRUCTIONS FOR TABLE 6 – PART I: Pick your eight most important life domains from those in Table 3. Enter one of each of these life domains on the top line of a column in Table 6. If you earn or spend money, please include the life domain *Source of Income* (or *Conscious Service* should that be more appropriate) at least once.

INSTRUCTIONS FOR TABLE 6 – PART II: Place at least four of your important values from Table 5 under each of your eight life domains. There is no need to prioritize life domains or values.

Table 6 – Most Important Life Domains with some of Your Most Important Values:

Your Life Domain:	Your Life Domain:	Your Life Domain:	Your Life Domain:
Value:	Value:	Value:	Value:
Value:	Value:	Value:	Value:
Value:	Value:	Value:	Value:
Value:	Value:	Value:	Value:
Your Life Domain:	Your Life Domain:	Your Life Domain:	Your Life Domain:
Value:	Value:	Value:	Value:
Value:	Value:	Value:	Value:
Value:	Value:	Value:	Value:
Value:	Value:	Value:	Value:

PART 5 – Ordering Your Life Domains:

MQ: Now you will arrange your life domains in a hierarchy according to the order of their importance to you. Please note that you are now separating structures in awareness that may have long been controlled by concealed conditioning. Therefore, a little difficulty is normal. Remember, if you earn an income or incur living expenses, please be sure to include the life domain *Source of Income* at least once in this ordered hierarchy. Take your time with this exercise. If you find it difficult to determine which of your life domains is the most important one, then allow the first, second, or third-place life domains to exchange places a few times, until one of them seems to be more stable in the primary slot or until you find an order with which you are comfortable.

INSTRUCTIONS FOR TABLE 7: This is an ordered list of your life domains. Using the same eight life domains from the previous Table 6, place the life domain that you consider to be most important in the Number 1 position and so on down the list to the last position. To begin placing your life domains in order, if you prefer, you can begin by completing the Number 8 position as the least important and work up the ordered list to the Number 1 position as the most important of your life domains.

Table 7 – Ordered List of Your Life Domains:

Life domain number 1: _____ (The most important to you)

Life domain number 2: _____ (2nd most important)

Life domain number 3: _____ (3rd most important)

Life domain number 4: _____

Life domain number 5: _____

Life domain number 6: _____

Life domain number 7: _____

Life domain number 8: _____ (Less important to you)

PART 6 – Ordering Your Values:

MQ: In this part of the exercise you will arrange your values into a single hierarchy in order of their importance to you. This is similar to the previous exercise, so arranging your values into a single group order can also be challenging. A reason for this difficulty is that values have long traded positions of importance during times of making major decisions. Conditioning has convinced you that this is normal. This exercise helps you identify how the ego-mind may be in control of your values to primarily suit its needs. This discomfort zone indicates an invitation of consciousness that you are already prepared to evolve to the next level of your development. You are only being asked to order your most important values and *not* the significance of the choices you make based on them. If you have a source of income or incur expenses, please include the value of *money* at least once in this table in its appropriate position of significance to you.

INSTRUCTIONS FOR TABLE 8: Place the value that you consider to be the most representative of who you are — your most important value — in the Value Number 1 position. If you like, start at the end of the list with your least important values, working your way up to your *Value number 1*. Please enter *only your most cherished eight values* here, regardless of how many you initially identified in *Table 5*.

Table 8 – An Ordered Hierarchy of Your Values:

Value number 1: _____ (The most important value to you)

Value number 2: _____ (2nd most important)

Value number 3: _____ (3rd most important)

Value number 4: _____

Value number 5: _____

Value number 6: _____

Value number 7: _____

Value number 8: _____ (Less important value to you)

PART 7 – Confirming Your Life Domains:

MQ: The decisions you make across your various life domains guide your most cherished intentions to fruition. Therefore, if you have an intention to be free or to express an existing realization, then a supportive value structure is required so that the awakened life may be your outcome. It is essential to align *who you think you are* with *who you are* in reality. *Who you are* is readily revealed by the ways in which you express consciousness across your life domains – regardless of your present level of development or achievements thus far.

EVOLUTIONARY POINTER: Awakening compels you to confirm that *who you think you are* is not wholly embedded in the veiled impressions of the ego-mind.

MQ: You will begin by verifying evidence for your particular life domains. This is important, because to sustain the conditions for awakening, you have to ensure that your existing life domains are capable of allowing you to be *who you want to be*. Recall an earlier quote:

"Once your ego's values have become objectified in your awareness, then you are in a position to begin to freely choose: Is that who I want to be or not?"

Without true objectivity on the structure of your values, concealed conditioning will continue to manipulate your decisions and hence your destiny.

P: Let me see if I am clear on the instruction. In this part of the exercise, I will determine the amount of time — in hours per week — that I spend expressing myself in each of the eight life domains I chose as the most important ones in Table 7. But, is it really necessary to gain such a degree of clarity about what I do with my time?

MQ: Yes, it is, if you genuinely aspire to awaken. Here is an example from a lower level of development than the intention of this particular exercise: When Bill Gates formally retired from the leadership role of Microsoft in July 2008[9], he had promised his successor, Steve Ballmer, that he will spend two-and-a-half hours per week working with the search and advertising team. How's that for exactness?

P: Okay. That is precise!

MQ: Therefore, confirming evidence for your life domains really threatens the ego-mind's control of your destiny. Since it may respond forcefully and in outright defiance of your desire for authenticity and transparency, there are several important aspects of this confirmation that we will discuss, before you set about doing the exercise.

The New Delhi Cab: At the end of a meditation retreat in India, I was sharing a taxi back to my hotel with a full-time student of the Western teacher who led this event at a local ashram. This student was expounding the teachings of enlightened potential so fluently that I was convinced that he, too, was fully awakened. I felt honored to be in his presence, and I asked him how he was applying these wonderful teachings on a day-to-day basis. He went on with unreserved excitement about how great his life was. In particular, he told me he had found a career opportunity as a software engineer soon after abandoning his old life to move closer to his teacher. He also recounted how his new employer gave him permission to attend these long retreats as long as he made up the time later.

But, to me, this interpretation seemed incomplete and somewhat disconnected from the vast scope and unlimited potential of the enlightenment teachings we had been immersed in over the past ten days. Not to mention, he had been a student of this work for eight years. As I sat there, wondering how to respond, it came to my mind that the issue was not that this person had a job; after all everyone needs money. What caught my attention were the glaring contradictions between these teachings of infinite possibilities that he professed to understand and embrace, and the cautious and reserved ways he seemed to be going about the manifestation of that majesty in other aspects of his life! He was talking up a storm, but it didn't seem as if he was living that way at all.

So, I posed a hypothetical question. I asked him what he might do if the financial future of his teacher's organization depended solely upon him. I wanted to know how he might harness and blend these teachings of unlimited possibilities, trust and surrender, with his obvious charisma and business skills to deal with a real-life challenge such as the one I had suggested. Suddenly, the energy in the cab changed dramatically, and for a moment, I was actually frightened. Now, I was faced with an angry and frustrated man. He expressed what seemed like a well-rehearsed list of excuses for limitation — for *not* changing — because, as he said: *"I like things the way they are."* When he finished speaking, the car fell deathly silent. It was clear he had nothing more to say to me about this or any other topic. I turned around and peered through the crimson haze of a New Delhi dusk to see if we were close to our hotel. We saw each other a few days later at the airport. He ignored me.

P: You were not criticizing the efforts that this man was making in his spiritual seeking?

MQ: Not in the least. I was just asking him to imagine evidence for the teachings he thought he was following. But, can you see that beneath his range of spiritual knowledge, the unhealthy-ego and a significant amount of shadow were still in control of his life?

P: And this is not about the amount of time he spends at work versus time spent at retreats?

MQ: No. It's about waking you up to the possibility that if you consider yourself to be a spiritual person, if you think like a spiritual person, have spiritual friends and talk like a spiritual person, yet simultaneously there's a gap between the uncompromising wisdom you claim to cherish and the ways in which you live, you may be unknowingly compromising with concealed conditioning instead.

Degrees of Giving
MQ: As you begin to look at how you split your time across your

various life domains, it is important to note that the hours you spend performing works of charity on a part-time basis are best included in the life domains of *Volunteering, Relationships* or *Religion*. If, however, your philanthropic efforts are carried out on a full-time basis, regardless of the cost to your life situations, self-image, public image or social status, and if the objectives for such devotion include the complete resolution of the issues you support, then those hours may be included instead as part of the life domain of *Conscious Service*.

EVOLUTIONARY POINTER: A vocation in which you are consciously co-creating a new reality for those in need — regardless of the personal inconvenience of doing so — transcends and includes a career or hobby that is intended to make you feel good about your place in the world.

MQ: It is good to note, too, that the life domain of *Conscious Service* will only contain those hours you dedicate to the spiritual development of *other people* and to the evolution of consciousness in culture.

P: Which means that the time I spend in self-development, personal healing, overcoming addictions, or activities that encompass my personal *quest* for meaning and purpose, are more appropriately allocated in the life domains of *Spiritual Seeking, Religion* or *Hobbies*?

MQ: That is correct.

The Value of Money

MQ: The life domain of *Source of Income* and the value of *money* are favorite stomping grounds of concealed conditioning. There is nothing at all wrong with earning or spending money. Both are essential aspects of modern life. But, if awakening is your objective, it is critical to pay special attention to how you spend your time and attention in relationship to the life domain of *Source of Income* and the value of *money*. To get started, please ask yourself these questions:

1) Is the job that supports myself and my family purely a means to an end?
2) Is my *Source of Income* a vibrant expression of my most creative potential?
3) Do I work for an organization whose principal mandate is the evolution of consciousness and culture?
4) Do I work with a company that produces a service or product that is specifically designed to help its customers harness the power of the human potential, beyond individual and collective conditioning?
5) Is my career related to the development and implementation of awakened business practices, awakened parenting, or to integral medicine, integral law or integral politics?
6) Is my company involved in the development of sustainable tools and technologies to preserve the biosphere or the advancement of the noosphere[10]?
7) Is my career related to the cultivation of subjective or inter-subjective awareness, as a thinker, trainer, teacher, writer, coach, consultant, or a guru, a pandit[11], or as an artist?
8) Have I figured out a way to integrate how I earn my primary living with a myriad of emerging business practices in the field of consciousness development?

P: What can I learn from my responses to these questions?

MQ: A positive answer to any question, except the first one, indicates the significant absence of concealed conditioning in your life domain *Source of Income* and your value *money*.

> EVOLUTIONARY POINTER: One expression of the truth and aliveness of an awakened perspective is that there is no longer a difference between *who you are* in the life domain *Conscious Service* and *what you do* in the life domain *Source of Income.*

P: Have awakened people figured out a way to combine both life domains?

MQ: Yes. If your work is simply a means to an end, then the hours you spend at that job is evidence for your life domain *Source of Income*. And, there is nothing wrong with that, because it is perfect for that level of development. On the other hand, if your primary source of income is derived from a career that is devoted to the evolution of humanity's potential, then the hours you spend at 'work' would be more appropriately represented in the life domain of *Conscious Service*.

> EVOLUTIONARY POINTER: Evidence of an awakened life includes unification of the gap between your 'spiritual' life and your 'work' life.

P: Closing this gap in reality is important because the ego often convinces me there is no gap.

MQ: That's it! The unhealthy-ego always insists that your 50-hour grind is essential to the evolution of consciousness, regardless of the type of work you do or the objectives of your company. For example, the ego's dharma suggests that holding a spiritual attitude in the boardroom or chatting about yoga in the break room is the *pinnacle of your contribution* to the evolution of humanity in your career. Again, there is nothing wrong with doing these things. Please remember, though, that the goal of this exercise is to liberate your value structures from the influences of concealed conditioning, not to deny every effort you may make, no matter how small, to raise the consciousness of the planet.

P: Okay, so this is why I seek evidence for my eight most important life domains, regardless of my current stage of development?

MQ: Yes. The beauty and bravery of any effort toward greatness is always to be admired. You need to be vigilant; however, to see that the unhealthy-ego does not paint your mundane, solely-for-the-sake-of-the-salary job as the best you can do with your liberated perspective. So long as the malicious ego remains in charge of the means of your financial sustenance, infinite potential will remain buried deep within you. This is because your attention is being drained by continuously having to support a self-image as an individual whose current career is the fullest expression of his potential, when that is *clearly not the case*.

Madison's Story: After many years of spiritual searching, Madison finally met a teacher who truly challenged her attachment to the ego-mind and the separate sense-of-self. In the presence of her teacher, Madison felt all was possible – even her own awakening. Madison studied with this teacher for several years and she eventually awoke to her full potential during a residential stay at her teacher's center. The joy was indescribable, relief was profound, and the potential immense! After about ten days in this awakened state, Madison returned to her home. In the following few years, she wrote an amazing book describing the intimate details that led up to her awakening. Madison secured a few high-profile endorsements and a wonderful publisher who distributed her book worldwide.

Madison's company, which was her only source of income at that time, was also expanding. She provided landscape architect services to the rich and famous. A few months after the release of the book, she had a conversation with her brother, Tony. He asked Madison about the relationship between the fantastic potentials she revealed in her book and the possibility of sustaining herself from a full-time career that was more closely related to the evolution of consciousness than providing beautiful gardens to wealthy people.

Madison replied, "I think there is a very direct connection between committing to the kind of perspective that my book points toward and living a really creative life. I don't make a distinction between my current career and my desire to raise the consciousness of humanity. As far as earning an income by teaching or coaching on a full-time basis, starting a foundation or whatever, I really have no idea. If I was Wayne Dyer or Eckhart Tolle it might be possible, but otherwise that's a rough road. I believe that my normal routine gives me a lot of chances to relate my vision. I also have a magazine series coming out about my landscaping, so I think I will be in a great position to share my realizations with ordinary folks in an ordinary way." Then Tony said to Madison, "But most well known teachers and authors started with nothing. Ken Wilber washed dishes for ten years while he wrote his first few books and Eckhart Tolle was near homelessness before he self-published a few thousand copies of his first book, *The Power of Now*."

Madison did not reply, so Tony continued, "If you had a preference between continuing to run your garden design business as usual, or starting a new venture that was directly related to sharing human potential, which would you choose?" Madison immediately picked the latter, and added, "I am motivated to show other people that inspiration, monetary success and enlightened awareness are not in disagreement with one another, but fully support each other. But now is not the time to make any radical changes to my main source of income, and besides, my husband would be dead set against any sort of change like that."

Tony was a little surprised by his sister's response. He pressed on. "There is nothing quite as powerful as a living example, right? If you are not willing to take that leap then who might be more prepared?" Madison, thought about his question for a while, but never replied.

P: This is very similar to the last story – Madison is unwilling to make any changes to her full-time job to help others awaken. But, not everyone can be successful at running retreats or coaching and writing books. Why can't she do both – build gardens and participate in the evolution of consciousness and culture at the same time?

MQ: Of course, this would be an excellent intermediate step, to eventually evolving into a career that would allow her to express her awakening on a consistent and permanent basis. But, did you notice she said, "I really have no idea"? Who do you think that was talking – the voice of immeasurable potential in her or the unhealthy-ego?

P: Okay, you got me there, but...

MQ: Wow! You are putting up quite a case here for Madison.

P: Yes, I am. I feel this is very important for my own understanding and awakening. I know many people who grapple with this very question.

MQ: So do I.

P: Is Madison not using common sense? Do you think there is a cap on the enlightenment market?

MQ: That's hilarious! Common sense is commendable, but being unknowingly embedded in conditioned limitations at the same time as professing an awakened perspective, is an entirely different matter.

P: But, is what you are pointing toward not too utopian? I mean, who will pick up the trash, or keep our streets safe, or work for our governments?

MQ: I don't think we have to be worried about that for now, considering that only about two percent of the world's population is at a transrational or postrational level of development, with only a few thousand individuals beyond that. The 'enlightenment market' is wide open. Who will lead the way if our pioneers are content and comfortable in their ways?

EVOLUTIONARY POINTER: Part of awakening to your full potential is to explore all of your discomfort zones, across all of the four quadrants, until the little-self has been completely objectified in your awareness.

P: Okay. It is clear that the malicious ego can hide itself, even after years of study, lots of 'spiritual' life experiences, and a book on the topic of awakening! Therefore, how can I determine if the glorious expression of my infinite potential is unknowingly being restricted in regard to my primary career?

MQ: Answer these questions:

1) Is it impossible to imagine having another career other than the exact one you have?

2) Do you sometimes find it easy to describe how you use your primary career as a means to bring the potential of conscious evolution to others?

3) If you became financially independent, would you continue to work without monetary compensation in the exact same job or career that you are currently in?

4) Does your job allow you to take full responsibility for the co-creation of a new reality?

5) Does your job allow you to engage — on a full-time basis — in the exploration of consciousness and the evolution of humanity beyond the conditioned mind?

6) If you discovered an authentic opportunity or possible career path that was solely related to the evolution of consciousness, would you accept that role, risk or challenge regardless of the support level of those who are nearest and dearest to you?

7) If your current work with the evolution of awareness in other people is sustained by a separate part-time career whose income is essential for your survival, are you actively engaged in the devel-

opment and implementation of an exit strategy, so that you may apply yourself full-time to the work of the evolution of awareness?

8) If you understand that your current work/job/career is *neither* the clearest expression of your creative abilities nor fully related to the evolution of consciousness and culture, are you actively engaged in the development and implementation of an exit strategy?

MQ: A 'no' answer reveals the possible presence of concealed conditioning in foundations of your current career.

P: I am still struggling with this concept. The structure of our society does not allow everyone to have a career dedicated purely to the evolution of consciousness.

MQ: This is true, but everyone does not need to have a career dedicated purely to the evolution of consciousness. Whether that ever happens or not, is not the point. What is most important is that those who have already become aware of this wonderful option do *everything* in their power to make that a reality! After all, a new world includes evolved social structures in which careers in the evolution of awareness are commonplace. But, who is going to create that?

P: That's my responsibility.

MQ: Yes, that's what you *do* when you awaken. That is one meaning of evolutionary enlightenment. What you are struggling with is the image of personal enlightenment that the ego's dharma has painted all over the inside of your awareness. When you remove those blinders, you see the amazing potential of what we are speaking of here.

Now we will get back to the exercise of confirming your life domains.

PART 7 – Confirming Your Life Domains - continued:

MQ: Discovering *who you are* begins by uncovering what you do with your time. It can be challenging to determine how you dedicate your time across a complex life. Therefore, please be flexible with yourself during this exercise.

INSTRUCTIONS FOR TABLE 9: Using the same life domains from Table 7, determine the number of hours that you engage with each life domain over the course of an average week. There are about 100 hours available for your discretion after normal amounts of sleep and other essential activities. Because overlapping of your various life domains is to be expected, do the best you can to separate out the amount of time you spend interacting in each life domain.

For example, if you spend nine hours per day in preparation, commuting and working at a job that is an essential source of income and not directly related to the development of awareness in others, then you can place 45 hours — 5 days x 9 hours — in your life domain of *Source of Income*. If you work in any way with the development of awareness in other people, as discussed above, include those hours in a life domain of *Conscious Service* or one with a name that suits that area of your life.

If you spend three hours every day consciously interacting with your partner/spouse/children, then place 21 hours — 7 days x 3 hours — as evidence in your life domain of *Marriage* or *Family*. Note that sleeping under the same roof as another person is not usually a conscious interaction.

Table 9: Evidence in Hours for Your Life Domains:

Your life domains (in the same order as *Table 7*)	The time you spend expressing yourself in this life domain
Life domain number 1: _____	_____ (hours)
Life domain number 2: _____	_____ (hours)
Life domain number 3: _____	_____ (hours)
Life domain number 4: _____	_____ (hours)
Life domain number 5: _____	_____ (hours)
Life domain number 6: _____	_____ (hours)
Life domain number 7: _____	_____ (hours)
Life domain number 8: _____	_____ (hours)
Total time*:	_____ (hours)

*Total time should be close to your weekly waking hours, which is on average 100 hours.

PART 8 – Evidence for Your Values:

MQ: In this part of the exercise, you seek out evidence for your decision-making structures – your values. Use the same hierarchy of your eight most important values from Table 8.

The challenge of identifying evidence for your values is similar to providing evidence for your life domains. But, now you are operating at a much more intimate level. This is the level of the actual structures by which you make decisions. Therefore, it can be demanding to confirm the expression of individual values in time, because the preexisting structures in collective consciousness that permit clarity of values are only beginning to stabilize in your own awareness. And secondly, the ego-mind is not going to voluntarily release its grip on the current arrangement of your values.

INSTRUCTIONS FOR TABLE **10**: Please use the same ordered list of values from Table 8 to complete the left side of this table. Then fill in the number of hours associated with each one of your values to the right. For example, if you included *fun* as one of your values in Table 8, and you spend one hour per day surfing the web or watching your favorite TV shows, and roughly five hours per week socializing with your friends then include a total of 12 hours as confirmation of the time spent expressing that value.

Table 10: Evidence in Hours for Your Values:

List your values (in the same order as *Table 8*)	Hours representing the clear expression of this value across *all* your life domains.
Value number 1: _____	_____ (Hours)
Value number 2: _____	_____ (Hours)
Value number 3: _____	_____ (Hours)
Value number 4: _____	_____ (Hours)
Value number 5: _____	_____ (Hours)
Value number 6: _____	_____ (Hours)
Value number 7: _____	_____ (Hours)
Value number 8: _____	_____ (Hours)
Total time*: _____ (Hours)	

*Total time should be close to your weekly waking hours, which is on average 100 hours.

Note to the reader: Considering that you may be decentering a lifetime of conditioning in your decision-making structures, it is perfectly normal to experience difficulty in quantifying the time you spend consciously expressing your most important values. As always, be gentle with yourself.

PART 9 – Comparing Your Life Domains:

MQ: In this part of the exercise, you will compare your *ordered list* of life domains from Table 7 with those same life domains arranged by *hours of expression* from Table 9. Please note that this exercise may alter the order of your life domains, so pay attention to the instructions.

INSTRUCTIONS FOR THE LEFT-HAND SIDE OF TABLE **11**: Please copy the exact same list of ordered life domains — *in the same order* — from Table 7 to the left side of the table below.

INSTRUCTIONS FOR THE RIGHT-HAND SIDE OF TABLE **11**: By referring back to Table 9, place the name of the life domain that has the *most* evidence in hours in the *life domain 1* position on the right-hand side of the table below. Continue doing so until you have entered each of your life domains from Table 9 all the way down to *life domain 8*, which will contain the name of your life domain that has the *least* number of hours of those in Table 9.

Please note that it is possible that the order of your life domains on the right will appear in a different order than those on the left. You will have the opportunity to interpret the results later.

Table 11 – Comparing Your Life Domains:

Your Ordered Life Domains: Taken from Table 7 in the *same* order.	Your Most Evident Life Domains: aken from Table 9, arranged from the most to the least time spent.
Life domain 1: _____	Life domain 1: _____
Life domain 2: _____	Life domain 2: _____
Life domain 3: _____	Life domain 3: _____
Life domain 4: _____	Life domain 4: _____
Life domain 5: _____	Life domain 5: _____
Life domain 6: _____	Life domain 6: _____
Life domain 7: _____	Life domain 7: _____
Life domain 8: _____	Life domain 8: _____

MQ: Are the life domains on the right in the same order as the ones on the left? Frequently what you *do* with your time (the right side) can be dissimilar from *what you think you do* (the left side). This reflects the presence of concealed conditioning. Remain with any dissimilarity. Acceptance is the doorway to transcendence.

PART 10 – Comparing Your Values:

MQ: The ego controls your destiny by convincing you that the existing arrangement of your values is destined to lead you to an awakening. The ego-mind tries to convince you that your values are already arranged in such a way as to allow the fullest expression of your potential. Therefore, this exercise often reveals how concealed conditioning is manipulating the arrangement of your values to exclusively suit *its* objectives.

EVOLUTIONARY POINTER: A conditioned arrangement of your values cannot guide your intention to awaken.

INSTRUCTIONS FOR THE LEFT-HAND SIDE OF TABLE 12: Copy your values, *in the same order*, from Table 8, to the left-hand side of the table below.

INSTRUCTIONS FOR THE RIGHT-HAND SIDE OF TABLE 12: Using your values from Table 10, place the value that has the *most evidence in hours* in the *Value number 1* position and so on down the list to the last position. Please note that this may change their order.

Table 12 – Comparing Your Values:

Your Ordered Values: Taken from Table 8, in the *same* order.	Your Most Evident Values: Taken from Table 10, arranged from the most time to the least time spent.
Value number 1: _____	Evident value 1: _____
Value number 2: _____	Evident value 2: _____
Value number 3: _____	Evident value 3: _____
Value number 4: _____	Evident value 4: _____
Value number 5: _____	Evident value 5: _____
Value number 6: _____	Evident value 6: _____
Value number 7: _____	Evident value 7: _____
Value number 8: _____	Evident value 8: _____

MQ: After you have completed both sides of Table 12, compare your *ordered values* on the left, to the list of *most evident values* on the right. Are they in the same order?

P: And what if they are in a different order?

MQ: Often, your presumed values, (the ones on the left), vary greatly from your most commonly expressed values, (the ones on the right). If the evidence for the expression of your values (the list on the right) conflicts with what you think your values are (the list on the left), you have succeeded in identifying the influence of concealed conditioning in your values.

P: This is how the ego-mind controls my decisions, by controlling my values.

MQ: Exactly! This discovery gives you the opportunity to consciously rearrange your most commonly expressed values. You will see how to do this by the end of this chapter. This rearrangement compels you to make choices in a new way, and in doing so you reclaim consciousness that otherwise would be consumed in dealing with challenging outcomes in the future because of making decisions in the present based upon the ego's arrangement of your values.

EVOLUTIONARY POINTER: Continued reclamation of your awareness leads to awakening.

P: Therefore, by finding evidence for values that I consider to be nearest and dearest to me is the only way to know that I am *living* them. If I cannot find proof of their manifestation in my life, then the only place they exist is in the mind of the ego.

MQ: And there is nothing wrong with this at all. It is correct at that level of development. If, however, your interest is in awakening, it is great to know about this influence of the ego on your values. The awakened life emerges as the relationship to the experience you are already having. New evidence is continually unfolding according to how you choose to respond to life. Remember that the goal here is to distinguish which values you are relying upon to make decisions that are manifesting your intentions as your destiny.

P: Now I really understand the following quote you mentioned earlier in the chapter. *"Once your ego's values have become objectified in your awareness, then you are in a position to begin to freely choose: Is that who I want to be or not?"* I have to clearly see my values before I can decide if that is *who I want to be or not.*

MQ: Yes. Take a moment now to review the life domains on the right-hand side of Table 11 and the values on the right-hand side of Table 12. Is that who you want to be or not?

The Values of an Awakened Person

MQ: The intentions of a liberated person are compelled by a vision of humanity's penchant to inflict unneeded suffering upon itself. Naturally, when you awaken, you strive to show others that a more peaceful way of *being* and *becoming* is possible. Collectively, millions of people simultaneously overlook their most glorious potential. When you perceive this with awakened compassion, you arrange your values *for the sake of humanity.*

EVOLUTIONARY POINTER: Wisdom blends the perfection and imperfection of the world, *as it is*, which reveals a direct connection between values, intentions and outcomes.

P: Can you give me an example of a primary value of an awakened person?

MQ: A primary value might be *freedom* – guiding his intention *to be free from the attachment to ego-mind.* This would be a primary value of a person in the traditional sense of personal enlightenment. An awakened person could also have a primary value of *evolution or development* – guiding his intention *to participate in the evolution of consciousness and culture.* Such a leading principle would represent a person whose main interest in life is helping other people become integrated, free-functioning human beings. This represents a higher stage of development and is also referred to as evolutionary enlightenment.

P: And just like you and me, an awakened person has many life domains, correct?

MQ: Yes and many different values. Nonetheless, all of his most important decisions are arrived at by the use of a *single hierarchy of values*. Such a conscious arrangement of his decision-making-structures is initially the key to his liberation. This is because this arrangement is completely capable of guiding his objectives to sustain the conditions for an awakened life.

P: The *single sphere of values* that an awakened person uses to guide his decisions is radically different to the way in which the values of an un-awakened person are structured, even though the latter may also have an intention to live a liberated life.

MQ: Yes.

EVOLUTIONARY POINTER: Believing that you are going to awaken, and having a value structure that is capable of permitting that outcome, are two entirely different matters.

P: You mentioned that the value structure of an awakened person reveals that his primary interest in life is helping other people become integrated, free-functioning human beings. Does this mean that he does this all of the time?

MQ: No, that would be impossible. Fifty-one percent is fine. Before you learn how to construct a single hierarchy of your own values to guide your awakening, let's look at why an intention to awaken based on a conditioned arrangement of your values, is rarely sufficient to produce that result.

The Conflict of Multiple Value Spheres

MQ: Are you beginning to see the problem with multiple value spheres and competing primary values spread across many different life domains that are competing for your attention?

P: Yes.

MQ: The ego-mind is naturally identified with the values of your culture. This happens long before you are even able to or allowed to make a major life decision. Because of conditioning, 'your' values are distributed into numerous spheres that support distinct life domains. You have relied on these structures to make decisions for so long that they now routinely operate without question.

P: This is the realm of conceptual-free-will.

MQ: Yes. This offers no possibility of release from unnecessary conflict and confusion.

EVOLUTIONARY POINTER: Conceptual-free-will is inherently inclined to support the separate sense-of-self, which leads to elevated levels of unnecessary emotional and psychological suffering.

MQ: Conceptual-free-will is the decision-making process that is based solely on a conditioned arrangement of your values. Cultural conditioning distributes values into various spheres that are capable of supporting distinct life domains. Each one of these separate value groups contain many values and several key values. For instance, the life domain of *Relationships* can contain dozens of values, but several values of primary importance, such as *love (feeling), fun, honesty* and *money*. This means that the leading principle can change its position of importance within a particular life domain, depending on the situation in which a decision is necessary.

For example, an offer of a promotion at work promises a salary increase and a corner office, but it also puts you in a position of having to boost profitability by increasing productivity and reducing costs. Your decision about this opportunity draws into play such values as *money, ambition* and *popularity* in your life domain of *Source of Income*. These three values may switch positions at the top of this life domain until you finally make a 'decision'.

P: Do the primary values at the top of one life domain come into conflict with the primary values at the top of a different life domain when I have to make an important decision?

MQ: Yes, this also happens. Using the same example of a promotion at work above, you can see how your decision about this opportunity calls up such values as *money* and *popularity* in your life domain of *Source of Income* and in your life domain of *Family*, the prospect of working extra hours and increasing your level of stress has to be weighed against important values such as *happiness* and *bonding*. Other life domains, such as *Hobbies, Health and Relationships*, and their associated key values, may also be considered before you make your final decision.

P: This is cause for much stress and indecisiveness?

EVOLUTIONARY POINTER: Procrastination is often the result of the clash of multiple values across multiple life domains. When you can't decide what's most important to you, it just looks as if you are delaying action, when in fact you simply can't decide what your *most important* value is going to be.

MQ: Other typical responses to complex choices can be to 'weigh your options', 'consider all scenarios', 'rate your preferences' or 'meditate on it'. You also may look to the past for patterns, consider your fears and desires of the future, consult your spouse or life partner, peers, popular culture and maybe even ask the *I Ching*[12] or your local *Tarot* reader for guidance.

P: All in all it seems that the ego's arrangement of my values is perfectly suited to creating much unnecessary emotional and psychological suffering around major life decisions.

MQ: Yes, that is exactly the point. Agonizing over big decisions implies that the malicious aspect of the ego-mind is overriding your values. Endless deliberation empowers the lesser-self to sustain itself by draining your consciousness, thus allowing it to direct your destiny while you are busy struggling with options. After you order and re-order your possibilities — in and across different life domains — you eventually select a value as the basis for your final decisions.

P: And the ensuing outcomes mirror the conditioned structures used to make that choice.

MQ: Yes. This is the basis for conceptual-free-will, which creates the illusion of free will. *"No one can serve two masters; for either he will hate the one and love the other, or else he will be loyal to the one and despise the other."*[13] Accessing the flow of conscious-free-will, on the other hand, is based on a awakened arrangement of your existing values. A primary value is assigned to the first position of that single value sphere. This primary value is one you know that is capable of guiding your intention to awaken to fruition.

P: Okay. I can also see how multiple groups of values inhibit the discovery and expression of my full potential because it is often impossible for me to abide by my decisions after I make them.

MQ: Yes. Conceptual-free-will inhibits complete accountability for your choices.

EVOLUTIONARY POINTER: 'Changing your mind' means that the malignant ego-mind just switched the value upon which you based your original decision.

MQ: In conditioned conversations, such a switch is often expressed as, "That situation is no longer relevant to me" or "My priorities have shifted since I made that decision," or simply "I don't know what I was thinking when I made that choice." This is the unhealthy-ego speaking through its host as it shuffles values around to *its* sole advantage.

P: Therefore, competing groups of values and conflicting primary values strewn across multiple life domains prevent me from being responsible for my decisions and subsequent actions.

MQ: This is true. You are never going to 'decide away' unnecessary suffering until you identify the ego-mind in your decision-making structures. As you awaken, it becomes apparent to you that the first big decision you ever made — independent of your parents — was a product of the ego-mind, the result of conditioned intentions, and based on the existence of multiple groups of values and conceptual-free-will. Have you been making choices in this way ever since?

P: I hope not.

Karen's Story: Here is an illustration of multiple hierarchies of *ordered* values distributed across distinct life domains. For the sake of this demonstration, I only selected the four most important life domains of this individual. In this example, Karen is in her late thirties and has two young sons. Both she and her husband work full-time in the advertising industry. They have a comfortable, yet busy, life with many friends.

Table 13 – Real–Life Example of Life Domains with Values Inserted

Life Domain: Source of Income *Primary* Time: 40 hrs	Life Domain: Family *Number 2* Time: 25 hrs	Life Domain: Relationships *Number 3* Time: 10 hrs	Life Domain: Spiritual Seeking *Number 4* Time: 6 hrs
Value 1: Money	Value 1: Love (feeling)	Value 1: Commitment	Value 1: Honesty
Value 2: Responsibility	Value 2: Joy	Value 2: Sharing	Value 2: Gratitude
Value 3: Security	Value 3: Money	Value 3: Honesty	Value 3: Responsibility
Value 4: Creativity	Value 4: Responsibility	Value 4: Fun	Value 4: Growth
Value 5: Learning	Value 5: Honesty	Value 5: Responsibility	Value 5: Love (selfless)
Value 6: Self-reliance	Value 6: Sharing	Value 6: Money	Value 6: Sharing
Value 7: Honesty	Value 7: Security	Value 7: Entertainment	Value 7: Money
Value 8: Travel	Value 8: Comfort	Value 8: Travel	Value 8: Well-being

MQ: It is clear that the life domain of *Source of Income* is primary to Karen. Note that several of her values repeat across her four most important life domains. This is to be expected. Karen depends on her job as a sole source of income, but she also has significant expenses in her life domain of *Family,* and to a lesser degree in her life domain of *Relationships* and *Spiritual Seeking*. This means that her value of *money* repeats in each life domain in an appropriate position within that value sphere.

P: I see that Karen's life domain of *Spiritual Seeking* indicates a primary value of *honesty*, which is also repeated in all of her life domains.

MQ: Yes. Notice, though, that this value of *honesty* is in the seventh position in her life domain of *Source of Income* and in the first position in her life domain of *Spiritual Seeking*. There are times at work when Karen cannot be completely truthful with her clients and her manager, so she downgrades her value of *honesty* so that *money* can remain in the primary position of her career. This is because, in the life domain of *Source of Income,* Karen *values* her salary more than she does being sincere.

P: By allowing her to shuffle values in this way, the unhealthy-ego gives Karen the illusion of true free will.

MQ: Yes. And the voice of fear reminds her that if she tells the truth at work she may lose a client, get into trouble with her boss, or she might even get fired. When Karen speaks to her sons, however, about the importance of *honesty,* she does so knowing that, beyond a cool cliché she has no idea what she wants to share. Karen sounds wise to her sons and to her spiritual friends when she talks about honesty. But, trading values as she does when she feels the need to at work keeps Karen awake at night as she tries to figure out the real answer to this question: *Who am I?*

The Values of an Awakened Person – Part II:

MQ: An awakened person's decision-making structure is based on a *single* hierarchy of values. This single group of guiding principles consistently includes a *Conscious Competent Value* in its primary position. This primary value is consciously selected because it is capable of directing their clarity of intention to sustain an awakened life.

P: And it is with this conscious arrangement of their values that an awakened person is capable of manifesting an awakened life *by choice.*

MQ: Exactly! The arrangement of their values is capable of guiding their intention to be free from all unnecessary emotional and psychological drama. This arrangement of their guiding principles allows them to directly access conscious-free-will at the time of making important choices.

EVOLUTIONARY POINTER: A highly integrated individual is indivisible from their primary value.

P: This also means that an awakened person can instantly recount their first value?

MQ: With great consistency and clarity. They may, however, have some difficulty telling you what their second and third values are. Other values on the single hierarchy of an awakened person can, and do, change positions with each other, depending on the particular situations about which decisions need to be made. The primary value on their single list of values is fully complementary with freedom from individual and collective conditioning, and the evolution of consciousness in culture.

EVOLUTIONARY POINTER: The major choices that an awakened person makes provide unswerving and tangible proof of this unified arrangement.

P: Therefore, having a single hierarchy of values, which at all times has the *same* primary value, ensures that I am always worthy of trust because I trust myself implicitly to make great decisions.

MQ: That's it. And, the profound implication of implicitly trusting your own choices is that you empower your capacity to unreservedly trust in the process of life.

P: My choices evolve the process of life.

A Single Hierarchy of Values:

MQ: Table 14 is an example of the values of an awakened person arranged in a single hierarchy.

Table 14: An Awakened Person's Single Hierarchy of Values:

Value number 1:	Evolution / or Development / or Freedom
Value number 2:	Money
Value number 3:	Love (feeling)
Value number 4:	Commitment
Value number 5:	Honesty
Value number 6:	Responsibility
Value number 7:	Joy
Value number 8:	Sharing
Value number 9:	Gratitude
Value number 10:	Security

MQ: The values in position 2, *money*, through to position 10, *security*, are completely arbitrary. They were compiled by taking the second and third place values from the example of Karen above.

P: Therefore, an awakened person shares some of the same values as an un-awakened person.

MQ: Yes, of course. This is important so that you may survive and thrive in this world. The big exception is their most important or primary principle. In the case of the awakened person, a conscious competent value occupies the first position in a single hierarchy of values.

EVOLUTIONARY POINTER: *"When thine eye is single, thy whole body also is full of light."*[14]

MQ: Is not your 'eye' that 'single' conscious competent value? The awakened person uses the conscious competent value to guide all-important decisions. Because they know this principle is capable of guiding their intention to live an awakened life – that is always their outcome.

P: I see now that freedom *is* a choice.

MQ: Yes, it is. By allocating a conscious competent value to guide your intentions of *being* and *becoming* a living example of awakened potential, you bring that outcome within your volition. This is the fundamental process of conscious-free-will.

Assigning your highest priority in life ends all seeking.

1   Mahatma Gandhi.

2   *Seven Spiritual Laws of Success* by Deepak Chopra. New World
    Library, 1994.

3   Harper & Row, New York, 1990.

4   Excerpted from a speech the author gave at ENPP 3rd Annual
    Conference, Portugal, 2006.

5   Lamsa Translation of the Holy Bible - John 12.25.

6   The Matrix Trilogy – Distributed by Warner Bros.

7   These are based on the four quadrants developed by Integral
    philosopher Ken Wilber. For more, see: *A Brief History of Everything*,
    Shambhala Publications, Inc., 1996.

8   Andrew Cohen.

9   Fortune magazine, European Edition, July 2008.

10 The sphere of human thought. For more see the work of Teilhard de
    Chardin.

11 A scholar who is deeply immersed in spiritual wisdom.

12 *Book of Changes* is one of the oldest of the Chinese classics. It is a
    system of symbols that are used to identify order in chance events.

13 New King James Version - Spirit Filled Version - Matthew 6.24.

14 King James Version - Luke 11.34.

Chapter 11

THE THIRD INSIGHT

RECALL YOUR ORIGIN OF ONENESS

"When you are unable to find tranquility within yourself,
it is useless to seek it elsewhere."[1]

Being in Stillness

MQ: To temporarily transcend thought and little-self awareness requires the development of both *cognition* and *consciousness*.

P: But, the path of awakening is not all intellect and theory. Is this correct?

MQ: You are right. Expanding your capacity to take different perspectives, which is one definition of cognitive development, is equally as important as increasing your capacity to understand emptiness, which is to experience consciousness directly.

Therefore, if the nature of enlightenment can be defined as the intersection of the psyche and consciousness at the edge of pure creativity, we now need to take a look at...

P: Enlightenment?

MQ: No, that's for you to *co-create* as the process of life, by means of the relationship you have to the experience you are already having in the company of other people who have also awakened to individual and collective conditioning.

P: We will speak of developing the capacity to understand emptiness and to experience consciousness directly.

MQ: Yes. Earlier in the book, we spoke of consciousness as the ground of all being, the simple awareness of being or the capacity to be aware. Now, we will discover what happens when consciousness focuses on consciousness.

P: God looking in a mirror…

MQ: Sees?

P: Only the mirror?

EVOLUTIONARY POINTER: God is a narcissist of Kosmic proportions. God looks in a mirror and from the depth of eternal emptiness and infinite potential *your* reflection appears.

P: God is the reflection of my infinite potential… I am the depth of eternal emptiness and infinite potential? Please continue.

MQ: Okay. There is a popular travel book called, *1,000 Places to See Before You Die*[2]. It no doubt offers a fascinating list of exotic locations that are worthy of experience. Yet, inside of you, an incalculable majesty awaits your attention without taking a single step or without circling the globe. We might title this humble volume: *One Place to See Before You Die*[3]. The rediscovery of this essential aspect of yourself does not require a large travel budget or demand that you take months of vacation time. Its recollection requires only *stillness*.

P: Stillness reveals my infinite potential?

MQ: Yes. The Third Insight is the key by which you may recall your origin of authentic joy, your source of already completeness, the state in which you have always been free. The Third Insight allows you to temporarily transcend thought and little-self awareness.

The Third Insight frees you from the stream of time, for a timeless moment, from all of your cherished opinions and the tribulations of this dual dimension.

P: The dual dimension is all the ways I currently recognize myself, but as that which I consider separate. For instance; me and the world, my relationships, my things, my memories, my plans for the future, my reflection in the mirror, my fears, my desires, the separate sense-of-self, the Ego, the ego, and my shadow…

MQ: Yes and even your enlightenment. The Third Insight describes a straightforward practice that allows you to take a *stance of stillness* in relation to the endless demands and attractions of this most intriguing, yet sometimes overwhelming dual dimension.

EVOLUTIONARY POINTER: The Third Insight reveals not so much all you *can be*, but that your inherent radiance is, in fact, your true quintessence. With the Third Insight, you recall that which is only the essential *You*, whole and complete just as you find You are.

MQ: Remember that Krishnamurti said, *"In the gap between subject and object lies the entire misery of humankind"*. The Third Insight is your key to melding this separation, uniting subject and object, activity and stillness, doing and being, the witness and consciousness as One, first in meditation, and eventually in all aspects of your perspective. The practice of stillness meditation outlined in the Third Insight points to the *rightness of being* you have so long intuited yet long missed. Once witnessed as your natural state, meditation ultimately emerges as your every waking moment.

EVOLUTIONARY POINTER: Then you no longer need to access Presence because you will realize that you can't ever escape your essential essence.

The Practice of Stillness Meditation

P: I have noticed that it is impossible to control the movement of my mind.

MQ: There is no need to try. Start your practice of *stillness meditation* by controlling the only thing you can – your body. In martial arts, the word 'stance' is used to describe a position of *readiness for engagement*. When in a stance, the practitioner is impeccably balanced and poised to respond, if required. No response is necessary when the sparring partner is only being observed. In meditation, you learn to sit completely still and be only the observer. You are not looking for anything in particular.

P: To continue this metaphor, as the observer in a stance, I don't care if my sparring partner is tall or short, small or large, black belt or yellow belt. I am not trying to make him anything other than how he appears to me.

MQ: Correct. In meditation, not looking for anything in particular becomes your *stance of stillness* in relation to the constant movement of the mind. The mind does as it pleases, but as long as you do not move your body you are assuming a position of objectivity. This is your silent statement of victory over the demands of the conditioned mind to always be moving.

EVOLUTIONARY POINTER: In the practice of *stillness meditation* there is to be no movement of the *body* whatsoever. A position of motionlessness leads to the significant quieting of the *mind*.

MQ: We mentioned earlier in the book that meditation is your natural state. This natural state first emerges when the conditions are created for that. The awareness of the body eases and recedes. Emotions slowly fall away. Thoughts become quieter and quieter. Persisting in physical stillness enables a great sense of wellbeing and joy to pervade your being. There is no activity now except silence, stillness and observation, more silence and stillness, deeper and deeper observation, and a delicate observation of effortless breathing – slowly and gently.

EVOLUTIONARY POINTER: *Who* is breathing is the timeless beauty in which no event has occurred or any damage has been done

---

MQ: You are breathing itself, there is no subject who is breathing, there is only breathing.

Eventually, even the tacit awareness of inhalation and exhalation slips away, without you noticing. The immutable state of *meditation* unfolds and now becomes wholly apparent as none other than your *Self*. You are now neither the observer nor the observed, for your awareness is merged with that which is observed. Consciousness awakens to itself in you as you. God is looking in the mirror.

EVOLUTIONARY POINTER: The state of meditation is apparent with great ease, as undeniably obvious perfection. You don't have to look 'here' or 'there' for it. You don't have to seek it in the 'now' or in some other 'moment'. *You cannot miss it!*

P: And where am 'I' during all this?

MQ: Your body is sitting right here on your cushions. Your attention is present and complete, beautiful and deep. You, your attention and the vastness of consciousness are one. And just like when you are fast asleep, safely tucked away in your bed, and the sounds of chirping birds eventually filter through to your attention, *you* are that noticing.

P: Yes, I am.

MQ: When you ask, "Who's paying attention?" the only answer can be: *I am.*

P: You mention that I can't miss the state of meditation?

MQ: Absolutely not. How could you miss your real face? The

state of meditation unfolds as a conscious reality when you are physically still, deeply at ease emotionally, and profoundly alert psychologically – in your sitting practice. Then the awakened life emerges as a conscious reality when you are physically active, deeply at ease emotionally, and profoundly alert psychologically – in your waking state. Can you see the connection and the subtle differences here?

P: Yes. The awakened life is meditation in action.

MQ: Stillness meditation, therefore, is the lifeline of awakened living.

EVOLUTIONARY POINTER: Meditation is a metaphor for enlightenment[4].

Meditation is Your Natural State

P: If meditation is the *natural state*, is it available to me at all times, even now?

MQ: Now and always. Not only is it always available, but, as we saw earlier, you can't get rid of it!

P: How can something so wholly available also be so utterly missed?

MQ: Here is a story that may shed a little light on that.

The Story of the White House: Many years ago I visited a beautiful part of western Massachusetts known as the Berkshires. I went there to take part in a weekend past-life regression workshop. A friend, who at that time was also an adamant seeker, invited me to stay at her home in the area. I arrived at her apartment on a dark wintery night. The next morning, I awoke to a striking sense of serenity. A pristine peace pervaded every aspect of my awareness, even my body seemed to tingle. This phenomenon was similar to the way I had often felt in the presence of a former teacher, a powerful master who would impart extremely high states of consciousness.

As I peered through an icy window at one December's dawn, I noticed there were many apartments just like the one in which I was staying. In the distance, and seemingly on the same property, was a large turn-of-the-century mansion. Since there were no visible signs of life in the big house, I could not tell if it was even occupied.

As the weekend progressed, the peace that enveloped me in my friend's apartment persisted. I asked her if she was aware of it, too. She said she was not. Then I asked her about the large house that was visible on the other side of the property. She told me she hadn't really paid any attention to it before and that she really knew nothing about the building. As a result, I forgot all about the big house that stood in the frozen mists just across the way.

I returned home to New York City and thought little of this weekend until several years later. Then one day I discovered a pamphlet of an internationally known and supposedly fully awakened teacher. His words spoke with great clarity about abandoning the struggle with emotions and thoughts. I was immediately attracted to his work, and after a little research, I found that this teacher was holding a short retreat at his home facility... in the Berkshires. When I told my friend I was coming up to her part country again, she was pleased to have me stay at her place, even though she would be away. As I planned my trip, I discovered that the address for the seminar I was to attend was on the same street as my friend's apartment.

Imagine my surprise when I arrived the morning of the retreat to find that this event was being held in the same big turn-of-the-century house I had seen years earlier from my friend's apartment. This location was the home — and international teaching center — of this renowned teacher and his large assembly of dedicated students. For many years my friend had lived right beside this location, looking directly at the big white house, without knowing of the potential that was there – in full line of sight, just a few steps across the garden.

MQ: The state of meditation is just like this, always available and in plain view. It is only because of the effects of concealed conditioning that you do not see it until — finally — you do!

P: The state of meditation is here as we are speaking?

EVOLUTIONARY POINTER: It's not so much that the state of meditation *is here now*. You don't have to look for it as there is nothing to be found because nothing's ever been missing.

MQ: Recall a time when you were in a bookstore in search of a specific item. You roamed the aisles, focused solely on your quest. Then, on a far-off shelf or from the corner of your eye, something grabbed your attention. As you approached, you realized you knew exactly what it was, and although it was not what you had been searching for, it was more than perfect. Furthermore, you couldn't imagine how you had forgotten about it or how many times you might have walked right past. It was just sitting there, awaiting discovery.

P: I've had this experience on more than one occasion.

MQ: Discovering meditation as the natural state is most similar. It is only your attention that has been absent without your leave, entangled with the ego-mind for a millennia. The fundamental state of meditation is present. In fact, it's *who you are*, so how can your truest essence 'go' anywhere? Don't be like the fish who's always looking for the water. Stillness meditation is like this: You stumble upon that which you know you are, yet had simply forgotten, with no memory of the loss. And though it was not the aim of your seeking, you find that its rediscovery is infinitely more than you ever imagined it could be. For now, you know you were never as two, because all that is found is You.

The Purpose of Meditation

P: In the world of duality, or the world of opposites, I already know who I am, what I am, and what I am not. I also know that I am *not* my full potential and that I am not reliably available to this state of Presence of which you speak.

MQ: In the gross state or waking state, all of the things you know about, don't know about, and don't know that you don't know about are important, but not exclusively so. You are just so conditioned to identify with the waking state that it becomes all you know and don't know. The most curious thing, however, is that the non-dual state is just as 'real' as this dimension. Did you know this?

P: I did not know this! The practice of meditation allows me to reconnect with a preexisting non-dual awareness in myself?

MQ: Yes, and in other words, it allows you to disconnect from the entire conditioned trance. The Third Insight reintroduces you as being originally not two, but one. Stillness meditation is the recollection of who you are at a non-dual level, beyond thought, knowledge, opinions and beliefs. The Third Insight is a reintroduction to your original state that has forever been whole, complete, perfect and ever gracefully as such.

EVOLUTIONARY POINTER: When consciousness focuses on itself, you become aware of the timeless *Self* that is forever beyond identity and image, fear and desire; unbound by physical birth and death. You realize yourself as the very ground upon which, and from which, all form unfolds and returns.

MQ: Meditation yokes or connects your attention to the part of yourself that has never been born and will never die. Do you know if the aim for your current practice of meditation also includes this particular intention?

P: No, I don't think so. I've been meditating because it makes me feel good.

MQ: Therefore, you may have been *unconsciously sitting on* your full potential as opposed to *consciously sitting in* your full potential!

P: This explains the tenet of the ego's dharma that tells us: *Meditation is for relieving stress and having peak experiences.*

MQ: Meditation most certainly eases anxiety, perhaps in anticipation of more of the same, but it is also used by the ego to try to get enlightened.

P: Wait a second. The ego can't get enlightened.

MQ: This is true, but that doesn't stop it from trying. Conditioning has filled you with so many ideas about meditation that great uncertainty arises as to its essential purpose. The malignant part of the ego is also convinced that if you or it just gets enlightened, all its worldly problems will disappear. And since the ego-mind prefers that you look like a little Buddha — and not act like him — you must be sure that your particular intentions for *being in stillness* are not smothered in the ill-advised directives of concealed conditioning.

P: Meditating according to the ego's dharma can never free me from suffering?

MQ: Not in a million lifetimes!

The Spiritual Encounter Junkie

MQ: Just like combat soldiers tend to get hooked on the high of the battle, in the ego's attempt to get enlightened, it frequently winds up with an addiction to spiritual experiences. Witness the shenanigans the next time you have an opportunity to attend an event with a spiritual teacher who is known to be very 'present' or truly in the 'now'. The unhealthy-ego can be seen jockeying for pole positions in the line outside and then competing with itself over the front row seats, which it would never admit to desiring. And immediately after such an event, the ego-mind quickly reverts the conversations to the dubious topics we covered in Chapter Seven, such as gossiping, sharing personal stories and defending cherished opinions. And, in all this, the hosts are mostly oblivious to the manipulation.

P: The ego's dharma calls this 'being spiritual'.

MQ: Indeed it does! I have to admit, though, as part of 'my conscious spiritual journey', I spent several years with a teacher who could flip into *Nirvakalpa Samadhi*[5] in a matter of seconds. And so forceful was the luminosity emanating from this man, that while dining with him, I often found it necessary to hold tightly to the edge of the table so I would not fall off the chair!

P: You're kidding!

MQ: No. And in the aftermath of spending time with him, I would be in a blissful state for days, where nothing mattered and nothing bothered me. I would also experience phenomenal psychic abilities, tremendous self-confidence and surges of unusual courage and bravado. But, while these experiences were astonishing, this teacher had no intention of transcending the malignant aspects of the ego-mind, simply because he knew nothing of its presence in him. Even though he had access to advanced states of mind, he was totally trapped in shadow and identification with the ego-mind. After a few days of my surfing the waves of non-dual consciousness, I would come crashing back to life as I once knew it.

P: That sounds like an incredible experience.

MQ: All but the crashing part!

EVOLUTIONARY POINTER: The lure of 'light' often turns genuine seekers in to guru-hopping spiritual encounter junkies. The unhealthy-ego has an unquenchable thirst for peak experiences.

MQ: For myself, it took a few years of tumbling off these highs to realize that all this 'spiritual' activity was just the ego-mind in me fortifying itself with metaphysical powers. It was doing this so that it could get more of what *it* wanted for me – bliss, money, image, power, sex, security, status and so on.

P: As a result, the unhealthy-ego keeps the hapless seeker moving from one peak experience to the next?

MQ: Forever, if you are not careful. While spiritual experiences can certainly loosen the ego-mind's grip on your motives and intentions, the ego knows this, too, and so it welcomes the pursuit of peak experiences rather than your genuine bid for transformation. This has a two-pronged effect. Firstly, spiritual experiences are taken as signs of progress on 'your path'. This is because you think that there's nothing more important than having more and more mystical encounters. Secondly, the hunt for additional numinous events becomes a priority over taking responsibility for your life situations that might resemble a 'personal' war zone. Therefore, conscious living and the attainment of higher and higher *stages of development* are discarded.

P: The ego is happy to get high and true transformation goes out the door.

MQ: Way out! This is exactly what the malevolent ego wants, and why the spiritual experiences you claim also require validation in subsequent actions. Otherwise, you and the ego will be on 'your conscious spiritual journey' for a long time. Here, you can only hope to awaken.

EVOLUTIONARY POINTER: If dramatic life changes, corresponding to the claimed intensity of a spiritual experience are *not* so apparent, it can also be the case that the ego's vision of impotent fireworks has been mistaken for a mystical immersion in the mind of the Kosmos[6].

P: Then, no change equals no experience?

MQ: No, not in the least. Mystical experiences are available at all levels of development. Children have spiritual experiences, as do tribal warriors, people who follow conformist religions and those at Integral stages of development can also experience higher states of consciousness. If you claim to have had a profound experience, yet there is little or no evidence of radical transformation, this points to the likelihood that concealed conditioning is still very much in control of your destiny at your particular level of development.

P: So I need to be careful that concealed conditioning is not the only one interpreting my spiritual experiences.

MQ: You can spend years having profound experiences — which is perfectly fine — but as long as hidden habituation is in the driver's seat, there won't be any noteworthy transformation, just significant amounts of superfluous suffering.

Going Beyond the Separate Self

P: Regardless of my current level of development, a spiritual experience can help me go beyond the separate sense-of-self long enough so that I may be compelled to change?

MQ: Yes. And this can occur the very first time you meditate. You don't necessarily need years and years of practice. When a spiritual experience takes you beyond the separate sense-of-self, in the Oneness you have so correctly intuited, the blind pursuit of conditioned living is temporarily quelled. This is because you see with clarity, perhaps for the first time. You realize that up to that instant you were living *unconsciously*, although you may have been under a self-righteous impression that you were living *consciously*.

EVOLUTIONARY POINTER: *"It is important to realize that the experience of the luminosity of mind, of the nature of mind, is not a profound realization in itself."*[7]

MQ: What makes an experience of luminosity profound is our interpretation of that realization.

P: Can just one taste of the nature of mind alter my entire perspective?

MQ: Yes, if interpreted in a way that permits such a shift.

P: How many different ways can I interpret a spiritual experience?

MQ: According to the Wilber/Coombs Lattice[8], mystical experiences can be classed according to at least 28 distinct, yet overlapping, interpretations. This means that you can understand a spiritual experience in such a way that it can act as a springboard to the awakened life. But, this also means that you can interpret a spiritual encounter in a way that fortifies an already conditioned perspective. For example, if an esoteric Buddhist, a devout Christian, a radical ecologist, and a scientist each have a profound spiritual experience during meditation, the first may interpret his experience as oneness with Buddha-mind, the second as being in the presence of Jesus, the ecologist may experience the encounter as oneness with the planet, and the scientist is very likely to see the entire experience as arising only in the right-side of the brain.

P: Which one is the right one?

MQ: They are all correct for the stage of development and perspective taken by the particular individual. But not one of them is complete. Become aware that there are many different ways to interpret a spiritual experience. Most often we view such an encounter through the lens of our cultural conditioning without even knowing that's what we are doing.

P: The brain is necessary to have a spiritual encounter, but I've always wondered if spiritual experiences happen only inside the brain.

MQ: To paraphrase Wilber, *divinity cannot be reduced to dopamine*! A refined level of self-reflective awareness, however, is also required to consistently experience your full potential in stillness meditation.

EVOLUTIONARY POINTER: You have to be careful to not deny the capacity to experience that which exists *beyond* the mind.

MQ: Simply because you may be unable to experience consciousness directly does not mean that this capacity does not exist in other people. Your inability to taste a direct experience of Self hardly gives you the right to refute the capacities and understandings of others who perhaps have developed themselves through years of self-discipline and willingness.

P: What is the stimulus for a spiritual experience?

MQ: In the context of stillness meditation, it begins with the ability to not pay attention to the constant movement of the mind. This can be learned if that is your interest and if you are not too indentified with your mind. Consider, also, this simple experiment: If I show you a physical object, like a flower for example, parts of your brain will respond to that stimulus. We can measure this activity using neuroimaging technology[9]. Spiritual experiences that occur during meditation also activate certain parts of the brain and these responses can be recorded by using this same technology. Universities around the world have studied this phenomenon extensively with the assistance of people who have years and years of meditation experience.

P: But, this work has done little to convince die-hard scientific rationalists.

MQ: And such data cannot be expected to do so. This is because signifiers such as 'Oneness', 'Suchness', or 'Buddha-nature' do not exist in the awareness of people at their level of development. Systems theory, for instance, may sound like gobbledygook to a member of an indigenous tribe, but does that also mean it does not exist in the awareness of another person who is more evolved intellectually?

P: I understand. So the brain responds to both interior and

exterior stimuli?

MQ: Yes. But while you and I can view the same physical object, we can only *tell* each other about our spiritual experiences. I can only describe my encounter to you and will do so according to the level of my development.

P: And just because I can't show you my capacity to disregard a busy mind does not mean that my experiences while doing so are also invalid.

MQ: Yes, that is correct.

EVOLUTIONARY POINTER: You cannot show me your spiritual experience and I cannot show you mine. We can only show each other the evidence for a shift in perspective according to our interpretation of those encounters.

P: Therefore, the brain is a mechanism that allows us to perceive a stimulus and, subsequently, register a measurable response.

MQ: Does the brain create the flower?

P: No. The flower exists independently of the brain, not in the brain.

MQ: Yes. And spiritual experiences are also registered by the brain and measurable with advanced technology, but that does not necessarily mean that they originate there.

Do not question whether spiritual experiences are real or not. Instead, question why you might not want to find out for yourself if they are real or not. Who do you think might want you to believe that the pursuit of mystical Oneness is a waste of time?

P: The ego?

MQ: Yes, because beyond knowledge, in the vast expanse of your True Self, the ego does not exist.

P: Therefore, it will refute anything that threatens its existence.

MQ: Exactly.

EVOLUTIONARY POINTER: Regardless of the source of mystical emptiness, the correct interpretation of an authentic mind-meld with Oneness always calls you to question the sanity of man and your place in that charade across all of your life domains.

MQ: Remember, if there's no call to radical transformation from such an experience, the ego is likely to continue amusing itself with idle fancies!

Elizabeth's Story: Elizabeth was in her late twenties when she suddenly fell quite ill. As her condition worsened, she was admitted to a hospital and placed in a six-day drug-induced coma. During this time, Elizabeth's heart stopped and was started several times.

Then she recovered just as quickly. No reason was ever found for her condition. She subsequently described a fantastic series of events while she was in the coma. She spoke of meeting deceased family members, reviewing aspects of her childhood in detail, and having deep and meaningful conversations with wise beings while soaring over fields of light and valleys of great majesty. Elizabeth also reported experiencing tremendous bliss, joy and peace.

While still glowing from her experiences, Elizabeth was happy to return home to her life but, she was also surprised at how rapidly the peace of her transcendent experiences dissipated. Troubled by her reversion to the former conflicts and frustrations, she confided in her spiritual teacher one day, "I thought these experiences were going to help me continue my healing process," she said. To which the teacher replied, "How can you be sure that the ego-mind was not on that flight of fancy with you?" Elizabeth retorted, "How could that be? My experiences felt so wonderful and seemed so real!" As Elizabeth waited for his response, she realized she had not reinterpreted any aspects of her complex life in the context of these great events. She had done nothing to change many of her complicated and draining life situations. "In light of your revelations, did you pursue a practice of meditation to rekindle the glory of your experiences?" the teacher asked her. And on consideration, she replied, "No". Then the teacher said, "If you had carefully considered the implications of your spiritual experiences, as profound as they were, maybe you might be helping others with *their* healing processes by now. Remember, the victim can also tumble down the rabbit hole."

EVOLUTIONARY POINTER: The ways in which you live have to reflect the ecstatic unions you have experienced. Otherwise you remain bound by the consequences of your past that are simultaneously draining your attention and your ability to trust in your future.

Be the Witness of the Ego-Mind

MQ: As you create your own practice of stillness meditation, the good news is that if you have no experience with this discipline, you may be in a better position than someone who has been 'practicing' for years. Often what the ego calls 'an interest in meditation' obscures a strategy to give yourself and those around you a false impression of authenticity.

P: The unhealthy-ego doesn't want me to learn how to meditate correctly?

MQ: No, not in the least. It calls 20 minutes of shifting and scratching with your eyes closed, a meditation. The ego-mind's sole purpose in life is to support your thought-based sense of self. If you begin to only observe your thoughts and subsequently remain unresponsive to their demands that you move, what becomes of the ego's dominion over your poor soul? If you see that the ideations of the ego-mind are not entirely who you are, it loses command of you because now you clearly see you have choices that you didn't have before.

EVOLUTIONARY POINTER: The ego-mind is unable to face the inevitability of its own demise in your awakening or in your physical death. Yet, *you* can be with both in great confidence.

P: The objectivity of the thinker ultimately reveals the impotence of the unhealthy-ego.

MQ: Yes. And the ego knows this, too. Therefore, by disregarding its rants and raves to always be moving during your meditation practice, your attention rests instead upon that which has always been right in front of you... *pure stillness.*

Meditation and No Attention to Thinking

MQ: In Chapter Five, we discussed *conditioned attention to thinking* as the state most prevalent in humanity. This is the un-awakened state in which the thoughts present in awareness are generally taken to mean something about the thinker. The way in which an awakened person relates to the content of his mind is through *awakened attention to thinking*. This is to be fully at ease, regardless of what thoughts happen to be present in awareness. Awakened attention to thinking offers freedom from the constant struggle with the mind. Awakened attention to thinking allows you to pick and choose from the thoughts that are arising in your awareness, selecting only those that will help manifest your intention to evolve. In one way or another, every awakened person has passed from paying *conditioned attention* to *no attention* to *awakened attention* to thinking.

P: Therefore, to move from *conditioned attention* to thinking to *awakened attention* to thinking I must first practice *no attention* to thinking.

MQ: Exactly. And stillness meditation teaches you how to do

this.

P: By facing the busyness of my mind in the controlled environment of stillness meditation, I can then reinterpret the effects of my culture on my thoughts when the meditation is over and I am engaging in daily activities.

MQ: Yes. You can do this by learning to pay *no attention* to the content of your mind in stillness meditation. In practice you get to see that the thinker is not just the thoughts. This frees you from an unconscious identity with the mind.

EVOLUTIONARY POINTER: No attention to thinking bridges the gap between the un-awakened life and the awakened life.

MQ: *No attention* to thinking begins by sitting perfectly still. It is the art of releasing your focus from all thoughts, feelings and sensations regardless of their nature, persistence, or promise.

P: In order to develop clarity on the flow of my thoughts, I have to first let go of them all.

MQ: Yes, just as every awakened person has done.

EVOLUTIONARY POINTER: Meditation teaches you how to recognize the unreasonable fears and desires of the ego-mind in your daily life so that you can just *let them be*.

MQ: When you recall your origin of oneness in meditation, you also display an unusually high level of balance and stability in everyday life. Such a perspective does not make you immune from pain or suffering, but you are free from the constant battering of the neurotic mind. Being truly skilled in the art of meditation leads to a life of great peace.

P: Always. The reason I ask, is that I know several people who have been meditating for years who have lives that are still quite messy, if you know what I mean?

MQ: *Messy* means that there is still much unneeded emotional and psychological suffering?

P: Yes.

MQ: This is a common problem that occurs because the ego's dharma tells us that meditation is the great cure all and that this practice can heal your shadow. In Chapter Two, we defined shadow as the aspects of yourself that you have denied or repressed that show up as painful emotional responses to external stimuli.

EVOLUTIONARY POINTER: Meditation does not cure your shadow, nor is it supposed to.

MQ: To meditate is to disregard everything that is arising in your awareness. But, everything includes any shadow you might have, too. Therefore, people who meditate regularly can also have very messy lives. The problem is that during meditation, they are disregarding aspects of themselves that they have *already* denied in the waking state. Let's say you deny you are an angry person and you create a shadow with that repression. In other words, subjective anger is made into 'its' anger. Then, as you project your shadow in a futile attempt to be rid of it, you may encounter angry people all around you, or you may experience the world as an angry place. Subsequently, as a symptom of your shadow, you suffer from bouts of depression. Consequently, if sadness or anger arises in your meditation, you will disregard it there, because that is what you are supposed to do with everything that arises in your meditation. But, if that appearance of sadness or anger is a symptom of your shadow and you continue to disregard it in your meditation *and* in your everyday life, the symptoms of that shadow will only get worse. So in some cases, meditation can make your shadow worse.

P: I remember this earlier quote from Ken Wilber in regard to the shadow and Freudian Ego:

"…try transcending the ego before properly owning it, and watch the shadow grow."

MQ: Therefore, as you develop your practice of stillness meditation, ensure that you are also paying attention to the arising of your emotions *before* and *after* your practice. You do this to see if they are a reflection of your shadow. If this is the case, then you can follow the instructions in Chapter Two to heal those symptoms[8].

Disregarding a Founding Thought

MQ: Before we come to the instructions in stillness meditation, imagine for a moment that you are listening to a world-famous classical guitarist in a Gothic cathedral in Europe. You are completely at ease and your attention is resting lightly on the sense of rightness of the moment. Suddenly a thought such as this appears – *I must make a bank deposit!* This is a *founding thought*. And if you're not in touch with who is paying attention, when such a thought pops into your awareness, its presence can initiate a long series of other thoughts. So, there you are in a beautiful cathedral with a melody of strings reverberating through the granite arches. What do you do with this founding thought? Do you expand on it, following it as far as it goes? Do you start thinking about how much money you have, how much you want to put in the bank, if that deposit will be cash or checks, where the nearest branch might be, the name of your favorite clerk and so on? Do you pull out your organizer and write down a to-do? Do you immediately stand up and leave for the bank?

P: No, not at all.

MQ: That's correct. You calmly witness the presence of the *founding thought* and then, effortlessly glide your attention beyond its edge, back to the object of your awareness – the rightness of that very moment.

EVOLUTIONARY POINTER: Your natural ability to be aware of a *founding thought*, but not run with it, means that you are already in touch with the *observer* or the *witness* of your thoughts.

MQ: Knowing this helps you stabilize your practice. Additionally, the conditioned mind uses flashes of insight to get you to ramble off in thinking, or even to stop meditating and jot down some notes. Be confident that you can release all such ideas. They are already attracted to your awareness and they will appear again in your mind later, after your meditation.

Stillness Meditation

MQ: Stillness meditation is to be okay with what 'is'. In stillness meditation, there is nothing *to do* as you come to rest in that present moment, as the *one* who knows no need to judge.

EVOLUTIONARY POINTER: Stillness meditation occurs when there is no movement of the body.

P: Does stillness meditation require effort?

MQ: Sometimes it does and sometimes it does not. Meditation can occur spontaneously. And when it does, all you have to do is gently relax and pay attention. Should this not be your experience, however, then you may need to make a little effort. Presence sometimes takes a little practice. Making effort in the context of meditation, is to allow resistance to practice to become another object in awareness, so that you may disregard that, too. Struggle with resistance and it wins. *Effort*, in the context of this specific instruction, means remaining still so that you don't start moving your body again. The only effort is toward maintaining physical stillness.

P: What if my mind is busy. Should I try to stop my thoughts?

MQ: Stillness meditation is not about trying to stop your thoughts, pushing your thoughts away, replacing your thoughts, or becoming aware of the gaps between your thoughts. It is not about focusing on the sensations of the body, watching a candle, repeating a mantra, praying, counting your breaths or focusing on the gaps between your breaths.

P: Yet, these practices can be helpful as I prepare for complete stillness.

MQ: Yes, of course, they are all valuable skills. But, as you begin this practice of simple stillness, you are learning to be with your body, emotions and thoughts, and the many requests for you to be anything else but still. Being with *what is*, in stillness meditation, is your only challenge. Stillness meditation is to move safely beyond the reach of the lesser-mind, for a little while, at least. Your capacity to disregard any demands to move also implies that you are the master of your body-mind.

P: But, surely I must be in control of my body!

MQ: Stillness meditation shows you just how much your mind controls your body, how the ego keeps us in flight from *what is*, from the present moment, from now, from the consequences of our actions in the past, and from our thoughts of the future. The ego-mind keeps you running away from yourself until you can run no more – death. In meditation, you notice just how hard the ego in you tries to prevent you from sitting still. Therefore, it is important to know that you are in charge of yourself as opposed to the ego-mind being in charge of you. When you are able to sit perfectly still for ten, twenty, sixty minutes or more, then your presence is the dominant force of your body-mind – and not the ego's. This is good to know!

Sanjeev's Story: I was once invited to teach stillness meditation at a Sikh temple. After the class was finished, a young man approached me with a question. Sanjeev had a happy marriage and a successful career as a journalist with a major newspaper, so undoubtedly he possessed a high degree of personal power and initiative. He said that he enjoyed meditation but found it impossible to sit still for very long. I asked him to remember if he was ever brought to a point of great irritation and frustration in a situation, in the office with a co-worker or a superior, or perhaps while driving, that took all of his personal willpower to not respond with anger, or even physical action. He pondered for a moment and then described a few instances. I then asked him what he did with the thoughts that were pushing him to react with outrage or even brute force. He said that he was able to control his response, despite the presence of thoughts, emotions, and justifications, because such an outbreak would have not been at all appropriate. I then asked him to relate his obvious ability to manage his actions in these situations to when he was attempting to sit still in meditation. Now he realized that he possessed the power to pay no attention to certain thoughts, and disregard others. In this knowing, I suggested that he return to his practice of meditation with great confidence.

An Instruction in Stillness Meditation

MQ: The following is an outline of the instructions for stillness meditation:

1)   Remain totally motionless.
2)   Start with ten minutes per day, working up to at least an hour.
3)   Sit comfortably on a chair or on the floor with pillows.
4)   Keep your back straight, but not taut.
5)   Your eyes can be closed or partially open.
6)   Breathe as you normally would – *be the breath.*
7)   Release all affirmations and mindfulness exercises.
8)   Draw no conclusions about the quality of your meditation

during practice.

9) Be the observer of your thoughts.

10) Realize the observer of no thought and *be no thought*.

1) Remain totally motionless, just as Buddha sat still under the Bodhi tree:

MQ: Stillness meditation speaks not of the goal, but of the practice. This is the *single most essential* aspect of this practice. Therefore, it is frequently the most misunderstood instruction of stillness meditation.

EVOLUTIONARY POINTER: The name *stillness meditation* is your first indication of the importance of maintaining a physically still body.

MQ: There is to be no movement at all. Movement and stillness meditation are mutually exclusive. Because it is impossible to control the mind, the only option you have is to control your body. Therefore, if there is movement, there cannot be stillness meditation. So, when you settle into your stance of stillness, there is to be no twitching, shifting, fidgeting, sighing, laughing, crying, grimacing, swallowing or paying attention to the sensations of the body. Note: The voice of the unhealthy-ego says that complete physical immobility is impossible and it invents all sorts of reasons for you not to remain still. These can range from the mythical fly on your nose, to the *kundalini*[10] snake in your spine, the monkey on your back, your chakras[11] pulsating light, or the fact that your mouth naturally waters so you that you have to keep swallowing. Ignore all of these distractions during your meditation. With just a little practice, you even lose the awareness that there is a 'you' who is being still.

> EVOLUTIONARY POINTER: Rest evenly in the stillness beyond physical movement.

2) Frequency:

MQ: Start by sitting for ten or fifteen minutes each day. First thing in the morning is best, simply because the mind tends to be quieter at that time. The goal is to eventually be motionless in practice for an hour or so. Make a point of meditating as often as possible. Note: The unhealthy-ego is the one who arranges your daily schedules so that you are too busy, too tired or have too many interruptions to sustain a regular practice. It does not want *you* to meditate. When you say, "I *can't* meditate," that 'I' is not *you* speaking; it's the ego.

3) Sit comfortably on a chair or on pillows on the floor:

MQ: Pick a comfortable place to meditate. This can be on a chair, a mat or pillows on the floor. Be patient and take your time to find a seating arrangement that is most conducive to extended periods of physical stillness. If your leg falls asleep, all that means is that you are cutting off the blood supply. Simply raise your cushions a little. Once you have the right sitting position and combination of pillows, you will find that you can quickly settle into that pose every time. Note: Stillness meditation is not about 'pushing through the pain' or 'sitting in the pain'. The key to a successful practice is taking your time to figure out a comfortable position so you can meditate and not just torture yourself. If, however, you have been diagnosed with back injury or nerve damage, you may need to apply a little extra effort to easing your attention from that area of your body. The ego-mind concocts physical pains so you are never still for more than a few minutes. Disregard its suggestions to move. Moving during practice is not stillness meditation, it's just movement.

4) Keep your back comfortably straight:

MQ: Sit in an upright position, keeping your back comfortably straight but not taut. This may take some trial and error to get it right. You do not want your back to be too tight and erect, nor do you want to slouch. Find a comfortable medium that suits you. If possible, it is best to not lean against a chair back or a wall. Allow your face, shoulders and entire body to relax. Rest your hands lightly in your lap. Note: The unhealthy-ego often employs drowsiness or tries to convince you that you are falling backwards, forwards, or listing to one side to make you stop meditating.

5) Eyes closed or partially open:

MQ: Relax your eyes. If they close, that is fine. If they remain partially open, that is fine, too. There is no need to watch a candle, a stone, or other objects. Note: The unhealthy-ego is going to tell you that it's too bright or too dark or that you should stop because you have nothing to focus your attention on. Focusing on *no-thing* except being still is the whole point.

6) Breathe normally:

MQ: Breathe normally through your nose. Release any specific attention to the breath and all breathing exercises. There is no need to count your breaths or focus on the gap between them, the point at which the airflow changes direction, or the temperature difference between exhaling and inhaling. Just breathe. Be just the breathing itself. Realize that there is no subject who is breathing, only the breathing. Note: The ego uses a fear of apnea, which is cessation of breathing and hypoxia, which is under-breathing, as reasons for you to hyperventilate and stop your practice.

7) Release all affirmations and mindfulness routines:

MQ: Allow all thinking and non-thinking exercises, visualizations, positive pictures, sacred places, chanting, and all objects of mental and emotional desire to fall away. Note: The conditioned mind always wants you to be running some mental routine and as long as you agree to that, it wins your attention.

8) Draw no conclusions about your meditation during your practice:

MQ: The time to interpret your meditation is *after* the event. *Not during*. The time to draw conclusions about your practice is *after* your practice. *Not during*.

P: Did you repeat this on purpose?

MQ: Yes. The reason I said this twice is so that you will understand that the time to think about your meditation is *after* the event. *Not during*. Therefore, as you engage in practice, don't worry about how you are doing, because that's thinking. You can forget about whether it is good, bad, hard, easy or somewhere in between, because that's paying attention to your thoughts. The quantity and quality of your thoughts has no bearing on your ability to meditate, because that's all thinking. While in practice, those qualifications, as well as all your opinions about those qualifications, are completely irrelevant. Drawing conclusions about your meditation during your meditation is not meditation; that's thinking. Therefore, all estimations and commentaries about how well or poorly you are doing *during* your meditation can safely be disregarded. *No attention* to thinking is the only 'routine'.

EVOLUTIONARY POINTER: Proclaiming advancement during stillness meditation is only a sign of deterioration.

MQ: You can, of course, share your experiences after your meditation practice ends. In fact, that is one of the tools of interpretation: learning to think and speak with great clarity about the subjective realization you had during your meditation. But, think about it and elaborate on it *after*, not during, your practice. Since the primary role of the ego-mind is self-protection in thinking, your meditation practice is to let go of control of the thought process completely, but for a short time. Let it run wild and observe. Pay no attention to where it goes. If your mind feels busy, let it be. If your body feels uncomfortable, let that be. If you feel as if you are having a great meditation or a horrible meditation or if you are unsure, let that be also. Judge not your experience during meditation, no matter the experience. Don't be distracted by bliss, joy or ecstasy either, because ultimately, those are just experiences.

EVOLUTIONARY POINTER: Realize that if you didn't draw the conclusion that your experience in this very moment is not exactly the awakened life, it would be.

MQ: The ego-mind also emerges from consciousness.

9) **Realize the observer of your thoughts:**
MQ: Meditation hones a preexisting skill to recognize a founding thought and to let it be. Your inherent ability to be aware of a founding thought, but not run with it, means that you are already in touch with the observer of your thoughts. In the practice of stillness meditation you are getting in touch with that observer, instead of being exclusively focused on all those wonderful and necessary objects in your awareness. This immeasurable context that is endowing you with the ability to perceive its serenity, is also already *full and complete*. This is the vast depth of Presence in which everything already appears. There is no need for adjustments, alterations or additions.

EVOLUTIONARY POINTER: The observer is concealed behind the compulsion to constantly roam in thinking.

MQ: The observer *includes*, but is not defined by or attached to the struggle with the thinking mind. This serene and subtle essence is your *stance of stillness*. In the complete absence of opinions about *what is*, the meditative state unveils. It is so obvious you don't have to be constantly looking for it or answering the ego when it asks, "Is this it, is this it, is this it, are we there yet, are you enlightened yet, are we enlightened yet?" Be the observer of those questions, because the observer is already free and already *one*.

EVOLUTIONARY POINTER: Your job is to simply sit, don't move and discover *who is observing*.

---

10) **Realize the observer of no thought and *be no thought.***
MQ: All that remains is the gentle awareness of the observer. When that silent watcher is only aware of stillness, the observer and that which is being observed unite. When the *subjective* (the silent watcher) and the *objective* (the no-thing of simple stillness) merge, when you, the observer, become one with the observed thought-lessness, your original state of oneness explodes resplendent as the unequivocal *Allness of Being*.

EVOLUTIONARY POINTER: You are beyond form and formlessness, yet include all of that.

MQ: When you allow your attention to rest on that inclusiveness, you realize that *you* are that vast *Suchness* in which all experiences arise and then fall away. *You* and boundless space are One without detection. That you were not this in the past and that you will always be this in the future is recalled as your eternal home. This is your own most intimate Self. With extended diligence in practice you, too, may realize the profound implication of these words from Ramana Maharshi: *"That which is not present in deep dreamless sleep is not real."*

P: Thank you.

MQ: You're welcome.

Wisdom and Emptiness

> EVOLUTIONARY POINTER: Wisdom is the ability to understand emptiness.[12]

P: Ultimate wisdom is unattainable.

MQ: Yes. And by continually reinterpreting your reality, the paradox of volitional wisdom places the future of humanity in your hands.

Beloved
Let us know
What light first saw and said
When it discovered
You[13]

1   Francois de La Rochefoucauld (1613–1680).

2   By Patricia Schultz. Workman Publishing Company, 2003.

3   Copyright – CELF, Worldwide. 2005.

4   Andrew Cohen (www.andrewcohen.org).

5   A highly advanced state of consciousness.

6   The Kosmos includes the physiophere, the biosphere, the noosphere, and the theosphere.

7   The Dalai Lama

8   For an in-depth study of shadow and meditation see, Integral Spirituality by Ken Wilber, Published by Integral Books, 2007.

9   New York Times, March, 2008.

10 Corporal energy that is coiled up at the base of the spine.

11 Energy centers in and out of the body.

12 Ken Wilber.

13 Hafiz – Great Sufi Master.

Chapter 12

THE FOURTH INSIGHT

RELATE AS YOUR FULL POTENTIAL

"The confidence which we have in ourselves gives birth to much of that which we have in others."[1]

A New World

MQ: With renewed objectivity on previously hidden habituation, we realize that the possibilities presented in this final chapter are not simply wishful thinking, but a tangible reality available to us as we walk an uncommon path.

The Fourth Insight is a spontaneous emergence. It supplants a formerly conditioned trance with the sweet intimacies of freedom from all unnecessary emotional and psychological suffering. The appearance of the Fourth Insight is entirely dependent upon the extent of our engagement with the preceding three Insights. The Fourth Insight encompasses every aspect of our lives. Its emergence becomes the foundation for our engagement with other people as *living examples* of the infinite creative potential inherent in each of us.

> EVOLUTIONARY POINTER: The Fourth Insight reveals the possibility of a new world.

MQ: As the Fourth Insight unfolds, our reasons for *being* and *becoming* are strikingly dissimilar from those who are still confined by conditioned perspectives and the excessive limitations of the ego. The evolution of consciousness and culture is of primary, yet not exclusive, significance to us. We express our eternal motives to the best of our abilities in our work and in our relevant relationships. Sharing our realizations of the Fourth Insight with other people creates the possibility of manifesting a new reality on a global scale. This new way of interacting confirms our availability to merge with, and contribute to, the unity consciousness which is just beginning to become visible in our world.

P: There exist interactions that are already leading toward a new reality?

MQ: Yes. Though in their infancy, the unified efforts of highly aware individuals offer great hope of a way of life which transcends and includes both the functional and the dysfunctional aspects of all previous levels of development. These associations promise new ways of *being* and *becoming* in harmonious community beyond personal and culturally-based conflict.

P: Has an adequate shift in consciousness taken place in our world yet? Are we now in a position to adequately impact the grave issues we now face by sustaining these five conditions for sufficient periods of time?

MQ: Not yet.

P: Are we even close to the home stretch?

MQ: No, not by a long shot. For example, take a look at *The New York Times* bestselling Non-Fiction and Advice book sections. These lists provide a curious snapshot of where the millions of people in the most evolved country on the planet are currently placing their attention. Recent bestsellers reflect a great interest in business, politics, and getting what you want in regards to money, love, and specific subjective states of awareness. Therefore, though development through all levels is most important and unavoidable, we are a far cry from a new earth!

The solutions to the problems we are facing appear when hundreds and thousands of people are capable of uniting in a state in which the following five conditions are simultaneously present:

1) There is objectivity on the separate sense-of-self and the culturally-created-self.
2) There is a conscious release of the limited topics and agendas of the ego-mind.
3) There is surrender of attention, for a time, to the pure intentions of the union.
4) Actions are taken primarily for the sake of humanity and secondarily for personal gain.
5) Actions occur without attachment to the outcome.

MQ: Such unity emerges as *collective individualism* – this is you and I together as One Self in an awakened relationship, acting in harmony with the energy and intelligence that created the universe, for the sake of all sentient beings at all levels of development.

Awakened Relationships

MQ: With the emergence of the Fourth Insight, we are drawn to and naturally attract those with whom we share the magnificent vision of a new world. Since our decision-making structures are based on a *single* hierarchy of values, which consistently includes a *conscious competent value* in its primary position, we are capable of directing our clarity of intention to sustain an awakened life and to share that with others. Such unions of evolved individuals are called *awakened relationships*. Awakened relationships greatly advance the collective consciousness of our planet for the benefit of current and future residents. Awakened relationships begin to form between two or more *whole* or *complete* individuals and are characterized by joy, enthusiasm, respect, devotion, creativity, autonomy, cooperation, service, passion, power, and wholesome direction.

> **EVOLUTIONARY POINTER:** Awakened relationships emerge with other people who recognize us by the same light that is shining in their own courageous hearts.

MQ: When awakened relationships smile upon us, *awakened love* becomes a reality, too. By its own nature, awakened love is unlimited, absolutely fulfilled and fulfilling. Awakened love arises when the inherited motives for 'exchanging love' are transcended and included in our most important interactions. With awakened love, all things are possible – from peace in our homes to peace in the world! Awakened love is visceral, physically expressed, and exists as a deep sense of *knowing* that permeates all of our interactions. Where awakened love flows, it greatly surpasses the levels of closeness, bonding and caring in all former relationships.

> **EVOLUTIONARY POINTER:** Awakened love emerges as the capacity to evolve our consciousness by contributing to the spiritual development of humanity.

MQ: Participants in awakened relationships are fully self-expressed, self-sufficient and they seamlessly combine agency[4], judgment, empathy, commitment, communion, spontaneity and sacrifice in service of a higher purpose. An awakened relationship is a limitless well of resourcefulness, reaching far beyond the capacity and expectations of the individuals who are involved – often in the most delightful, challenging and surprising ways. The contribution of each individual in an awakened relationship is fully acknowledged and nourished by the other participants for being *exactly* who they are. To openly give and receive this kind of acceptance is extraordinary. And, of course, there is one more facet of awakened relationships, which is simply amazing...

EVOLUTIONARY POINTER: Awakened relationships are absolutely free from *personal* conflict. This reveals the possibility of perfection in the human form, right in your own home.

MQ: The joyous relief of relationships free from personal anguish acts as evidence that an advancement in awareness has occurred and also evidence of the emergence of the Fourth Insight. As mentioned in the Introduction, Eckhart Tolle said that a sign of a true shift in consciousness is that your relationships with other human beings become peaceful and that *"conflict dissolves in your presence"*.

A Continual State of Resolution

MQ: Awakened relationships are always in a state of complete resolution. There are never any 'loose ends' or unsettled matters between the partners. In fact, the possibility of personal conflict no longer even exists. Consider *that* for potential!

P: You mention this throughout our conversation here. Why are relationships without personal anguish so entirely possible?

MQ: Awakened relationships are devoid of strife because of the communal objectivity of the unhealthy-ego by each of the partners. When this recognition is jointly present, the absence of all unnecessary emotional and psychological conflict is effortless. In fact, it is completely taken for granted. Also present in an awakened relationship is an advanced awareness, if not a complete absence of, shadow. Therefore, what we normally recognize as personal arguments, bickering, unhealthy competitiveness, negative self-consciousness, one-upmanship, breakdowns, unreasonable demands, flare-ups and temper tantrums are now thoroughly absent.

P: When the center of attention in our relationships shifts from ego to evolution, unnecessary suffering in those interactions ends.

MQ: Yes.

EVOLUTIONARY POINTER: Awakened people care *marginally more* about their partners, the state of their relationships, and the efforts and creations of those relationships than they do about their subjective experiences.

P: As a result, the partners in an awakened relationship do not need, nor wish, to position themselves strategically, spread rumors, gossip or feed off disparities in any way.

MQ: No, not in the least. Because an awakened relationship tends toward a state of continual resolution, the partners do not leverage any aspects of arising disagreements to project their shadows. Their interest and attention is on something far more significant than ridding themselves of pent-up feelings.

P: So, the persecutor, enabler, rescuer and the victim, at the personal level, disappear from those relevant relationships.

MQ: Yes indeed! They are transcended and included in our new understanding. This is why awakened relationships offer the possibility of creating a new world. The resolutions we seek can only exist when we interact for consistent periods of time in a context that is beyond the root of conflict — the notion of separateness — and at that same time completely share our life skills as unique individuals.

P: Otherwise, my partners and I are going to be consumed with the agendas of the unhealthy-ego and the fortification of our self-images.

MQ: Yes, continually and forever.

P: But, isn't divergence and disagreement necessary for growth in our relationships?

MQ: Yes, indeed it is, for development on an individual level as well as for the relationship itself. We will examine four instances in which growth at this level can occur in awakened relationships a little later in this chapter. Such divergences, however, are related to the *product* or *direction* of the relationship, or to a change in the level of *participation* of an individual, or to the *function* or *leadership* of a group. As we will discover, these variances have absolutely nothing to do with 'personal conflict'.

EVOLUTIONARY POINTER: *Necessary suffering* for the sake of humanity, between partners in awakened relationships, is not at all the same as the *unnecessary suffering* we have experienced in our relationship because of our unwitting attachment to the ego-mind.

MQ: It is vital to grasp that variances in awakened relationships are completely devoid of the exploitation that is commonly found in un-awakened relationships and the 'power-plays' and manipulative strategizing inherent in many business relationships. An awakened relationship exists on a completely different plane from those types of interactions at the level of ego-identity, therefore, no comparison is even possible.

P: Beyond the attachment to ego-identity we are all on the same wavelength!

MQ: Yes. And together we can make decisions for the sake of the *whole*.

EVOLUTIONARY POINTER: The emergence of awakened relationships calls for our willingness to trust in our partners and our individual decisions, as much as we trust in the process of life.

MQ: Awakened relationships are fully available to us as an indication of our genuine aspirations to be the transformation we want to see it in the world, and also as an indication that a shift in our subjective consciousness has actually occurred.

The Beginning of Awakened Relationships

P: As the Fourth Insight unfolds, do awakened relationships occur of their own accord?

MQ: Awakened relationships naturally appear when we consistently express ourselves in our long-term interactions as the *same unified individuals*, regardless of the former basis for those associations. And in other situations, with a little effort, awakened relationships are crafted between two or more willing individuals.

P: What do you mean by *willing*?

MQ: Willing to live an awakened life of authentic joy in the constant discovery and expression of potential. Willing to come together beyond the separate sense-of-self. Willing to let go of the ego-identity in the company of others. Willing to endure a little difficulty for the sake of the evolution of consciousness and culture and to allow continual development at the level of the individual, the relationship, and the joint purposes of those relationships.

EVOLUTIONARY POINTER: In awakened relationships we come together for the sake of others.

MQ: When we unite with other people in this context, we certainly leverage our past experiences to design and sustain those unions, but our primary objectives are not for personal gain, though the participants more often than not derive a great sense of individual satisfaction in the work they are doing and they can also earn a decent living.

P: And I am sure that awakened relationships are also light

hearted and fun...

MQ: Of course they are! Awakened relationships include all the familiar facets of normal human interactions. They do not preclude swapping cordial banter at the café, hanging out watching a movie with our families, or enjoying a good bottle of wine with some friends. Awakened relationships always invite *more* depth, *more* closeness, *more* caring, *more* compassion, *more* love, *more* sentiment, *more* pain, *more* grief and subsequently, *more* loss.

> EVOLUTIONARY POINTER: Awakened relationships introduce us to the fully-alive perspective of the human experience.

Acknowledging Perspectives

P: As the Fourth Insight suffuses our ways of being, does everybody we know acknowledge our passion for authenticity, trust, truth and responsibility? And do they respect our wishes to come together beyond personal conflict?

MQ: In many cases, yes. A subjective awareness of the infinite possibilities of human consciousness in togetherness with other people, however, does not necessarily imply a similar level of interest in this wonder by our peers.

> EVOLUTIONARY POINTER: There are always those who are more interested in preserving the old ways than in co-creating the *new*. You may be looking directly at the solution to what the Buddha called *duhkha*[2], while its hosts are completely unaware of their plight.

P: Despite our suggestions that alternative ways of being are indeed a tangible new reality, other people may wish to remain at their present levels of development.

MQ: This is true. With the unfolding of the Fourth Insight, we discover that we are living in a different world – one of limitless possibilities. Simply because this is our experience does not mean that others are also willing to embrace such dynamic clarity.

P: Therefore, it is not just that our worldview has shifted or that we see things in a different way?

MQ: No. We are living in a *new world* of infinite and incredible promise. Some people, however, are unwilling to give up their attachment to suffering or they are simply intimidated by our call to transparency. Their perspectives, therefore, are to be accepted, regardless of the personal consequences of doing so. Since we have all denied, at some time in our lives, the invitations of consciousness to evolve, we must embrace those who cannot even glimpse the new reality that is our world. Judgment implies that all interpretations are correct for those particular levels of development.

The Retriever's Story: A man took his new hunting dog out for the first time. The retriever seemed to be doing fine, but when a duck the man was hunting fell into the lake, the dog ran to the edge and stopped. He then proceeded to walk on the water, retrieving the duck and placing it back at his master's feet. The man was stunned. Later in the day, another duck fell in a river and the dog once again walked on the water to retrieve the bird. The hunter invited a friend along on a hunt the next day. Both men watched in silence as the retriever crossed over the water to the bird and returned with it safely. The hunter then said to his friend, "There is something unusual about this dog." His friend nodded fervently and said, "That's for sure. Your dog can't swim."[3]

P: As the Fourth Insight stabilizes in our awareness, do the wily tactics of the unhealthy-ego continue to disturb our new understanding?

MQ: Once we have reached this stage of our development, the ego-mind in us, and in other people, is fundamentally incapable of shaking the ground upon which we stand.

P: This is a wonderful relief.

MQ: Absolutely! The spontaneous emergence of the Fourth Insight implies that a profound shift has taken place at the level of consciousness. Because we see that there is no going back to the old ways, the uncommon path draws us forward, together with other people working on all levels of understanding, in the co-creation of a better way of being. As we express awakening potential in our most important interactions, we are aware of, yet completely undisturbed by, the movements of conditioning.

This gives us great confidence, especially when facing those who are blinded by their own evolution as beings with self-awareness. Because we no longer have an active interest in the plight of the unhealthy-ego, we communicate with the lesser-self in other people for shorter and shorter periods of time. We do this, not to belittle these individuals, but because we no longer understand the language of constraint. To us, it sounds as if these people are speaking in an ancient tongue.

P: We remember what it was to speak like this, but we no longer understand it?

MQ: The words we understand, but the compulsion to share them is now unintelligible to us!

Nonviolent Communications and Awakened Compassion
MQ: The manner in which we communicate amongst our relevant relationships reveals that the expression of *awakened compassion* for all humankind is possible.

EVOLUTIONARY POINTER: The consistency with which we access and share awakened compassion allows us to effortlessly disengage from conditioning in others without judgment, regret or karmic consequences.

MQ: This revitalized way of interacting is also known as *nonviolent communication*.

P: Therefore, the capacity to come together with other people in a setting that transcends and includes the ego-mind is the essential key to *compassionate conversation*?

MQ: Yes.

EVOLUTIONARY POINTER: Nonviolent communication is fully realized when the unseen forces of individual and collective conditioning are no longer manipulating us.

MQ: Nonviolent communication is described as a method of interacting in which we connect with the human spirit in another person. It is also a way of conversing in which the connection and the quality of speaking and listening are most important.

P: Does nonviolent communication also allow everyone's needs to be equally valued?

MQ: While the connection you make with the human spirit in another person is essential, whether everyone's needs are equally valued is not so important to the objectives of awakened relationships. The fact that everyone's needs are equally valued is not as critical as *who* is communicating and *who* is determining those needs. Is that *you* or the *ego-mind in you*? Being proficient in compassionate communication also means that you are accomplished at recognizing if it is only the ego in you or the ego in another person that is demanding that its needs be met. Awakened relationships are completely free from personal conflict because to be truly skilled at communicating nonviolently, implies that you are also capable of relegating personal needs to second place.

P: And to respond directly to the ego makes us accomplices to suffering?

MQ: Yes. This we discussed in the chapter about relationships. It is one reason why awakened people are incapable of communicating for very long with another individual who is lost in conditioned speaking.

P: Therefore, our capacity to infuse our dialogues with awakened compassion is crucial?

MQ: Yes. This is especially true when it becomes clear that it is only the ego-mind in the other person that is interested in being heard.

P: And what happens in such cases?

MQ: It is only a matter of time before the responses of an awakened person — sincerely based on nonviolent communications — are perceived as being *violent* by the ego in the other person.

EVOLUTIONARY POINTER: A truly nonviolent dialogue with an awakened person is labeled by the ego as violent so that it may deny the possibilities for liberation being presented in that conversation to its host.

MQ: And to defend its position of restriction, the ego interprets the requests of the awakened person for its host as irrational, unreasonable or impossible. Its predictable reactions also reveal that the ego only pretends to admire and support compassionate communication. What is mostly going on in ego-based interactions is a feeding session for the self-images of the individuals involved. This is far removed from the truth of nonviolent communications.

P: As a result, a person who is unknowingly tethered to an ego-identity always defends personal conflict in a relevant relationship?

MQ: Not exactly. The human spirit is capable of great love. It is the unhealthy-ego in that person that portrays personal conflict in relevant relationships as acceptable.

P: A subtle, yet profound distinction.

Awakened Love is Perfectly Conditional

MQ: Awakened relationships emerge when we care more about the spiritual development of other people than we do about the 'personal' requirements or challenges of those engagements. Therefore, in such relationships, love is vast and deep, yet only finite amounts of the ego-mind's arguments for limitation are tolerated. Though the level of concern we feel for other people is profound, the degree of caring is not unconditional. The compassion of truly awakened people is unlimited. But, they choose to limit their inter-actions in relevant relationships when it is clear that an exclusive identity with ego in the other person has yet to be transcended and included. Therefore, they do not feed or create more suffering for that individual.

P: But the splendor of unconditional love is rarely expounded in this way!

MQ: That's because the ego's dharma tells us: *Unconditional love implies that unnecessary suffering is to be repeatedly forgiven.*

EVOLUTIONARY POINTER: Awakened people are wholly incapable of tolerating repeated transgressions at the level of ego-mind as the perpetrator or the victim.

MQ: As you can imagine, the lesser-self dislikes the truth of awakened compassion. The self-righteous pleas of the misbehaving ego for 'compassionate' understanding are led by two of the most popular slogans of its dharma: *'Do not judge'* and *'We are all equal'*. To justify its addiction to unneeded anguish, the covert ego constantly seeks absolution for its own wrongdoings by not reproaching the irrational behavior of others.

P: So, the ego assumes that awakened people should maintain resolute empathy for all un-awakened people at all times?

MQ: Yes. And, make no mistake, those who have awakened do

just that! In fact, it's one of their reasons for *being*. But, let's be very clear about something: The transmission of awakened compassion is not what the unhealthy-ego wants nor cares about. It only wants to be placated without any requirements that its host evolves beyond the current level of development. As we saw in Chapter Seven, the ego revels in idiot compassion, simply because that form of concern is devoid of any requests for resolution and responsibility.

P: I can see that from the ego's position, the expression of *awakened compassion* is often interpreted as being judgmental, aloof and uncaring.

MQ: I'm afraid so. After years of suckling on idiot compassion, the unhealthy aspect of the ego often responds with belligerence when the stabilization of our awakenings removes its favorite source of sustenance – worthy opponents with whom to do battle with over a never-ending list of personal issues and an ear for its superfluous afflictions.

EVOLUTIONARY POINTER: Have no doubt – awakened love is perfectly conditional.

MQ: Though awakened people judge others by the level of awareness as evidenced in their choice of words and actions, they do not condemn those at lower stages of development. For they too, had to pass through many degrees of evolution in order to release and express their full potential. The Fourth Insight reveals that the transmission of awakened love heals all those who listen, but it does not affirm those who are unwilling to let go of unnecessary suffering, even though we may care deeply for their predicament. It is important to allow those rights of passage to all and in their own timeframe. As it says in the Bible, *"Come after me, and let the dead bury their dead"*[7]. But it is also important not to have your precious vitality exhausted in the process.

The Purpose of Awakened Relationships

P: How do you summarize the purpose of awakened relationships?

EVOLUTIONARY POINTER: Awakened relationships stimulate effects that are of primary benefit to humanity and of secondary benefit to the individuals involved.

MQ: The point of awakened relationships is to allow for the emergence of an *endeavor* or *creation*, which serves humanity first. The endeavors or creations of awakened relationships are concepts, processes, services or physical items that emerge from the unified efforts of the participants. Such outputs are directly related to the evolution of awareness and the welfare of humankind. In the context of the development of human awareness and potential, such endeavors and creations currently take the forms of conscious networking groups, awakened philanthropic efforts, university-based and public educational seminars, and a vast array of other media in the field of conscious evolution. Beside traditional conscious learning retreats or integrally informed think tanks, the creations of awakened relationships also include teleconferencing and online video series that suit this genre of development at the level of awareness. There are also many such creations currently being developed and implemented in the area of medicine, law, politics, art, and also in the areas of awakened parenting and awakened business practices.

P: I can see how all of these efforts are the beginning of a new world.

MQ: Yes, the beginning. The early pioneers in these areas provide much evidence that it is possible to come together with other people for the sake of humanity, even though a financial base for this type of work has yet to fully stabilize. In other words, it's hard to make money when your sole focus is the evolution of human potential. But, we are working on that, too!

P: So the possibilities for the endeavors or creations of an awakened relationship are limitless.

MQ: Yes. Which bring us to the first instance of divergence in awakened relationships. This emerges because of the intimate concern of the participants for the endeavors, creations, or products of their interactions. Therefore, disagreements in awakened relationships can arise in regard to how the efforts or outputs can best be designed, explained, branded, promoted, delivered, sustained, integrated or evolved.

P: The conflict is not related to the subjective states of the partners, how one person might view the 'quality' of the interaction, nor is the anguish in defense of the cherished opinions of any one of the participants.

MQ: No, not in the least. The divergence is in the best interest of the productivity of the relationship and how that can be most efficiently directed in the service of humanity. The second form of conflict can appear when an individual has succumbed to the limitation of deeply embedded conditioning. This often emerges because of the continual development that is required for awakened relationships to sustain itself. For instance, an individual might have difficulty working with or they might completely disown the healthy manifestations of male compassion – this is the voice that requires discipline, sharpness, ruthless compassion and tough love. Or, an individual might have problems with the healthy manifestation of the voice of female compassion – this is the voice that nurtures, cares and embraces without restrictions or requirements. At the outset, the person might see the voice of male compassion as uncaring and even uncompassionate, until they realize the necessity and beauty of this part of the self. In the case of the voice of female compassion, the person may see it as too weak or ineffective. In this period of development and acceptance, a certain degree of disruption can occur in the group's energy.

The third form of conflict in awakened relationships appears as a group function is being refined because of expansion or contraction. The restructuring of teams often interrupts comfortable patterns and compels new learning curves. Despite these difficulties, awakened groups can be surprisingly fluid, so organizational changes can be implemented with a high degree of cooperation despite the stress of role redefinitions and evolving mandates.

P: Is the way in which disagreement is approached in awakened relationships different from 'conflict resolution' at the level of an un-awakened relationship?

MQ: Yes, it is very different. Challenges in awakened relation-ships are attended to immediately. Groups and sub-groups that are comprised of awakened relationships are wholly capable of uncov-ering the core of the issues at hand and resolving them in a most direct and efficient manner. As the road to resolution is navigated, participants frequently have strong feelings and also sense the emotional states of their partners.

But, since the lesser-self no longer needs to be affirmed, and conditioned beliefs no longer need to be defended, each of the participants manifest their intentions to investigate and transcend conflict for the sake of the union and output of their community. The discussions of resolution take place in an environment which is jointly sustained in conscious stability by each of the individuals.

P: Even though strong emotional states exist subjectively, the partners no longer manifest these sentiments as the painful symptoms of 'personal' conflict.

MQ: Yes. That level of ego-based wrangling in our interactions is simply gone.

'What You Do' versus 'How You Feel'

MQ: In awakened relationships, objectivity on the presence of emotion as shadow, or not, as the case may be, empowers the realization that *how we feel* is slightly less important than *what we do*. What we do is the only thing that matters to the co-creation of a new society. We won't know what a new world feels like until it is co-

415

created.

P: But, without denying any aspect of our humanity?

MQ: Yes, of course, without denying any of our feelings. In awakening, it's not *what we think* or *how we feel* that really and truly matters, it's how we treat other people. Do you think that while the world-renowned spiritual master, J.K. Krishnamurti, was on one of his extended speaking tours, his audience members truly cared about his subjective emotional states as he was giving one of his many great presentations? Please be honest.

P: I would say that there may have been a passive caring for his wellbeing. But, a deep, critical concern on behalf of the audience about his subjective emotional state — as long as it did not interfere with his glorious teaching — I think not.

MQ: I admire your honesty.

EVOLUTIONARY POINTER: When it's time for darshan[5], all eyes rest on what the master says and does, not particularly how he or she happens to be feeling in that very moment.

MQ: What we *do*, therefore, as awakened people is far more important than how we happen to feel when we are taking actions in any given situation. As we embrace the blessings of the Fourth Insight, we find that the eternal motives and intentions by which we express ourselves together with other kindred spirits are no longer about the ideas and dreams of the little-self.

P: I can imagine this is of great comfort?

MQ: To no longer be trapped in the images of our former selves, yes indeed it is! This is what Lama Ole Nydal, founder of over 500 Diamond Way Buddhist centers, said:

EVOLUTIONARY POINTER: *"I hardly have any private or complicated stuff in my life. I seem to have deeply promised to express certain activities when I'm in this world and these I joyfully fulfill. Protecting and developing beings on all levels, is constantly on my mind."*[6]

MQ: The *un-awakened* see suffering, poverty, global warming and terrorism as indirectly related to who they are, and ask with great empathy, "What can I do about this, I'm only one person?" The *awakened* see suffering, poverty, global warming and terrorism, as essential aspects of who they are and understanding the possibilities of awakened relationships, declare with great empathy, "What *can't* I do about this, together with other people?"

Natural Hierarchies

P: How does a leadership structure emerge in larger groups of awakened relationships?

MQ: Awakened relationships are based on a natural hierarchy of leadership, which simply means that the most evolved person leads. Leadership structures are constructed according to levels of consciousness and the reality of each person's life experiences and skills. This allows a natural chain of command to evolve that is based on the development of the awareness of each individual.

P: This is quite the opposite of imposed hierarchies that are currently predominant and necessary in our world; such as those enforced by psychological, emotional and physical force, intellectual capacity, financial wherewithal or political power.

MQ: Indeed it is. For example, government by these methods is a natural level of development beyond which we can evolve. It is only from stable democracies that are based on unnatural hierarchies, that we springboard to a more evolved form of administration. This brings us to the fourth form of divergence in awakened relationships, which appears when a new leader or management structure is emerging in core or satellite groups. While such situations can affect the mission of the entire organization, the affected director ensures that the progress and evolution of the team and its endeavors are more important than their own particular role as the leader. In a context of *nonviolent communications,* an existing leader navigates the evolving management hierarchy for the best interests of the group. In this way, an affected director can graciously step aside or will enter their revised role as efficiently as possible, and without the need to defend the self-image of their former role. Because of their level of dedication to working together *as one,* the entire team structure can quickly return to its focus and purpose, which is the evolution of humanity's potential.

EVOLUTIONARY POINTER: An awakened master is always overjoyed to find a student who is more evolved than they are.

Three Experiences of Collective Consciousness

MQ: The Fourth Insight reveals to us the glorious possibilities of awakened relationships, awakened love, awakened compassion, nonviolent communications, natural hierarchies, and the fundamental absence of personal conflict. This enables the basis for collective individualism, which is the emergence of the One Self, the experience of consciousness in an inter-subjective context that is shared by many.

EVOLUTIONARY POINTER: Collective individualism is the wholly conscious experience of the 'Higher We' in action for the sake of humanity.

MQ: In awakened relationships your partners are not seen as separate, but as unique expressions of the same consciousness that is you. You and your colleagues are *as one*. Because of this, when two or more whole individuals come together in awakened relationships, a state of collective consciousness becomes apparent. This state arises naturally or it can also be driven by the intention of the participants. The ability to participate in such collective efforts further unifies the participants and guides them as they co-create the future.

P: But, can't I lose control in such a state of collective individualism?

MQ: No, not in the least. Who's asking that question anyway – you or the ego in you? Because of concealed conditioning, experiences of collective consciousness are often confused with trance-like states, out-of-body encounters, being psychic, channeling various entities or communing with 'angels'. Hidden beneath this false concern for your wellbeing is an ego-motive that is trying to dominate your destiny. Such interpretations of collective consciousness, as mentioned above, are rooted in aspects of cultural conditioning and have yet to be transcended.

P: Are the experiences of collective individualism *personal*?

MQ: They are actually better than that. They are transpersonal or *personal-plus*! Only the ego-mind runs away from this level of true intimacy with other human beings. The phenomena of collective consciousness take many forms and their effects are infinitely broad-ranging.

EVOLUTIONARY POINTER: Diaspora's[8] triumphant homecoming is in collective individualism.

MQ: We will now examine three significant categories of collective consciousness experiences: *Event-Driven*, *Restorative*, and *Spontaneous*.

Event-Driven Collective Consciousness

MQ: Event-Driven Collective Consciousness experiences are the most common. The motives for this type of unity can include fun, entertainment, creativity, self-identity and defense at the tribal, ethnocentric or national level. Lower manifestations can appears as 'mob-mentality' and more positive emergences as 'group bonding' is the 'high' that sweeps through a sporting arena during critical or climactic moments.

Event-driven experiences of collective consciousness occur in suitable conditions and appear regardless of the level of consciousness of the participants. For instance, when Portugal's soccer team lost to Greece in the final match of the European Cup, different collective experiences permeated each country. In Portugal, it was reflected in the dejected faces and movements of every person. In Greece at the exact same time, this event-driven unity manifested as triumphant elation!

Another emergence of event-driven collective consciousness brought together the population of Spain on two occasions. The first instance was sparked by the Prestige oil tanker catastrophe. This event united legions of strangers who worked from sunrise to sunset to save hundreds of miles of coastline from permanent desecration. These volunteer groups worked effectively, cohesively, tirelessly and without pay. They toiled under extreme conditions for many months with little personal interaction.

Another major emergence of collective consciousness in that country occurred after the terrorist attacks on 3/11 in Madrid. Three days after this tragic event this unity resulted in the election of the trailing second place government party, even though the incumbents were expected to win by a massive majority. A year later, however, the power of this tragic event had all but dissipated. Citizens of other countries got over this event in a matter of a few months.

In the aftermath of 9/11 total strangers came together in honor and support of one another on the streets of every city and town in the United States. This unity generated an unprecedented level of caring and compassion, which was felt around the globe. Unfortunately, event-driven experiences of collective consciousness tend to fade rapidly.

P: What do you mean by 'fade rapidly'?

MQ: In the years following that fateful day, except for a small core of concerned citizens worldwide and on its anniversary, that subject has faded from daily awareness. Despite the considerable effect of event-driven unity on the thoughts, emotions, actions, and interactions during such occurrences, rarely are those transformations permanent. Looking back from today it is difficult to find evidence for significant changes in the lives of the millions who were shocked and awed by the events of this day. For the vast majority, life has returned to normal. The greatest guilt of 9/11 is that a great opportunity was missed to make essential changes. Those topics that consumed your attention prior to 9/11 do so again today – the price of oil, the housing market, the next election, the latest Hollywood gossip. Look to your own experience. Is there an overwhelming amount of tangible evidence available today to prove that significant and fundamental transformations occurred in your relationships, career, in the ways you treat yourself, and in your daily routines, as a direct result of 9/11?

P: I feel more compassionate and my thinking will never be the same.

MQ: Okay. A shift in your subjective experience can only be verified by a shift in your actions. Have your core motives, values and intentions for being, becoming, and interacting been significantly and irrevocably altered to a point where the *you* of today, as evidenced by your actions, is completely dissimilar to the *you* of pre-9/11.

P: Well, when you put it that way, not really.

MQ: Where is the evidence that 9/11 changed us forever?

P: Have you flown into the USA recently?

MQ: I have been flying in and out of the USA on a regular basis since 1986. Though significant changes have occurred in US Official

Policies, there is little of significance about an extra five minutes on a security line at the airport or the fact that I can't bring my toothpaste on board a flight? The question here is not pride in one's country, it is to be able to provide confirmation for the changes *you think* have already occurred in *you*. The amount of evidence for change is directly proportional to the amount of change.

EVOLUTIONARY POINTER: The ego resists every possibility of change, but it is especially averse to the likely emergence of a new reality that ultimately challenges its rule.

MQ: To help that nation get over the shock of these tragic events, people were encouraged to go back to life as normal. *"Live your lives and hug your children"* was the request issued to the American public by their President, and *"I ask your continued participation and confidence in the American economy,"*[9]. The unhealthy-ego, clearly shaken by the veracity of sudden death was relieved to go back to the mall.

P: But, isn't our confidence and participation in the economy essential?

MQ: Yes, of course it is. The current economic structures empower our capacity to awaken and evolve beyond them. But, as we have seen in Chapter Ten, our exclusive fascination with this stage of development must be transcended and included if we are to free our values and our destiny from concealed conditioning. The tragic events of 9/11, however, clearly portray the forceful aversion the ego has to allowing us to change to any significant degree.

P: Therefore, radical transformation only comes from within our relevant relationships because event-driven experiences of collective consciousness are generally incapable of influencing the ego, but only for a few minutes, weeks or months.

MQ: Yes. Since event-driven responses generally appear when certain conditions overwhelm the realm of self-interest, we respond to them in the immediate aftermath from the perspective that is beyond the personal. 'We' temporarily becomes more important than 'I'. Notice, though, that after the shock of such events dissipates, they are always described from a personal perspective; how such an event affected 'me'.

P: Therefore, when my attention is lost in an event-driven collective 'high' or 'low', pathological narcissism can be temporarily transcended.

MQ: Transcended for a few seconds or perhaps weeks if the situation is profound enough. Pay attention the next time your favorite team scores in an important game or a natural tragedy overwhelms the frenzied pace of the ego's control. In those very moments you taste a little bit of freedom, and almost immediately that state begins to dissipate.

P: Because the ego takes over your attention again.

MQ: Exactly.

Restorative Collective Consciousness

MQ: An occurrence of *restorative collective consciousness* requires the existence of more advanced motives in a significant number of the participants than in the previous category. These advanced motives are generally related to self-development or healing. The emergence of restorative collective consciousness also requires direct interactions between the participants in this specific context of development, as opposed to simply being a spectator, witness, or victim in the case of event-driven experiences. For example, when people come together in the face of a common struggle, with shared motives of support, healing and growth, a tangible and curative energy fills the space around them. Those who attend Alcoholics Anonymous or other Twelve-Step groups speak of powerful communal experiences and the spiritual presence that often envelopes such gatherings.

EVOLUTIONARY POINTER: Amazing grace appears when people come together with the purpose of creating a community of mutual support in the face of overwhelming difficulties.

MQ: The appearance of a restorative collective presence is a direct result of the combined motivation for the gathering. When the group faces the destructive agendas or seeks out the hidden potential of its individuals together, the ensuing conversations, actions and relationships emerge as a living expression of collective intelligence at the level of personal healing.

P: Do those involved in an experience of restorative collective consciousness engage in ego-identity during such an event?

MQ: Not necessarily. While we find awakened people every-where, the goal of this type of gathering is to let go of an addiction to certain ways of being and not the addiction to ego-identity. Therefore, the location of the participant's center of attention is somewhat irrelevant. Although transcending the ego is usually not the objective of restorative collective consciousness, this type of self-healing can certainly encourage aspirations for awakened living.

Another example of restorative collective consciousness takes place in a foundational course offered by an international self-help organization: Landmark Education. Thousands of people throughout the world have participated in these engaging events. In one particular workshop, each of the participants join their class-mates in a profound recognition of the joy and harshness of the human experience. In a unique group exercise each individual is overwhelmed by a sense of non-difference between *self* and *other*. A short-lived, but extremely moving collective experience of unity, acceptance and healing emerges everywhere in the room. This occurs despite the fact that the attendees hardly know each other's first names. The relationships that form in that room during this exercise last for years afterwards. For many people this can be their first taste of collective consciousness that was not event-driven, such as by a sporting occasion, music concert or natural calamity.

Though generally perceived as being personal and interpreted at the level of ego-mind, experiences of restorative collective consciousness transcend tribal, ethnocentric and national identities while they are occurring. Because the group's primary motivator is healing and self-development, differences and opinions at the level of gender, race and creed also fall away, at least temporarily.

MQ: We will now look at the next form of collective unity, which is *called spontaneous collective consciousness.*

P: Okay. Before we move on I want to summarize the previous two forms.

MQ: Sure.

P: The first category — the experience of event-driven collective consciousness — commonly emerges because of tribal, ethnocentric or national levels of ego-identity. Therefore, such an emergence is based on an exclusive attachment to the individual ego and/or the culturally-created-self. The second category — the experience of restorative collective consciousness — does not particularly require that any person in the group have objectivity on the ego-mind. Therefore, in restorative collective consciousness, the focus is mainly about sharing personal history, overcoming personal issues and grappling with the afflictions of ongoing emotional and psychological suffering.

MQ: Good! We can see that both the experiences of event-driven and restorative collective consciousness are heavily influenced by the ego-mind and the separate sense-of-self at the individual, ethnocentric or nation-centric level.

P: Yes. And because of this focus, the outcomes of event-driven or restorative collective consciousness experiences are limited by concealed conditioning.

MQ: This is true. The results of such events are invariably dictated by the ego-mind, simply because the majority of the participants are operating with conceptual-free-will.

Spontaneous Collective Consciousness

MQ: The experience of spontaneous collective consciousness occurs when we temporarily go *beyond* ego-identity in a group setting by using conscious-free-will. This experience of collective unity, also known as *awakened mind*, is a tangible experience of unity consciousness based on the ability of the participants to temporarily disengage from ego-identity. This experience is not event-driven or related to the work of recovery, healing or little-self development.

> EVOLUTIONARY POINTER: Awakened mind is the medium of discourse by which we co-create the future for all humankind.

P: The experience of spontaneous collective consciousness sounds quite dissimilar to the previous two categories.

MQ: Yes, completely different. The experience of spontaneous collective consciousness only emerges when we withdraw our attention from an exclusive identity with the ego. Remember, we can't co-create a vivid new world with the same point of focus that has taken us to this particular highpoint in our evolution as a race.

> EVOLUTIONARY POINTER: The 'Higher We' only unfolds between two or more individuals who are willing to temporarily release the separate sense of self in each other's company.

MQ: In the experience of spontaneous collective consciousness, while dynamic unity and creativity commands our attention, we are simultaneously fully alert, in charge and at ease within. Awakened mind coexists perfectly with our memories, emotions, learned knowledge, past experiences and life skills. This experience of spontaneous collective consciousness requires that only the ego-identity is purposefully placed to one side, at least in the interim, in each of the participants. A special event or wide scale calamity is not required to spark an experience of this collective unity.

EVOLUTIONARY POINTER: The experience of spontaneous collective consciousness appears when the intention of a group is to transcend all aspects of ego, together, for a period of time.

P: But, if awakened mind is the direct experience of *consciousness* beyond ego together with other people, then that means there are two ways in which we can experience consciousness?

MQ: Yes. Isn't that fascinating!

P: Indeed. Tell me more, please.

MQ: The first way to experience consciousness is in our meditation. This is the experience of consciousness in a *subjective* context. We are the *subject* and we are experiencing consciousness by ourselves. The second way to experience consciousness is in an *inter-subjective* context – meaning together with other people. During the experience of consciousness in an *inter-subjective* context, we still retain our individuality, of course, but our subjective awareness has merged with the collective awareness that is developed by the intention of each individual to go beyond ego-identity, together as a group. For a time, there is no 'I' other than the *one* we are sharing with the other participants. The collective individual or 'Higher We' is the unifying consciousness joining each of the participants together. Just like in the experience of Dennis Genpo Merzel's Big Mind Process[10], we see many human forms as the perfect vehicles through which consciousness can express itself, most effectively as *One*, for the sake of humanity.

P: These are two vastly different experiences of consciousness!

MQ: Absolutely!

P: Is there another way to describe this difference?

MQ: Think of it like this: Meditation is the experience of consciousness in a subjective context that is often described as the experience of *eternal beauty* in *silence, stillness and being*. We can also experience consciousness in an inter-subjective context, but now that same *eternal beauty* is experienced actively as *conversations, actions and becoming*.

P: One is not better than the other, just different?

MQ: Yes.

EVOLUTIONARY POINTER: Spontaneous collective unity is consciousness awakening to itself with the full use of our entangled minds and our life skills, with the capacity to engage in conversations and physical actions with other people whom we recognize as essentially non-different to who we are.

P: Do participants literally need to be in each other's physical presence so this spontaneity, enthusiasm and cooperation may unfold?

MQ: That is ideal, but not essential. They can be connected by a video or phone conference. All that matters is that the concerns of the ego-mind are released from the topics of conversation in a group situation, even for a short time. Then awakened mind appears.

'Flow' and Awakened Mind

Awakened mind can also be likened to the greatly studied aspects of *flow* described by author Mihaly Csikszentmihalyi who says that flow is *"the freedom of complete absorption in activity."*[11] Such states are highly pleasurable — ecstatic even — and all actions, including words, seem to be directed by a 'higher' aspect of being. Artists, athletes and other accomplished individuals often report states of *flow*.

P: Awakened mind is the 'down-home' version of flow?

MQ: Exactly! And, unlike the 'spectator separation' aspects of traditional flow, awakened mind can include those present into the exact same awareness of creative expression. So, to continue with that metaphor, not only would we be in awe of the 'slam-dunk'[12], we would know how it feels, and be capable of contributing to the next move.

P: It is so liberating to discover that resting just beyond the edge of exclusive self-interest in everyday conversations is our natural capacity to access awakened mind and the experience of spontaneous collective consciousness.

MQ: The emergence of awakened mind also levels the playing field in regard to personal history, intellectual prowess and financial wherewithal.

P: But, it is only the great equalizer to the degree of our participation?

MQ: Yes. The more we can allow the attachment to the ego-mind to fall away for a while in the presence of our peers, the more we can play. The meek shall indeed inherit the earth.

We will now look at two ways in which the experience of awakened mind manifests:

1) Spontaneous Right-Speech.
2) Spontaneous Right-Action.

Spontaneous Right-Speech

MQ: When consciousness animates our words, awakened mind emerges as spontaneous right-speech. Awakened mind can flow during breakfast, while cooking at the barbeque and during meetings in the boardroom. Awakened mind brings us together with our peers as *one* in dialogue. Such conversations are full of energy, an undeniable sense of joy, direction, precision and are replete with possibility. A new world appears when more of us become skilled at communicating at this level of simplicity beyond the ego-mind. Its emergence is up to us!

P: Can I assume that the expression of awakened mind is enhanced by the personality of each individual?

MQ: Yes, of course. Since each person is unique, the multiplicity of their pasts are leveraged and expressed individually, yet for the sake of the collective. The degree to which each person participates in this collective experience determines the depth and direction for all involved. And as soon as the topics of the ego-mind are reintroduced, awakened mind withdraws to the un-manifested state. Despite its considerable power and its ability to enliven the participants, awakened mind offers no resistance whatsoever to the deliberate, unconscious or accidental reintroduction of the ego-mind. Awakened mind transcends, yet includes, each person in the group. This brings in to being a highly infectious state of awareness that is exponentially superior to the combined wisdom of the contributors.

P: This sounds fascinating. What might a script of such a conversation be like?

MQ: Imagine coming together with our best friends in a situation in which each one of us had let go of our personal stories, personal agendas, the need to be affirmed, the need to be right, all stresses, anxieties, worries, all fears of change and of the future, and all our perceptions of limitations. Imagine offering ourselves to the fullest of our capabilities, though absent from the gathering was any requirement to be better than another individual. Imagine that the reason we all did this was not so much to feel the sheer joy and elation of bonding at this level, but to work together as one coherent group on a project of primary benefit to humanity and of secondary benefit to us as individuals.

Spontaneous Right-Action

MQ: Though the expression of awakened mind begins in simple dialogue, it also manifests with its own wholesome agendas and direction. Since each person in an awakened relationship has equal access to the direct experience of consciousness, in this dynamic – we merge with the group to do the work of Oneness. Spontaneous right-action emerges as the endeavors, creations, products or outputs of awakened relationships. Our active participation in awakened relationships produces spontaneous right-actions that are perfectly directed by this exquisite awareness. A buoyant trust and confidence rejuvenates and enlivens us to the degree of our contribution. Yet, despite this seamless unity, we retain our unique personality and the ability to harness our individual and unique life experiences for the sake of the team. When awakened mind is present as spontaneous right-action, our primary concern is to allow that infinite creative potential to direct our life skills for the sake of the community and its particular goals.

EVOLUTIONARY POINTER: The emergence of spontaneous right-speech and spontaneous right-action provide further evidence of the appearance of the Fourth Insight in our lives.

Initiating Awakened Mind – Six Questions

MQ: Awakened mind emerges when conditioned topics of conversation and their related words are withheld from the dialogue. The only other qualification to sustain this unified field of exchange is our interest in exploring our depth beyond the personal in communion with other people.

P: This means we can 'dial up' an experience of consciousness when we wish?

MQ: Yes, and why not? The expression of awakened mind is a result of conscious-free-will and is not dependent upon our personal history or location. There must be two or more individuals present for awakened mind to emerge in reality. It is better to have a relevant relationship with the other person, but that is not essential.

EVOLUTIONARY POINTER: When objectivity on the ego-mind is combined with a wholesome interest in expressing our full potential, awakened mind appears as spontaneous right-speech and subsequently as spontaneous right-action.

MQ: To begin, one person should ask the other(s) the following six questions:

1) Is the creation of the conditions for awakened mind our responsibility?
2) Is awakened mind available to every willing individual present?
3) Is the expression of awakened mind within our volition?
4) Is the location in which awakened mind emerges relevant?
5) Are our current personal circumstances or personal histories relevant to the emergence of awakened mind?
6) What are the qualities, features, and nature of awakened mind?

MQ: By allowing ourselves to answer the first five questions somewhat as follows, we are creating the conditions for awakened mind to emerge as our responses to the sixth question:

1) Yes, it is our responsibility to create the conditions for awakened mind.
2) Yes, awakened mind is available to every willing individual present.
3) Yes, the expression of the awakened mind is a conscious choice.
4) No, the location in which awakened mind emerges is not relevant.
5) No, our personal circumstances or personal histories are not relevant to the emergence of awakened mind.
6) Awakened mind is our innate ability to communicate in a context that is free from conditioned limitations and beyond the words

and topics of the ego-mind. To respond to the sixth question, start by describing the qualities and potential we feel in that very moment for the dialogue in which we are engaged. The expression of awakened mind begins by using individual words to describe its qualities, features, components and nature. If we only use single words at the beginning, that is fine. With practice, fully formed sentences will come along. Simply speak as the voice of awakened mind. For example, awakened mind is joy, lightness, without bounds, replete with potential and endless creativity...

MQ: Try this at home, with a friend or family member, play with it, and see what happens. It is okay to repeat these six questions as often as needed, using a different person to ask each time, if a larger group is present.

EVOLUTIONARY POINTER: Awakened Mind is the Fourth Insight in action!

P: And what if, as someone just starting out at this, silence is the only response?

MQ: This is perfectly fine and to be expected. Selective silence in a group setting is often a precursor to the clarity of awakened mind. Just be with the silence, yet watchful to allow the very first word of awakened mind to come forth.

P: We can also pay attention to the presence of awakened mind emerging in the dialogue between others in the group, right?

MQ: Yes. This is very helpful. Simply being present to awakened mind in conversations helps us witness and eventually manifest its depth. If one person in the group has prior experience with awakened mind, they can stabilize the experience once it emerges. As we progress in this practice, we will notice that awakened mind appears in a conversation, then comes and goes, and in just a few words, it can be brought right back again.

Daniel's Story: Daniel was invited to the 40th birthday party of his friend, Jordan. As he circulated at the party, he noticed that most of the conversations were about football, golf, cars, boating, the economy, with some stories of weddings and baby showers. When Daniel finally had the chance to talk at length with his friend, Jordan asked what he had been up to over the past few years. Daniel told Jordan of his awakening to concealed conditioning, how all emotional and psychological suffering had come to an end, and how, over the period of a few years, he had completely changed his career from accounting to running awareness training programs at local universities. The air of this conversation had suddenly become light and crisp! As the two friends spoke, an older gentleman joined them. Then a conversation about the source of wisdom appeared and this dialogue quickly caught the attention of several people sitting around them. In a short while, each member of this group was engrossed in an enlivening the conversation. It was obvious to Daniel that awakened mind had spontaneously emerged. He could clearly see this by the words each person was using and the quality of the contribution they were making. A profound degree of levity, potential, and openness had pervaded the group, which was free entirely from the agendas of the conditioned mind. Then someone began to share a concern that by acting on his wisdom, he often incurred great critique from a friend (who was not present). Immediately, the lightness dropped away as awakened mind exited. Daniel suggested that this concern be reframed in such a context so that each member of the group could learn from it, since this was an issue that many people grappled with. The person thought for a while about Daniel's request and then he continued to speak, but this time about the fact that accepting responsibility for wisdom is a matter of our interest in doing so, and not directly related to the opinions of those who do not share or believe in our desire to evolve.

Awakened mind had once again returned. Jordan looked over at Daniel and simply smiled.

P: *Awakened mind* is literal.

MQ: Yes!

EVOLUTIONARY POINTER: Consciousness wakes up to itself in us, in the other, and in the shared experience. It is the force of creation, the 'Higher We' or One Mind walking and talking together.

P: Is this experience of awakened mind commonplace?

MQ: Not yet. Awakened mind has yet to stabilize as an autonomous emergent. According to the spiritual teacher, Andrew Cohen, the appearance of what he calls the *Authentic Self* must still be orchestrated with great effort. One of his life goals is to stabilize this emergence that has appeared on many occasions since 2001 in groups as large as 50 of his most dedicated students and partners. The work of Dennis Genpo Merzel, founder of the *Big Mind American Zen* Organization and the *Big Mind Process,* allows participants to easily access collective individualism by calling on particular 'voices'. With Merzel's work, by speaking from the voice of *Big Mind* or the voice of the *Fully Functioning Human Being,* even those who have little or no experience in meditation or other aspects of spiritual development can easily taste this unity consciousness. Therefore, the Big Mind Process offers additional tools to access, expand and evolve collective individualism. With active engagement in this process, each participant gains access to this dynamic of awakened mind. This produces spontaneous right-speech and right-actions since each individual has temporarily gone beyond the identity with the separate sense-of-self, and has been swept up into a collective experience of vibrant trust that is enlivening the entire group.

People who have experienced Cohen's *Authentic Self* and the voice of Merzel's *Fully Functioning Human Being* describe a similar highly contagious and vibrant state of awareness that is exponentially superior to the combined wisdom of the contributors.

God and the Goal of Evolution

P: Does this fully functioning human being you speak of here transcend and include the idea of the mythic God?

MQ: Yes. This is not a new concept. Here are a few quotes on this point:

"God is the goal of evolution. It is God who is the source of the evolutionary force and God who is the destination. It is a very old idea, but, by the millions you run away from it in sheer panic. For no idea ever came to the mind of man which places upon you such a burden. As long as you can believe that godhood is an impossible attainment for yourself, you don't have to worry about your spiritual growth...you can relax and just be human. You can do your bit toward assuring yourself a comfortable old age, hopefully complete with healthy, happy and grateful children, and grandchildren; but beyond that you need not bother yourself...God's responsibility must be your own. It is no wonder that belief in the possibility of Godhead is so repugnant." from *The Road Less Traveled*[13] by Scott Peck

"God does not want you to become a god; he wants you to become godly—taking on his values, attitudes, and character." from *The Purpose Driven Life*[14] by Rick Warren

"Evolutionary Enlightenment is the most challenging spiritual endeavor because in it there is no promise of escape. Too many of you still secretly hope that one day you will be released from this process and able to rest forever." from spiritual teacher, Andrew Cohen

> EVOLUTIONARY POINTER: The tools to access awakened mind are fully available. It's important to actively create the conditions for the emergence of unified communities for the sake of others. The path we take is unimportant. What matters is that we participate.

The Man in the Rain

MQ: A man was walking in the street one day. Without warning, the skies became dark and it started to rain heavily. Having no cover from the rain, before long, he was soaking wet. Close by, another man standing on a great balcony completely dry, motioned to him, "Come over to the balcony. Here the vistas are long and you can be dry and warm. From here, you and I can also speak of the possibility that one day all this darkness may end". The man, standing in the rain, looked over and said, "I don't trust myself so I don't know that I can trust you. You want to speak with me about this crazy possibility. You are dry and warm while I am wet and cold. I think I can find an umbrella somewhere to try to shield myself. This is real life out here". There was no response from the man on the balcony so the first man continued, "Besides, I think I like the rain and the cold, I have become so accustomed to its relentlessness. I may have to change my whole way of being if I am to live the rest of my life on such a splendid balcony just so I could help someone like me who is lost in the rain... I am sorry, but I am busy right now and I can't accept that kind of responsibility." As he finished his last sentence he thought to himself, "There has to be another way," but deep down he also knew that he didn't want to accept the uncommon path. Then suddenly, and without warning, there was a heavy gust of wind and the man in the street disappeared into the sheets of rain.

The Tears of the Bodhisattvas

"Freedom manifests as compassionate activity, as agonizing concern. The Form of Freedom is sorrow,

Unrelenting worry, for those struggling to awaken. The Bodhisattvas weep daily; the tears stain the very fabric of the Kosmos in all directions."[15]

The Awakened Life

MQ: As the limitations of concealed conditioning and conceptual-free-will fall by the wayside, the Fourth Insight joins you with others who have also awakened. Now we are united in a vision to manifest and stabilize a new reality for the sake of humanity by the power and grace of conscious-free-will based on shared values and pure intentions. The rate at which our lives move appears to speed up, and even though our perspective is vast, time seems short. There is much to do. We are a species that may be running out of time and this is a race we cannot afford to lose.

Awakening holds the key to a new world for all of us. Allow your soul to hear this evolutionary call to awaken to dignity, transparency, authenticity and most of all – *Conscious Service.*

Do you choose the awakened life?
If you don't, then who?

1 Francois de La Rochefoucauld (1613 - 1680).
2 Very often translated as 'sufferings'.
3 Adapted from Taking Flight by Anthony de Mello: Random House, New York, 1990.
4 The condition of being in action.
5 Receiving spiritual teachings or insight.
6 Lama Ole Nydahl: Western teacher and founder of over 500 Diamond Way Buddhist meditation centers.
7 Lamsa Translation of the Holy Bible – Matthew 8.22.
8 Diaspora: A dispersion of an originally homogeneous entity, such as a language or culture.
9 http://www.whitehouse.gov/news/releases/2001/09/20010920-8.html
10 There is a great book called Big Mind / Big Heart, by Western Zen Master, Dennis Genpo Merzel, which describes the many voices that make up the self in a most unique way.
11 Flow: The Psychology of Optimal Experience by Mihaly Csikszentmihalyi - Harper Perennial, 1991.
12 A term from basketball; to shoot the ball through the hoop with great force.
13 Simon and Schuster,1978
14 Zondervan, 2002.
15 A Brief History of Everything by Ken Wilber: Shambhala, 2000.

Selected Bibliography

A Brief History of Everything – by Ken Wilber, Shambhala, 2 Edition (2007)

Boomeritis – by Ken Wilber, Shambhala (2003) Up From Eden, New Edition – by Ken Wilber, Quest Books (1996)

Integral Spirituality – by Ken Wilber, Shambhala (2007)

Atman Project – by Ken Wilber, Shambhala (2003)

Sex, Ecology and Spirituality – by Ken Wilber, Shambhala; Rev Sub edition (2001)

One Taste – by Ken Wilber, (2000) Grace and Grit – by Ken Wilber, Shambhala (2001)

Freedom Has No History – by Andrew Cohen, What Is Enlightenment? Press (1997)

Embracing Heaven and Earth – by Andrew Cohen, What Is Enlightenment? Press (2000)

Enlightenment is Secret – by Andrew Cohen, What Is Enlightenment? Press (1995)

Who Am I, How Shall I Live – by Andrew Cohen, What Is Enlightenment? Press (1998)

Living Enlightenment – by Andrew Cohen, What Is Enlightenment? Press (2002)

The Promise of Perfection – by Andrew Cohen, Moksha Press (1998)

Big Mind / Big Heart – by Dennis Genpo Merzel, Big Mind Publishing (2007)

The Path of the Human Being – by Dennis Genpo Merzel, Shambhala (2005)

The Gospel of Saint Thomas - by Jean-Yves Leloup, Shambhala (2003)

The Road Less Traveled – by Scott M. Peck, Simon & Schuster 2 edition (2002)

The Power of Now – by Eckhart Tolle, New World Library (1999)

Stillness Speaks – by Eckhart Tolle, New World Library (2004)

Power VS Force – by David R. Hawkins, Hay House (2002)

The Pope's Children – David McWilliams, Gill & Macmillan (2005)

Beyond Knowledge – by Jean Klein, Non-Duality Press (2006)

Meditations – by Marcus Aurelius, Modern Library Edition (2002)

Walden – by Henry David Thoreau, Castle Books (2007)

The Little Prince – by Antoine de Saint-Exupéry, Harcourt Children's Books (2003)

Bhagavad Gita – by Three Rivers Press, Stephen Mitchell Translation (2002)

Dhammapada – by Shambhala Pocket Classsics, Thomas Byrom Translation (1993)

Tao Te Ching – by Lao Tzu, Harper Classics, Stephen Mitchell Translation (2002)

Book of Awakening – by the 14th Dalai Lama, Thorsons (2003)

The Awakened One – by Sherab Chodzin Kohn, Shambala (1994)

The Feeling Buddha – by David Brazier, Fromm International (1998)

Art of War – by Sun Tzu Shambhala, Thomas Cleary Translation (1988)

Flow – by Mihaly Csikszentmihalyi - Harper Perennial (1991)

A Brief History of Time – by Stephen Hawking, Bantam Book (1988)

The Tibetan Book of the Dead – Oxford Press, Evan Wentz Edition (1960)

Tibetan Yoga – Oxford Press, Evan Wentz Edition (1958)

Autobiography of a Yogi – Parmahansa Yogananda, Self Realization Fellowship (1946)

EnlightenNext Magazine – EnlightenNext Inc? Press (Published 6 times per year)

For updated list, please visit
http://www.mickquinn.com/bibliography.htm

BOOKS

O is a symbol of the world, of oneness and unity. In different cultures it also means the "eye," symbolizing knowledge and insight. We aim to publish books that are accessible, constructive and that challenge accepted opinion, both that of academia and the "moral majority."

Our books are available in all good English language bookstores worldwide. If you don't see the book on the shelves ask the bookstore to order it for you, quoting the ISBN number and title. Alternatively you can order online (all major online retail sites carry our titles) or contact the distributor in the relevant country, listed on the copyright page.

See our website **www.o-books.net** for a full list of over 500 titles, growing by 100 a year.

And tune in to myspiritradio.com for our book review radio show, hosted by June-Elleni Laine, where you can listen to the authors discussing their books.

MySpiritRadio